Choosing the Nation's Fiscal Future

Committee on the Fiscal Future of the United States
Division of Behavioral and Social Sciences and Education

NATIONAL RESEARCH COUNCIL *and* NATIONAL ACADEMY OF PUBLIC ADMINISTRATION

THE NATIONAL ACADEMIES PRESS
Washington, D.C.
www.nap.edu

THE NATIONAL ACADEMIES PRESS   500 Fifth Street, N.W.   Washington, DC 20001

NOTICE: The project that is the subject of this report was approved by the Governing Board of the National Research Council, whose members are drawn from the councils of the National Academy of Sciences, the National Academy of Engineering, and the Institute of Medicine. The members of the committee responsible for the report were chosen for their special competences and with regard for appropriate balance.

This study was supported by Grant No. 07-90771-000-HCD to the National Academy of Sciences and Grant No. 07-90771-001-HCD to the National Academy of Public Administration from the John D. and Catherine T. MacArthur Foundation. Any opinions, findings, conclusions, or recommendations expressed in this publication are those of the author(s) and do not necessarily reflect the views of the organizations or agencies that provided support for the project.

International Standard Book Number-13:   978-0-309-14723-1
International Standard Book Number-10:   0-309-14723-9
Library of Congress Control Number: 2009943505

Additional copies of this report are available from the National Academies Press, 500 Fifth Street, N.W., Lockbox 285, Washington, DC 20055; (800) 624-6242 or (202) 334-3313 (in the Washington metropolitan area); Internet, http://www.nap.edu.

Suggested citation: National Research Council and National Academy of Public Administration. (2010). *Choosing the Nation's Fiscal Future*. Committee on the Fiscal Future of the United States. Washington, DC: The National Academies Press.

ERRATA

On pages 5-6, the sentence should read:

And it would allow spending on all other federal programs to be higher than the level implied by current policies.

On page 17, in the first full paragraph, in the second sentence:

Replace "the economy" with "per capita GDP"

On page 54, in Box 3-1, in the last two sentences:

Replace "0.3 percent" with "0.6 percent"
Replace "0.9 percentage points" with "1.8 percentage points"

On page 170, in note 26, in the second paragraph, the parenthetical sentence should read:

(The only exceptions are that Figure 8-1 and part of Table 8-1 use the baseline data in Chapter 9.)

Choosing the Nation's Fiscal Future
The National Academies Press, Washington, DC
2010
ISBN-13: 978-0-309-14723-1
ISBN-10: 0-309-14723-9

THE NATIONAL ACADEMIES
Advisers to the Nation on Science, Engineering, and Medicine

The **National Academy of Sciences** is a private, nonprofit, self-perpetuating society of distinguished scholars engaged in scientific and engineering research, dedicated to the furtherance of science and technology and to their use for the general welfare. Upon the authority of the charter granted to it by the Congress in 1863, the Academy has a mandate that requires it to advise the federal government on scientific and technical matters. Dr. Ralph J. Cicerone is president of the National Academy of Sciences.

The **National Academy of Engineering** was established in 1964, under the charter of the National Academy of Sciences, as a parallel organization of outstanding engineers. It is autonomous in its administration and in the selection of its members, sharing with the National Academy of Sciences the responsibility for advising the federal government. The National Academy of Engineering also sponsors engineering programs aimed at meeting national needs, encourages education and research, and recognizes the superior achievements of engineers. Dr. Charles M. Vest is president of the National Academy of Engineering.

The **Institute of Medicine** was established in 1970 by the National Academy of Sciences to secure the services of eminent members of appropriate professions in the examination of policy matters pertaining to the health of the public. The Institute acts under the responsibility given to the National Academy of Sciences by its congressional charter to be an adviser to the federal government and, upon its own initiative, to identify issues of medical care, research, and education. Dr. Harvey V. Fineberg is president of the Institute of Medicine.

The **National Research Council** was organized by the National Academy of Sciences in 1916 to associate the broad community of science and technology with the Academy's purposes of furthering knowledge and advising the federal government. Functioning in accordance with general policies determined by the Academy, the Council has become the principal operating agency of both the National Academy of Sciences and the National Academy of Engineering in providing services to the government, the public, and the scientific and engineering communities. The Council is administered jointly by both Academies and the Institute of Medicine. Dr. Ralph J. Cicerone and Dr. Charles M. Vest are chair and vice chair, respectively, of the National Research Council.

www.national-academies.org

NATIONAL ACADEMY OF
PUBLIC ADMINISTRATION®

THE NATIONAL ACADEMY OF PUBLIC ADMINISTRATION

The National Academy of Public Administration (National Academy) is a non-profit, independent organization of top policy and management leaders who tackle the most critical, timely, and challenging problems facing American government. With a network of more than 650 distinguished Fellows who lead the institution and guide its work, the National Academy is trusted across government to provide objective analysis and find practical, innovative solutions to management problems by bringing the best thinking and experience to bear on government problems. National Academy Fellows are elected by peers based on their impressive contributions to and experience in the field of public leadership and management. The Fellowship includes former cabinet officers, members of Congress, governors, mayors, and state legislators, as well as distinguished scholars, business executives, and public administrators. Individually, they are experts and trusted thought leaders; collectively, they are a national treasure.

Established over 40 years ago and chartered by Congress, the National Academy continues today to make a positive impact in America by helping federal state and local governments respond effectively to current circumstances and changing conditions. The National Academy is led by Kenneth S. Apfel and Timothy B. Clark, who serve as chair and vice chair, and Jennifer L. Dorn, who is president and chief executive officer.

www.napawash.org

COMMITTEE ON THE FISCAL FUTURE
OF THE UNITED STATES

F. Stevens Redburn, *Study Director*
Jane L. Ross, *Senior Staff Officer*
Mark David Menchik, *Senior Program Officer*
Kathy A. Ruffing, *Senior Program Officer* (March-November 2008)
Malay Majmundar, *Senior Program Associate*
Danielle Johnson Bland, *Senior Program Assistant*

Foreword

This report represents the outcome of a joint and shared effort between our two organizations: the National Academy of Public Administration (NAPA) and the National Academy of Sciences (NAS). In their respective spheres, these two institutions play important roles by bringing to bear expert advice on some of the most significant challenges facing our nation.

At the request of and with the support of the John D. and Catherine T. MacArthur Foundation and using procedures of the National Research Council, NAS and NAPA jointly undertook a 2-year study of the long-term fiscal challenge facing the United States. The work was performed by a stellar committee representing a diversity of disciplines and practices, a wealth of experience with the federal budget and various public policies, and a wide range of political and policy views. The committee has worked in harmony and forged a strong consensus under the leadership of its co-chairs, John Palmer and Rudy Penner. We thank them for their leadership and the entire committee for their extraordinary efforts.

No one reading this report can avoid being struck by the magnitude of the long-term budget challenge facing the federal government. Other studies have called attention to this challenge in similar terms. Uniquely, however, this study provides a framework that leaders and others can use to systematically consider a range of choices to put the federal budget on a sustainable course.

This report neither presumes nor recommends a particular path to a stable fiscal future. In a democracy, it is not the role of experts from outside the government to decide important policy questions, especially questions of this magnitude. That is the task of political leaders. And voters have the responsibility to engage in the issues, elect officials who understand the challenges, and then hold them accountable for acting responsibly.

As a group of experts, the committee is providing the basis for making policy decisions and their professional judgment about the key issues for our fiscal future. It acknowledges the differences in values and perspectives that must be reconciled in order to reach agreement. It illustrates the range, as well as the difficulty, of the policy choices that have to be faced. It also offers a set of analytical tools for weighing those choices, including practical tests that can be applied to budget proposals to determine their fiscal prudence.

Much is at stake. If we as a nation do not grapple promptly and wisely with the changes needed to put the federal budget on a sustainable course, all of us will find that the public goals we most value are at risk. This report will have served its purpose if its insights and analytical framework are widely used to support serious discussion of this most urgent question. We hope that it will receive the widest possible attention.

Ralph J. Cicerone
President
National Academy of Sciences
Chair
National Research Council

Jennifer L. Dorn
President and Chief Executive Officer
National Academy of
Public Administration

Acknowledgments

This study is the product of the generous support, hard work, and dedication of many organizations and individuals. The officers and staff of the John D. and Catherine T. MacArthur Foundation originated the idea for the study and provided its funding. They maintained strong support and interest throughout the course of the work.

Jennifer Dorn, president and chief executive officer of the National Academy of Public Administration; Lois Fu, senior adviser to the president of the National Academy of Public Administration; Michael Feuer, executive director of the Division of Behavioral and Social Sciences and Education (DBASSE) at the National Research Council (NRC); and Jane Ross, director of DBASSE's Center for Economic, Governance, and International Studies provided leadership in the development of the study and continued support through the study process.

We owe special thanks to our fellow committee members, who gave long hours to this project, providing not only in-depth analyses, but also drafts—and repeated redrafts—of text for the report. The members hold a broad range of views on topics related to this study, and they used those differences to explore a very wide range of policy ideas and to draft a report that would be useful to individuals and groups with diverse beliefs and priorities.

A great deal of the success of this project is due to its excellent staff, who performed innumerable analyses and produced many drafts of the report. We are especially indebted to our study director, Steve Redburn, who managed the overall work of the panel, led a complex set of analytic activities, and helped us to meet our deadlines. The fast pace of the work and the outstanding quality of the final product are due to an important extent also to the work of Mark Menchik, Malay Majmundar, Kathy Ruffing, and Danielle Bland. Eugenia Grohman, associate executive director of DBASSE, shared her extensive experience at critical points in the study process, especially in editing the manuscript.

Staff members of the Social Security Administration's Office of the Chief Actuary provided cost estimates on various proposals contained in the report's illustrative scenarios and reviewed text for completeness and accuracy. The Urban Institute-Brookings Institution Tax Policy Center contributed to the detailed analysis in the report by producing simulations of tax changes that were part of several illustrative scenarios. Barry Anderson and his colleagues in the Budgeting and Public Expenditures Division of the Public Governance and Territorial Development Directorate of the Organisation for Economic Co-operation and Development produced a study of the international experience with long-term budgeting.

This report has been reviewed in draft form by individuals chosen for their diverse perspectives and technical expertise, in accordance with procedures approved by the Report Review Committee of the NRC. The purpose of this independent review is to provide candid and critical comments that will assist the institution in making the published report as sound as possible and to ensure that the report meets institutional standards for objectivity, evidence, and responsiveness to the study charge. The review comments and draft manuscript remain confidential to protect the integrity of the deliberative process.

We thank the following individuals for their participation in the review of this report: Henry J. Aaron, Economic Studies Program, Brookings Institution, Washington, DC; Robert Greenstein, Center on Budget and Policy Priorities, Washington, DC; Edwin L. Harper, Public Affairs/Government Relations, Assurant, Inc., Washington, DC; Ron Haskins, Brookings Institution, Washington, DC; Peter S. Heller, Paul H. Nitze School of Advanced International Studies, Johns Hopkins University; James R. Horney, Center on Budget and Policy Priorities, Washington, DC; Philip G. Joyce, George Washington University; Lawrence S. Lewin, Executive Consultant, Chevy Chase, MD; Alicia H. Munnell, Carroll School of Management, Boston College; William Nordhaus, Department of Economics, Yale University; Marilyn Rubin, Department of Public Management, John Jay College of Criminal Justice; John B. Shoven, Department of Economics, Stanford University; and Theda Skocpol, Department of Government, Harvard University.

Although the reviewers listed above have provided many constructive comments and suggestions, they were not asked to endorse the conclusions or recommendations nor did they see the final draft of the report before its release. The review of this report was overseen by Charles F. Manski, Department of Economics, Northwestern University, and M. Granger Morgan, Department of Engineering and Public Policy, Carnegie Mellon University. Responsibility for the final content of this report, however, rests entirely with the authoring committee and the institutions.

John L. Palmer and Rudolph G. Penner, *Cochairs*
Committee on the Fiscal Future of the United States

Contents

6 Options for Social Security   105

7 Options for Defense and Other Domestic Spending   129

8 Revenue Options   143

Appendixes

**Appendixes A through G are not printed in this book;
they can be found online at
http://www.nap.edu/catalog.php?record_id=12808.**

Figures, Tables, and Boxes

TABLES

BOXES

Summary

The federal government is currently spending far more than it collects in revenues, and if current policies are continued, will do so for the foreseeable future. Over the long term, three major programs—Medicare, Medicaid, and Social Security—account for the projected faster growth in federal spending relative to revenues. No reasonably foreseeable rate of economic growth would overcome this structural deficit. Thus, any efforts to rein in future deficits must entail either large increases in taxes to support these programs or major restraints on their growth—or some combination of the two. The good news is that the nation now has many options to change course and put the federal budget on a different path. Taking steps soon to stabilize the nation's fiscal future will be less costly and difficult than acting later.

The Committee on the Fiscal Future of the United States was established under the auspices of the National Academy of Sciences and the National Academy of Public Administration, supported by the John D. and Catherine T. MacArthur Foundation, to carry out a comprehensive study leading to a set of plausible scenarios for the federal budget, to put it on a path toward a stable fiscal future. Members of the committee have quite varied backgrounds and perspectives on the budget. We disagree on many policy matters; but we are unanimous that forceful, even painful, action must be taken soon to alter the nation's fiscal course.

Without such action, the long-term mismatch between expected revenues and the estimated costs of government policies and programs will continue to require the government to borrow heavily. If remedial action is postponed for even a few years, a large and increasing federal debt

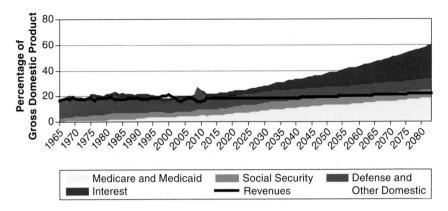

FIGURE S-1 The long-run budget outlook.

will inevitably limit the nation's future wealth by reducing the growth of capital stock and of the economy. It will also increase the nation's liabilities to investors abroad, who currently hold about one-half of the federal government's debt. If policies do not change, a large and increasing debt will expand the portion of the budget required to pay interest on the debt, especially if interest rates rise, and thereby reduce the resources available for all other government activities. Increasing debt also may contribute to a loss of international and domestic investor confidence in the nation's economy, which would, in turn, lead to even higher interest rates, lower domestic investment, and a falling dollar.

As shown in Figure S-1, the current trajectory of the federal budget cannot be sustained. Without a course change, the nation faces the risk of a disruptive fiscal crisis, a risk that increases each year that action to address the growing structural deficit is delayed. With delay, the available options become more extreme and therefore more difficult, and even more pain is shifted to future generations.

In the next year or two, large deficits and more borrowing are unavoidable given the severity of the economic downturn. However, action ought to begin soon thereafter—the committee believes that fiscal 2012 (which begins October 1, 2011) is a reasonable time to start—to first slow the rapid increase of the federal debt relative to the economy and then, over several years, reduce it to a more desirable level.

A first step toward dealing with the country's fiscal challenge is to specify a concrete test that can help to assess whether any budget is moving toward sustainability in a prudent manner. There are a variety of ways to measure fiscal prudence and numerous targets and time paths that could be connected to various measures. In order to design plausible scenarios to illustrate the implications of future policy choices, the committee selected a widely used metric as a reasonable (albeit not the only possible) indicator of fiscal prudence: the size of the government's debt as a percentage of the nation's gross domestic product (GDP). The key concern undergirding the committee's analysis is that under a continuation of current policies this ratio would continue to rise in the years ahead, with potentially harmful effects on current and future generations.

There is no magic number for the ratio of government debt to GDP; a smaller debt is always more manageable and gives a nation more ability to absorb unexpected shocks. A higher debt limits its choices and flexibility. The committee believes that the debt that will result if the United States continues with current tax and spending policies will be at a level that poses too great a risk to the economic welfare of the current generation and would impose an unfair and crushing burden on future generations. (The debt, which was about 40 percent of GDP just 2 years ago, is now above 50 percent and rising rapidly.) This is a judgment based on the committee's deliberations over the best available data, literature, understanding of economic policy and history, and analysis of possible scenarios. Given the additional risk of carrying a higher debt burden, the committee believes that the growth in this ratio must soon be limited, as shown in Figure S-2.

More specifically, the committee believes that some combination of revenue increases and spending restraints should be implemented soon to constrain the growth of federal debt as a percentage of GDP within a decade to a level that provides an appropriate balance between the risks as-

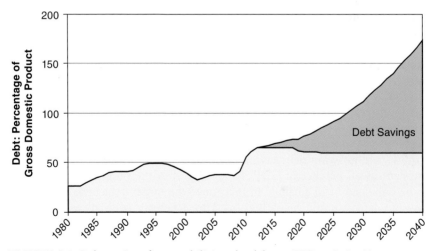

FIGURE S-2 Debt savings from stabilizing the debt-to-GDP ratio in 12 years.

sociated with a higher ratio and the additional difficulties of implementing policies that would be consistent with a lower ratio. The committee judged that a debt of 60 percent of GDP reflects an appropriate balance and is an achievable target within a decade—and is therefore useful to guide policy choices that will ultimately be made by elected leaders. This is a different ratio than the committee would have likely proposed under different circumstances. Indeed, it will surely be seen by some as too high and by others as too low. But the committee believes it is the lowest ratio that is practical given the fiscal outlook. A higher debt burden would leave the nation less able to cope with unforeseeable but inevitable shocks—such as international crises or natural disasters—requiring a vigorous federal response. It would put the nation closer to a point from which no politically credible path to sustainability could be constructed. Moreover, stabilizing the debt at a higher ratio implies a higher deficit, a greater draw on the nation's saving or more foreign borrowing, which will have a negative impact on future living standards. On the other side, a lower ratio would imply even more painful changes in tax and spending policies.

The rapid growth of federal spending for health care is the largest contributor to the nation's long-term fiscal challenge. Any reasonable path to fiscal sustainability will have to include reforms to reduce the growth rates of Medicare and Medicaid. The challenge posed by Social Security is far less problematic, but still substantial. Options for putting it on a sound fiscal footing range from sizable reductions in currently projected benefit growth to sizable increases in payroll taxes, with many possible intermediate combinations. Spending growth in many other areas of federal activity can be moderated, in part by curtailing or reforming less effective programs. Options that raise taxes substantially include significant reforms to make the tax system fairer and more efficient and include the introduction of new taxes on consumption.

These and other policy changes can be combined to produce a wide range of budget paths or scenarios that would bring revenues and spending into close alignment over the long term and to stabilize the nation's debt burden. The committee's different scenarios are intended as an illustrative, but by no means definitive or exhaustive, set of trajectories toward a sustainable fiscal future. The committee offers four representative scenarios that illustrate a wide range of available policy choices. Any of these paths would yield growing debt savings relative to current policies and stabilize the debt at 60 percent of GDP. To achieve this, the budget does not have to be balanced or in surplus. In fact, once the target debt ratio is reached, average deficits could be as high as 2 to 3 percent of GDP without debt growing faster than GDP.

The four illustrative paths show that many policy choices are available if action is taken soon. However, none of them is easy. If the choice is to continue all government programs at a level consistent with current policies, both spending and revenues would have to rise dramatically to prevent an ever-rising debt in relation to GDP. Given the inefficiency of the present tax structure, it would almost certainly also be necessary to change how revenue is collected. If, instead, the choice is to keep the federal government's share of the economy close to the level of the past several decades, the government would have to scale back what it does, and extremely difficult choices would have to be made about what social goals to pursue less vigorously and what programs to end.

Figure S-3 compares the committee's four illustrative paths.

1. *Low spending and revenue:* revenues are held near their recent average level of 18 to 19 percent of GDP, and spending is 2 to 3 percentage points higher than revenues. This path would require sharp reductions in projected growth rates for health and retirement programs, as well as reductions in the proportion of the economy's resources available for all other federal responsibilities.

2. *High spending and revenue:* spending and revenues are increased substantially, with spending eventually reaching one-third of GDP. Because this spending level is still less than under a continuation of current policies, it would require an eventual reduction in the rate of growth of health spending. It would, however, accommodate the spending needed to maintain currently scheduled Social Security benefits. And it would allow spending on all other federal programs to continue at the level implied by current policies—although if

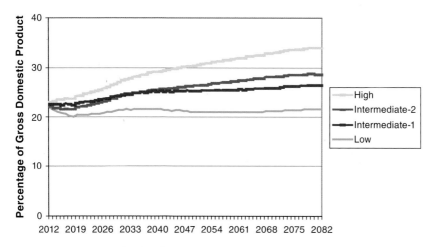

FIGURE S-3 Projected federal spending under the committee's four scenarios.

new initiatives were undertaken, then some program reductions would be required.

3. *Intermediate path 1:* spending and revenues rise gradually to about one-fourth of GDP and spending on the elderly population would be constrained to support only modest expansion of other federal spending. The growth rates for Social Security, Medicare, and Medicaid would be slower than under current policies. This path reflects the view that the federal government should make selective new public investments to promote economic growth, preserve the environment, and build for the future.

4. *Intermediate path 2:* spending and revenues would eventually rise to a little more than one-fourth of GDP. Spending growth for health and retirement benefits for the elderly population would be slowed but less constrained than in the intermediate-1 path. Spending for other federal responsibilities would be reduced. This path reflects the view that the government's implicit promises for the elderly are a higher priority than other spending.

The scenarios demonstrate that it is indeed possible to reduce the risk of financial disruption and put the budget on a sustainable course using the illustrative debt target of 60 percent of GDP and timeline to reach it. The choice of the starting date and timeline, as with the level of the target, will ultimately be a decision of elected leaders, taking into account the best information available to them when they must make budget choices.

The committee recognizes that this task is extremely difficult: the pain, whether cutting the growth of spending, increasing taxes, or both, must begin very soon, while the gain of avoiding a fiscal train wreck and its consequences is in the future and of uncertain magnitude. Although it may be natural to want to delay action, the committee has concluded that doing so would be costly and possibly perilous. With delay, revenues would have to be raised even higher or spending reduced even more to bring the debt to a prudent level while also incurring higher interest payments. With delay, also, the risk grows that the nation's creditors—especially, those abroad—will conclude that the United States has no plan to restore fiscal stability and will therefore demand higher interest rates or make other tough economic demands. The margin for error then would be smaller, and the options for corrective action even more painful than they are today.

The committee recognizes that fiscal sustainability cannot be achieved without major near-term policy changes, particularly forceful actions to slow the growth of spending in Medicare and Medicaid. Because of the difficulty of such changes, the committee proposes that elected leaders annually assess the country's progress and develop concrete proposals to place the budget on a sustainable path. To do so, the committee offers a framework that everyone can use to evaluate any proposed federal budget. Our framework of six tests can be used to hold leaders accountable for their proposed budgets:

1. Does the proposed budget include policy actions that start to reduce the deficit in the near future in order to reduce short-term borrowing and long-term interest costs?

2. Does the proposed budget put the government on a path to reduce the federal debt within a decade to a sustainable percentage of GDP? Given the fiscal outlook and the committee's analysis of the many factors that affect economic outcomes, the committee believes that the lowest ratio that is economically manageable within a decade, as well as practically and politically feasible, is 60 percent.

3. Does the proposed budget align revenues and spending closely over the long term?

4. Does the proposed budget restrain health care cost growth and introduce changes now in the major entitlement programs and in other spending and tax policies that will have cumulative beneficial fiscal effects over time?

5. Does the budget include spending and revenue policies that are cost-effective and promote more efficient use of resources in both the public and private sectors?

6. Does the federal budget reflect a realistic assessment of the fiscal problems facing state and local governments?

The President and Congress share accountability for putting and keeping the federal budget on a sustainable path. The Office of Management and Budget and the Congressional Budget Office—as well as private organizations—can make major contributions to the needed reassessment of the nation's fiscal course by regularly publishing projections of the long-term effects of the President's budget and of major alternatives. Those projections can be used to assess the extent to which proposals are sustainable by the tests above.

The current federal budget process does not favor forward-looking assessment and management of the nation's fiscal position. The committee finds that the present process gives too much weight to the interests of the current generation and too little weight to the interests of future generations. If the process is an obstacle to prompt correct action, then the first step in dealing with the fiscal challenge is to reform it.

The committee favors reforming the budget process to make it more far sighted and to establish a new regime of responsible budget stewardship. Under this new regime, leaders will be better prepared to take the political actions necessary to fairly represent the interests of the nation's children and grandchildren and to avoid the potentially serious consequences of continuing on the present path.

If action is taken soon, the country has a wide choice of options to help achieve fiscal sustainability. All are difficult; but if action is postponed, the options will be fewer and the choices will be even more difficult. With delay, the risk of a disruptive fiscal crisis will grow, and the standard of living experienced by everyone's grandchildren is likely to be lower than it is for people today.

The challenges are formidable, but not impossible. If the nation accepts sacrifices in the short run, it will be much stronger, safer, and more prosperous in the long run.

1

The Long-Term Challenge

It is simple arithmetic. The federal government's spending for current programs—already far in excess of current revenues—is projected to grow much faster than its revenues in the coming decades.

The cumulative effect of the fundamental mismatch between expected revenues and the spending implied by the federal government's policies and commitments will be a very large and rapid increase in the amounts that the United States must borrow to finance current spending. This spending will include growing interest payments to the individuals, institutions, and countries that provide the financing through the purchase of U.S. Treasury debt. In addition to this fundamental imbalance, there has been a surge of spending and a drop in revenues because of the 2008-2009 economic downturn, which added more than $1.5 trillion of debt in just 1 year, about $4,500 of additional borrowing for each U.S. resident. This temporary borrowing surge is of concern, of course; however, it is the much larger longer-term mismatch between projected spending and projected revenues implied by current policies that is the greater concern and the focus of this report.

Three major programs that primarily serve the elderly and many people of modest means—Medicare, Medicaid, and Social Security—are largely responsible for the projected growth of spending. Medicare and Medicaid have been growing faster than either revenues or the economy for some time, driven by enhanced benefits, rapid growth of health care costs, and, more recently, by aging of the U.S. population. Social Security spending will grow faster than the economy in the near future as baby boomers retire.

Those three programs already account for nearly one-half of all spending (excluding interest on the debt). The challenge posed by this growth of spending will be compounded by the projected slowing growth of the labor force that is a direct result of the aging of the U.S. population. The number of people who receive retirement and health benefits will increase just as the growth of revenues from income and payroll taxes slows down.

If changes are not made, the nation's debt is projected to surpass the immediate post-World War II record in less than 20 years, and it would be about seven times the size of the economy in 75 years. That, of course, is impossible. Long before the federal debt reached such a level, the United States would experience a financial crisis that would dwarf what the country has recently experienced, and with more lasting consequences.

The budgetary arithmetic may be simple, but making the necessary adjustments will not be. If policy changes are made, spending and revenues can gradually be brought into alignment, over several years. The required policy changes will entail some painful decisions, and action would have to begin soon. If such changes are delayed too long, it will not be possible to put the federal budget on a sustainable course before a fiscal disaster becomes inevitable.

In the face of the looming fiscal crisis, the John D. and Catherine T. MacArthur Foundation asked the National Academy of Sciences and the National Academy of Public Administration to undertake a comprehensive study to identify how to put the federal budget on a sustainable path; see Box 1-1 for the full charge to the committee. In response to that charge, the two organizations appointed our committee. (See Appendix H for biographical sketches of the committee members and staff.) The rest of this chapter discusses the size and nature of the budget challenge, how it arose, and its implications. Subsequent chapters discuss in detail how to approach solutions, what some major policy options look like, and how people of differing views might combine these options to put the budget on a sustainable long-term path. Chapter 2 provides a framework for thinking about how to address the fiscal challenge. Chapter 3 provides practical tests of fiscal prudence that can be applied to the federal budget or alternatives. Chapters 4 through 9 lay out major building blocks of possible corrective action—in three major areas of spending and in revenues—and then illustrate how such policy options can be combined in order to put the federal budget on a sustainable path. The results demonstrate that there are a wide range of possible ways to bring revenues and spending into alignment over the far horizon. Chapter 10 describes possible reforms of the budget process to make it easier to address the long-term fiscal challenge. Chapter 11 describes how citizens and leaders can use the results of this study as a basis for constructive analysis and discussion of alternatives.

BOX 1-1
Committee Charge

An ad hoc committee will conduct the following tasks and prepare a report.

1. Produce several baseline projections of the federal budget, deficit, and debt, based on existing information and on an analysis of the nature and extent of the nation's fiscal and economic conditions. The projections will be based in part, on data from sources such as the Social Security Actuaries, the Congressional Budget Office, and the U.S. Office of Management and Budget.
2. Produce a fiscal framework and set of guiding principles for the development of policy scenarios and estimates of the effects of selected budget options. The framework could include the target date by which the federal budget would achieve balance and the desired path to close the fiscal gap, which is the amount of spending reductions or tax increases needed to keep debt as a share of gross domestic product at or below today's ratio.
3. Identify values, preferences, and concerns that prior research has shown are shared by segments of the American public and use this information to assist in the development of several budget scenarios that are designed to reduce federal deficits or federal debt. The prior research should also take account of alternative views of the roles of individuals and employers in restoring the country's long-term fiscal health.
4. Develop several budget scenarios that will demonstrate various ways to address the fiscal challenge facing the national economy over the next several decades. The scenarios will deal with both the income and expenditure sides of the federal budget. The scenarios will be crafted to take into account information on values, preferences, and concerns of the American public and differing views of the roles of individuals and employers.
5. Identify and evaluate options to improve fiscal transparency and discipline in the federal budget development process.
6. Develop a report that will summarize the methodology and evidentiary base for the projections and provide an explanation of how different values and attitudes have been reflected in the policy scenarios. The report will not recommend a single solution to the structural deficit problem. Its conclusions will be limited largely to providing a framework for understanding the deficit issue and a rigorous methodology for analyzing different policy scenarios.

THE BUDGET OUTLOOK

Largely because of the severe downturn in the economy that began in 2008, the federal government borrowed $1.4 trillion in fiscal 2009 to pay for current spending, and it is expected to run an annual deficit in excess of $1 trillion for at least 1 more year. After the unprecedented deficits of 2009 and 2010, the economy's recovery will reduce the annual deficit, although it is likely to remain near historically high levels. But the debt, which was just over 40 percent of the gross domestic product (GDP) at the end of 2008 and approaching 55 percent just 1 year later, will continue to grow; see Box 1-2 on the debt and the deficit.

Using information as of June 2009 (Congressional Budget Office, 2009e) and projecting the likely effects of current policies, the long-term budget outlook if policies are not changed is bleak:

- By 2020, current policies would raise the federal debt to nearly 80 percent of GDP; see Figure 1-1, which also shows trends in spending and revenue from 1965 to the present.
- In about 30 years, if new revenues are not raised, and the three big retirement and health programs are not modified, those programs alone will consume all available federal revenues. Even sooner, their growth will intensify pressure to cut the portion of federal spending that is subject to annual appropriations, an array of programs that includes most of the core functions of government and many services and investments generally considered vital.

BOX 1-2
The Deficit and the Debt

The "headline" federal budget deficit (or, in some years, surplus), is the difference in a given year between what the government spends and what it takes in (revenues). The deficit is mostly a measure of the net cash flows to and from the U.S. Department of the Treasury. The deficit is financed by borrowing from the public (individuals, governments, and investors here and in other countries). The deficit was $459 billion for fiscal 2008 (the year ending September 30, 2008) and $1.4 trillion in fiscal 2009.

The debt is the cumulative amount the U.S. government owes. In most years, the annual deficit is a rough measure of the change that year in the federal debt. However, in fiscal 2008 and 2009 the federal government also borrowed to finance transactions related to the failure of major financial institutions. The publicly held portion of federal debt is that held by persons or organizations (foreign or domestic) outside the federal government. It excludes federal debt held inside the government, much of it in balances of the Social Security and Medicare trust funds dedicated to payment of future benefits. (The combined total of debt held by the public and held in government accounts is sometimes referred to as the gross federal debt.) Debt held by the public reached $5.8 trillion in fiscal 2008 and rose to about $7.5 trillion a year later, about $25,000 per person. A substantial fraction of the outstanding public debt matures each year and must be replaced by new borrowings at then-current interest rates.

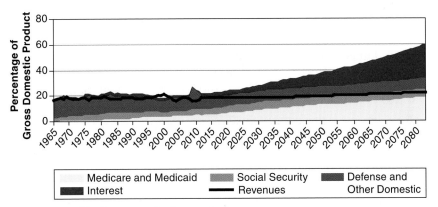

FIGURE 1-1 The long-term budget outlook.

- Through about 2035, Social Security spending as a share of GDP will grow significantly, reflecting the broad demographic trend of an aging population. It will grow more slowly thereafter.
- Medicare and Medicaid will consume an increasing share of GDP as per-capita health spending continues to grow at a faster rate than the economy. Federal health spending also will grow because the number of recipients will increase, even without legislation expanding program coverage, driven by the same aging demographic trend that affects Social Security.
- As noted above, if no action is taken to constrain or offset the growth of Social Security, Medicare, and Medicaid, if the tax rates stay near their current levels, and if other programs are held at their current share of GDP, the federal debt, deficits, and interest costs will explode over the long term. If all this were to occur, the federal debt would be more than seven times the nation's GDP in 75 years; see Figure 1-2.

These projections, which largely rely on the Congressional Budget Office (CBO) for estimates (although making a few different assumptions, see Box 1-3), are similar to those that others have made using similar techniques. They estimate the budget effects of current policies if they are continued over a long period—what is commonly referred to as a *budget baseline*; see Box 1-3. CBO's June 2009 long-term outlook reached the same basic conclusion as its previous updates, that "under current law, the federal budget is on an unsustainable path" (Congressional Budget Office, 2009e:1). The latest long-term projections from the Government Accountability Office (GAO), using somewhat different assumptions, also confirm that "the long-term fiscal outlook is unsustainable" (Government Accountability Office,

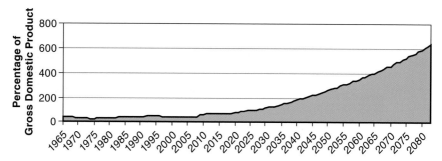

FIGURE 1-2 The long-term outlook for the debt.

2009:1). The U.S. Office of Management and Budget (OMB), in its annual long-run budget outlook published in April 2009, also says that "increasing health costs and the aging of the population will place the budget on an unsustainable course without changes in policy to address these challenges" (U.S. Office of Management and Budget, 2009a:191). In sum, our conclusion that a change of course is needed is not at all controversial among the government's experts, and private analysts agree (Auerbach and Gale, 2009; Cox et al., 2009; Moore, 2009). What is controversial is just how urgent is corrective action, an issue we address later in the report. Similarly, there will be controversy, even among those who believe that action is needed very soon, on what mix of spending and revenue policies should be pursued to close the fiscal gap.

BOX 1-3
Constructing a Budget Baseline

A baseline is useful for understanding the implications of current policies as they could play out over time and as a benchmark against which to measure the effects of proposed policy changes. A baseline is not a prediction—of course, no one can predict the fiscal future with much accuracy over even a few years. Nor is it a "realistic" projection in the sense that it unrealistically assumes no changes in policy. The study committee developed its baseline by making several modifications to baseline projections published by the Congressional Budget Office. In most cases, these modifications were to take account of likely congressional actions. Specifically, the committee's baseline assumes that Congress acts to extend expiring tax breaks that have bipartisan support, continues providing relief from the alternative minimum tax, adjusts for expected costs of operations in Iraq and Afghanistan, assumes modest increases (instead of sharp cuts that are in the law but Congress annually overrides) in fees paid to physicians by Medicare, and adds an expected cost for federal disaster payments.

If no major policy changes are made, debt service (the amount the U.S. government must spend each year for interest on the debt), which was more than $800 per person in 2008, would roughly double in those terms by 2020 at current interest rates. But average interest rates on government debt now are extraordinarily low, because of worldwide economic conditions: CBO and others project that, as the recovery proceeds, the government's borrowing rates will return to more historically normal levels, roughly doubling over the 10-year period. With debt nearly doubling *and* the government's average borrowing rate rising, spending for debt service in 2020 could approach $1,700 per person. And beyond 2020, the projected growth of the debt accelerates. Of course, uncertainties surround any budget forecast, especially over a long horizon; see Box 1-4. Each update changes the picture slightly, without changing the basic conclusion; for example, CBO's August 2009 update of its 10-year baseline increased the projection of cumulative deficits over 10 years by about $1.5 trillion relative to its March estimate (Congressional Budget Office, 2009a, 2009g).[1] However, this update does not change the committee's conclusion that if action is not taken soon the necessary and nearly certain result will be a larger discrepancy between revenues and spending and heavier burden of debt that eventually will require very sharp cuts in spending or very sharp increases in taxes. These, in turn, could have disruptive effects on many people and inflict severe damage on the economy or raise the risk of a severe financial crisis.

BOX 1-4
Uncertainties

The fiscal outlook could be worse than projected if:

- the economic recovery is weaker or slower than forecast, automatically increasing spending and depressing revenues;
- health spending growth is faster than projected;
- new or expanded spending programs are not fully offset by new revenues or cuts in other programs;
- annually appropriated spending (that is, other than for entitlements) grows with GDP rather than only with inflation, as assumed for the next 10 years;
- new crises—pandemics, wars, major natural disasters; major bankruptcies—demand emergency spending; or
- interest rates rise more than projected.

The fiscal outlook could be better than projected if economic growth is stronger than forecast, if health spending growth slows, or if interest rates remain lower than predicted.

A crisis could begin when, absent a credible plan to correct the fiscal mismatch, the nation's creditors—the people and institutions that hold the nation's debt—demand additional interest (or sell their dollar-denominated assets) to compensate for increased risk that the United States could default on its debts. Such a result seems unthinkable today, but so too, just 2 years ago, did the bankruptcy of General Motors and huge financial institutions. Although the "too late to turn back" date is unclear, it is clear that the clock is ticking. Certainly, the consequences of failing to address the fiscal challenge in time would be far more painful than those of acting to put the budget on a sustainable path. Fortunately, the nation still has reasonable options.

THE FISCAL CHALLENGE: HISTORICAL PERSPECTIVE

At the end of World War II, the size of the federal debt was a record 109 percent of GDP. So, in one sense, the United States has been here before. But in the immediate post-World War II period, the U.S. economy was growing rapidly. Rapid growth of the labor force after the war, combined with inflation that eroded the value of the debt principal, made the task of balancing the budget easier. The debt was reduced to about 25 percent of GDP by the 1970s. It rose again, to about 50 percent in the very early 1990s, but then reached another low—33 percent of GDP—in 2001. At the end of fiscal 2008, the federal debt was equal to about 41 percent of GDP, about where it had been in the 1960s and, again, as recently as 1999.

Yet there is a major difference in the post-World War II situation and the current situation. For one thing, labor force growth now is slowing (with the retirement of baby boomers) rather than accelerating. Furthermore, the debt incurred during World War II was owed almost entirely to average Americans; in contrast, today's debt is largely held by governments and foreign investors. Governments and other investors held less than 5 percent of outstanding Treasury debt in the 1960s, but they held nearly 50 percent at the end of 2008. Realistically, a large proportion of the trillions of dollars of additional debt that the federal government will accumulate in coming years will have to be funded from foreign institutions and investors.

If people are willing to lend to the U.S. government, as they have been, then the *current* debt burden is sustainable. However, looking farther ahead, it is clear that the budget is on an unsustainable course, as noted above: Social Security, Medicare, and Medicaid have been growing and will continue to grow rapidly. Arithmetically, these three programs alone largely account for the long-term problem. In 2008, Social Security paid about $612 billion to beneficiaries of its old-age, survivors, and disability insurance programs. Although Medicare health benefit payments of $460 billion were partly offset by premiums paid by the program's (mostly elderly) beneficiaries, net outlays were still almost $390 billion. The spending for Medicaid, the health program targeted for poor people, totaled just over $200 billion. Together, these three big programs in 2008 accounted for nearly 45 percent of federal spending (excluding interest on the debt).

Rapidly rising health care costs are at the core of the federal government's fiscal challenge. Although part of that rise results from predictable growth in the number of aged beneficiaries, more of it is attributable to the extent to which costs per beneficiary are expected to continue to grow faster than the economy (even after adjusting for changes in the age-sex mix of the beneficiary population), as they have in the past. If such "excess cost growth"—as it is called—continues as CBO and others project, the federal spending on health care alone will exceed the total amount collected in federal revenues within 50 years. There is little evidence to date to suggest that the growth of health costs will slow any time soon without major changes in health policy, and some changes, such as expanded health insurance coverage, could exacerbate the budget problem unless they are offset or paid for by savings in health care or elsewhere, or by new revenues (see Chapter 5).

The United States—like many other affluent countries—faces a steep demographic transition. There are several factors in the transition. People 65 and older, who currently make up 13 percent of the population, are expected to account for 20 percent by 2035. Over the same time, the expected patterns of retirement, immigration, longevity, and birth rates will result in a decline in the percentage of the population of working age. Over the next 20 to 30 years, aging of the population will be as important, or more important than, the projected growth in health care costs in driving up spending for the three major entitlement programs (Biggs, 2008; U.S. Office of Management and Budget, 2009c). Over a longer term, a 70-year horizon, aging and cost increases are expected by most analysts to play roughly equal parts in driving up spending for Social Security, Medicare, and Medicaid; see Figure 1-3.

The slowdown in workforce growth not only means a rise in the proportion of the population who are recipients of federal retirement and health benefits, but also a long-term slowing of economic growth. A smaller proportion of the population working also means that, absent other changes, federal income and payroll tax revenues will grow more slowly than they have in the past.

The long-term problem existed before the economic downturn that began in 2008, but the downturn has made it worse. The downturn has thus far affected the fiscal outlook in four main ways (not all negative). It has (1) temporarily reduced individual and corporate incomes and therefore tax collections related to personal income and corporate profits; (2) temporar-

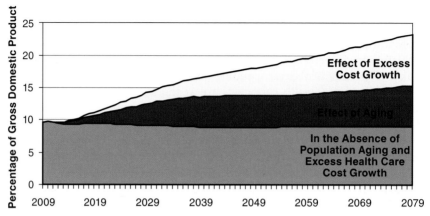

FIGURE 1-3 Factors in projected Social Security, Medicare, and Medicaid spending, 2009-2079, as a percentage of GDP.
SOURCE: Congressional Budget Office (2009e:12).

ily increased spending for economically vulnerable or newly unemployed people, their communities, and some sectors of the economy; (3) led to the "stimulus" legislation, including new temporary tax provisions and spending, and to a variety of new federal authority to provide financial support for or to rescue private financial institutions and provide relief for homeowners facing default; and (4) temporarily reduced inflation and interest rates.[2] The jump in deficits and borrowing resulting from the downturn may be only temporary, but the extra trillions of debt that will have accumulated in that period will be a lasting burden. This extra burden also makes the challenge of facing the much larger long-term deficits implied by current policies greater and more urgent.

The United States is not alone in facing growing gross government debt. The International Monetary Fund (IMF) has projected that the average public debt-to-GDP ratio in 2014 for 19 major industrialized countries would exceed their weighted average at the end of 2007, which was then 78 percent of GDP, by 36 percentage points of GDP; and that debt ratios for these countries would continue to grow over the longer term because of demographic forces (International Monetary Fund, 2009a:26). (These international comparisons include debt for all levels of government, not just the central or federal level, and internal as well as publicly held debt.)

CHANGING PATTERNS OF SPENDING AND REVENUES

Over the past 50 years, the federal government's budget has usually been somewhat out of balance—that is, revenues were less than spending (outlays). In fiscal 2008, the budget deficit equaled 3.2 percent of GDP. However, in fiscal 2009, the combination of falling revenues and higher spending because of the downturn have caused the deficit to swell to about 10 percent of GDP (4 percentage points higher than the largest previous deficit since World War II), rapidly adding to the amounts the federal government must borrow to finance its current spending. For perspective, in the 1970s the federal debt had fallen to about 25 percent of GDP; the 2009 deficit alone increased the debt by more than 10 percent of GDP.

Federal government outlays in 2008 equaled just under 21 percent of the size of the U.S. economy, almost the same proportion as in 1979 (U.S. Office of Management and Budget, 2009c). In fiscal 2008, the federal government spent nearly $3 trillion, about $9,600 for every U.S. resident; see Figure 1-4.

In 2009, federal spending spiked to 25 percent of GDP, higher than the previous post-World War II maximum of 23.5 percent, in 1983. Revenues dipped to 15 percent of GDP in 2009, a low not seen since the 1950s. In 2009, the deficit approached 10 percent of GDP, far above the previous postwar high of 6 percent in 1983, another recession year.

Social Security, Medicare, and Medicaid (as well as some smaller but similarly designed programs) are sometimes referred to as "entitlements" because their spending is determined by provisions of law establishing who is eligible and for what payments. These are part of a broader class of federal programs (commonly referred to as "mandatory spending programs") for which the level of spending is not determined through annual congressional appropriations; instead, absent a change in policies, spending

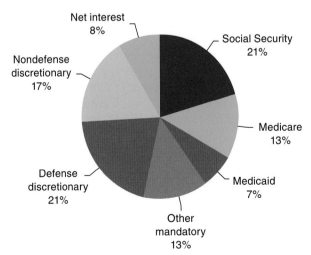

FIGURE 1-4 Federal outlays in fiscal 2008.

is largely determined by changes over time in demographic and cost factors. From 1962 to 2008, spending for the three large entitlement programs increased from 2.5 percent to 8.5 percent of GDP; see Figure 1-5A. As noted above, their costs are projected to continue growing faster than federal revenues and the economy in the decades ahead.

Over the same period, other noninterest spending declined from 15 percent to less than 11 percent of GDP; see Figures 1-5B and 1-5C. This diverse category of spending topped $1.4 trillion in 2008: about $610 billion for defense spending and $520 billion for nondefense spending. The category includes a wide range of programs (commonly referred to as "discretionary") for which spending levels are set annually by congressional appropriations. These include foreign aid, science and space programs, environmental protection, transportation, biomedical research, grants to states for education and social services, veterans' medical care, and the administration of justice. Although most of the programs are discretionary, the category also includes smaller entitlements (totaling about $400 billion)—food stamps, the Supplemental Security Income (SSI) program, the refundable Earned Income Tax Credit (EITC), federal military and civil service retirement, unemployment compensation, payments to disabled veterans, and farm price supports.

Defense and international spending, one of the largest components of this part of the budget, accounted for more than 10 percent of GDP 50 years ago and again at the height of the Vietnam War before falling to less than 5 percent 30 years ago and as low as 3 percent at the end of the 1990s (see Figure 1-5B). In 2008, as the United States was fighting wars in Iraq and Afghanistan, it had risen to just over 4 percent of GDP.

Because spending for federal programs other than the three large entitlements grew less rapidly than the U.S. economy from the early 1960s to 2008, the federal government was able to keep taxes stable and hold its debt in a sustainable range as a proportion of GDP. In other words, the high growth rate of the large entitlement programs for retirement and health over a long interval was offset by slower growth of spending for defense and some other programs. From 2008 on, however, it is hard to imagine how the anticipated continued growth of the large entitlements could be offset by further relative reductions in other spending. The large entitlements have grown even larger, and the smaller programs are now so small as a group that even eliminating them would not yield sufficient savings to offset future growth of the larger ones.

The government paid a net $253 billion in interest in fiscal 2008—the cost of servicing its debt less some interest earnings. This interest is paid to investors in U.S. Treasury bonds and other U.S. Treasury securities. The outstanding volume of the nation's publicly held debt was $5.8 trillion at the end of 2008 and reached $7.6 trillion a year later. The interest total

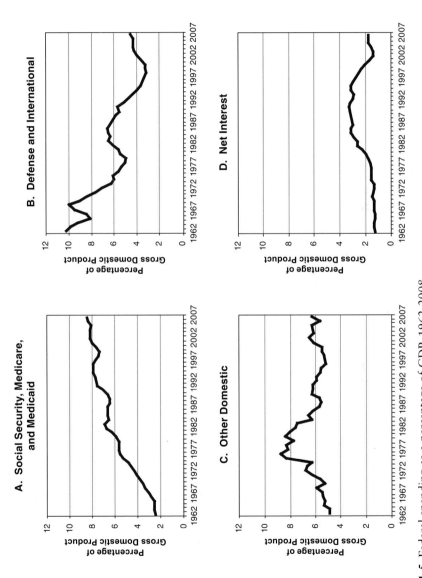

FIGURE 1-5 Federal spending as a percentage of GDP, 1962-2008.
SOURCE: Data from U.S. Office of Management and Budget (2009c:Tables 1.2, 3.1, 8.4, 8.5, and 8.7).

excludes interest income from debt held by federal trust funds, like Social Security; see Figure 1-5D.

In 2008, the government collected just over $2.5 trillion in revenues—equal to 17.7 percent of GDP, or about $8,100 per person. For almost three decades, two sources have accounted for about 80 percent of the money the federal government takes in: the individual income tax, which brought in more than $1.1 trillion in fiscal 2008, and social insurance (payroll) taxes, which brought in $900 billion in that year. Social insurance taxes are dominated by the 15.3 percent payroll tax that workers and their employers pay for Social Security and the Medicare Hospital Insurance programs. For most workers, in fact, social insurance taxes are higher than income taxes (Congressional Budget Office, 2007a). Corporate income taxes accounted for about $300 billion of the government's revenues in fiscal 2008. The remaining $170 billion came from excise taxes on gasoline, alcohol, tobacco, airline tickets, and other products and services; estate and gift taxes; customs duties; and miscellaneous receipts (chiefly the earnings of the Federal Reserve System); see Figure 1-6.

Because federal revenues fell far short of the $3 trillion in federal outlays in fiscal 2008, the government covered the gap by borrowing[3]—the "exploded" wedge in Figure 1-6. The deficit of $459 billion in that year amounted to 15 percent of total outlays and slightly more than 3 percent of GDP. On a per-person basis, it came to about $1,500 for each U.S. resident in 2008. However, the following year, as spending surged and revenues fell during the economic downturn, both borrowing and the debt increased significantly.

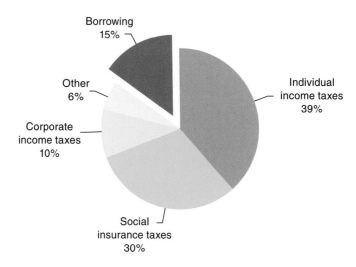

FIGURE 1-6 Federal revenues and borrowing in fiscal 2008.

Revenues, as a percentage of the economy, have stayed relatively constant since 1978. In fact, revenues have been remarkably stable in these terms over the past 40 years, never falling below 17 percent of GDP and only once (in 2000) exceeding 20 percent of GDP, despite many changes in tax policy and economic ups and downs. Missing from most discussion and representations of revenues is "tax expenditures," revenues not received; see Box 1-5.

The downturn that began in 2008 has at least temporarily caused major changes in both spending and revenues, especially for fiscal 2009. Spending rose sharply as the federal government stepped in to stabilize the financial sector and stimulate the economy. As incomes and business profits fell, so did revenues. The resulting very large increase in the deficit was financed with additional borrowing.

Few economic experts would forgo strictly temporary increases in federal spending, deficits, and debt in an economic downturn as severe as this one. Such deficits are countercyclical—they help moderate the societal effects of a recession that might otherwise be far harsher, and they may speed

---

BOX 1-5
Tax Expenditures

An invisible component of charts like Figure 1-6—because no one has figured out how to depict negative slices of pie—is tax expenditures. Also dubbed tax breaks, preferences, or loopholes, "tax expenditures" refer to departures from normal tax law that favor certain types of income or economic activity. Tax expenditures reduce the amount of money that the government collects from specified sources. Analysts debate how best to measure tax expenditures, but one commonly used measure is the annual loss of revenue resulting from each provision (assuming other parts of the current tax code are unchanged).

The Joint Committee on Taxation (2008a) lists more than 200 tax expenditures, led by preferential rates on dividends and capital gains ($150 billion in 2008), favorable treatment of pensions and other retirement plans ($120 billion), the exclusion of employer contributions to health insurance and similar plans ($117 billion), the deductibility of mortgage interest on owner-occupied housing ($67 billion), and the deductibility of state and local income, sales, and property taxes ($48 billion). This list of the top five tax expenditures omits the tax rebates paid as part of the economic stimulus effort, which the Joint Committee estimated at $95 billion in 2008, because those rebates are not a permanent feature of the tax code. Although tax expenditures reduce federal revenues and thus make government's role appear smaller by that measure, they have the same effect on the deficit as would equivalent spending for the same activities. If they were classified as federal spending instead of tax benefits, federal expenditures would have been about 30 percent higher in 2006 than OMB reported—slightly over 26 percent of GDP instead of 20.3 percent (Burman, Toder, and Geissler, 2008).

recovery. The long-term problem with such widely accepted temporary deficits during a short-term downturn is that they add to the accumulated debt. As two prominent economists have noted: "[E]ven if the recovery occurs as projected and the stimulus package is allowed to expire, the country will face the highest debt-to-GDP ratio in 50 years and an increasingly unsustainable and urgent fiscal problem" (Auerbach and Gale, 2009:13).

Interest rates on U.S. Treasury bonds fell dramatically during the downturn. This may indicate that buyers of federal debt do not as yet perceive a significant risk of a future explicit default or an implicit default through inflation. As many analysts have noted, the confidence that investors have in the strength of the U.S. economy and its ability to manage its fiscal affairs enables it to borrow in its own currency, and at lower rates than other countries in comparable circumstances. However, investors' confidence could falter as the government's fiscal outlook worsens. The mere fact that a larger share of the budget must be dedicated to debt service increases the risk that, at any time, if investors demanded sharply higher interest returns, interest spending could become a substantially larger (and obligatory) share of federal spending. Larger interest payments to investors both in the United States and abroad would quickly increase the deficit. To offset such an outcome would require either painful cuts in other spending or increases in revenue.

How the Nation Got Here

How did the United States get into this situation? Some critics blame policy choices made during the George W. Bush administration, especially the tax cuts of 2001 and 2003 and the expansion of Medicare to cover prescription drugs. Those tax cuts significantly increased deficits, and their indefinite extension for people with incomes below $250,000—as proposed by President Obama and assumed in the committee's study baseline—would increase annual deficits beyond what they would otherwise be over the next decade by an average of 1.3 percent of GDP.[4] Although those policy choices made the long-run fiscal outlook worse, the roots of the problem go deeper and carry no particular political brand.

The three large entitlements whose projected growth is largely responsible for the budget's unsustainable course are part of a major expansion of the federal government's commitments to provide income support and health insurance to the old and the disabled. This expansion has roughly paralleled similar social program growth in other affluent countries. These and other federal programs help limit income inequality and prevent severe hardship for millions; for those with more personal resources, they supplement those resources, reducing uncertainty and the risk of personal financial catastrophe.[5] They represent open-ended promises to future generations.

For both Social Security and Medicare, the primary sources of revenue for these programs grow with the economy, but the benefits grow with the size of the eligible population and other factors. Although the intention was—and is—to finance both programs in part from dedicated sources, the structure of both Social Security and Medicare creates the opportunity for benefits to outrun revenues (for details of the program structure and operations, see Chapters 5 and 6; see also Oberlander, 2003). As discussed above, the changing age structure of the population means that for at least the next two decades a smaller workforce will be supporting a growing retired population.

The growth of health care costs at a faster rate than the growth of the economy for a long period is another factor causing federal spending for Medicare, as well as other federal health care spending, to outpace dedicated revenue sources, including payroll taxes and premiums. As discussed in Chapter 5, the upward growth of Medicare costs has been driven largely by a broad dynamic that has caused all health care costs to rise faster than GDP over most of the last three decades—not primarily because more people were receiving care but mainly because on average the intensity and quality of care have increased. The same is true of spending for Medicaid, but this program does not have a dedicated revenue source.

Looking forward, it is difficult to quantify how much of the mismatch between projected spending and dedicated revenues for Social Security and Medicare is attributable to initial design, how much to subsequent expansion and other program changes, and how much to changing demographic and economic forecasts. In any case, their costs now far exceed early estimates. Medicare and Medicaid costs have grown at a rate similar to that of all health spending, which has been substantially faster than that of the economy. For example, when Medicare was enacted in 1965, it was then estimated to cost $3 billion a year (about $20 billion in 2008 dollars). In 2008, net outlays for a much-expanded Medicare program approached $400 billion. Tax expenditures for employer-provided health benefits have fueled the growth and generosity of private insurance plans, adding to the rising total of federal subsidies for health while reducing revenues.[6] And medical science has advanced to provide far better, but also far more costly, treatments and services. Given that Social Security and Medicare were known to be structured in a way that allowed their costs to grow faster than tax revenues, the difficult question is why policy makers have been so slow to address their lack of sustainability. Initially, unintentional underestimates of what Social Security and Medicare would cost may have set the stage for later underfunding of those long-term commitments. Yet continuing warnings of underfunding or shortfalls have been discounted or ignored.

Even in 2000, when the budget was in surplus and many were actually concerned about the rate at which the federal debt was being reduced, budget analysts warned of pitfalls ahead; the budget was already on an unsustainable path, with health and Social Security costs rising steeply outside the 10-year window conventionally used to assess the budget effects of policies (Congressional Budget Office, 2000; U.S. Office of Management and Budget, 2000). Since then, a succession of reports not only repeated the warning, but also outlined possible solutions to the looming problem (see, e.g., Rivlin and Sawhill, 2004). While the Social Security and Medicare program actuaries have projected and warned about shortfalls for a long time, such exercises for the whole budget were rarely done until about 20 years ago. The National Economic Commission, formed by the President and Congress in 1987 and reporting in 1989, was perhaps the first in a series of high-level independent bodies to call attention to the seriousness of the long-term budget challenge. Its findings were largely ignored. It was followed in 1994 by the Kerry-Danforth Commission, which also foresaw a long-term budget crisis. Kerry-Danforth, for example, concluded that, absent reforms, spending on five programs alone—Social Security, Medicare, Medicaid, and federal civilian and military pensions—would exceed federal revenues by 2030. However, its members could not agree on "any proposal to reform a system that it had in its own report concluded was 'unsustainable'" (Peterson, 2004:124).

CBO made its first long-term projections of the federal budget in 1996. Looking out to 2050, CBO noted that the expected increase in the number of beneficiaries of federal programs for the elderly and a slowing in the rate of growth of the labor force—combined with the anticipated growth in the per-person cost of Medicare—would put enormous pressure on the budget. Its report (Congressional Budget Office, 1996:xxii) said that if those pressures were not dealt with by reducing spending or increasing taxes, mounting deficits could seriously erode future economic growth. At about the same time, OMB published its first long-term projections. The fiscal 1998 budget (U.S. Office of Management and Budget, 1997:21) noted: "Despite the improvement in the outlook after the passage of OBRA [President Clinton's economic plan in 1993], serious long-run problems remain. Beginning around the year 2010 and continuing throughout the next several decades, the deficit would rise [under current policies], eventually reaching unsustainable levels."

A fundamental obstacle to dealing with the nation's long-term fiscal problem is that all solutions are painful. Thus, leaders who advocate them may well be voted out of office, especially if the voters are not well informed about the problem. Poorly informed voters are vulnerable to demagoguery, such as: (1) there is no long-run problem that cannot be solved by economic growth or immigration; (2) solving it through growth is possible only if you avoid any tax increases; and (3) any cut in promised benefits or increase in taxes will cause unacceptable suffering. These claims ignore the facts that one can get a long way to a solution by reducing the rate of growth of benefits, rather than cutting them outright, by raising taxes, or with a judicious mix of benefit reductions and revenue increases. That is, as detailed in Chapters 4-9, there are several possible ways to solve the nation's long-term fiscal problem that are less drastic than sometimes suggested, although it is important to emphasize that none is pain free.

It is generally assumed that electorates always prefer a combination of higher spending and lower taxes. Survey results and other evidence suggest a more complicated pattern of thinking (Modigliani and Modigliani, 1987; Schultze, 1992). Most Americans say that their taxes are too high (52 percent in a 2009 Gallup survey), although this proportion is lower than two or three decades ago. In a 2008 Pew survey, cutting middle-class income taxes was ranked 15th in importance in a list of 20 issues, although this survey was conducted prior to the current major recession. Another 2008 survey (by CBS and the *New York Times*) found that the public appears evenly split (43 percent to 43 percent) between those who favor a larger government that offers more services and those who favor a smaller government that offers fewer services. Other research shows that Americans object more to how their federal tax dollars are spent than to how much they pay (Bowman, 2009). Perhaps public opinion constrains leaders from acting unless or until the wolf is at the door, push comes to shove, or Scylla meets Charybdis (Weaver, 1986). Some observers have likened the lack of forceful action to address the long-term fiscal imbalance to a similar lack of forceful action in other major policy areas, such as climate change. Both the fiscal and climate problems exemplify a class of challenges that have enormous long-term cost—but pose no immediate pain—for the nation's welfare and people's way of living.

In addition to the dynamics of politics in a democracy, particular elements of the federal government's policy-making process seemingly work against a focus on solving the long-term problem. The reasons for this are several, including natural limits on rational behavior and the normal incentives facing decision makers, especially elected officials. In principle, a better-informed and integrated decision-making process can help overcome these natural limits. But, expert observers have not found that a substantial increase in information and analysis available to policy makers has had a demonstrable effect to date on the quality of budget decisions (Joyce, 2008). Reforming the budget process may help focus attention on long-term consequences of today's actions, thereby improving incentives for early action. Such options are discussed in Chapter 10.

Consequences of Inaction

One reason it has been relatively easy for most policy makers and the public to ignore the nation's fiscal problem is that, to date, the United States has had no difficulty borrowing to finance current spending. And borrowing is not necessarily a bad thing, any more than when a family takes out a mortgage in order to purchase a home. However, more resources spent to pay interest on debt means fewer resources available for other uses. And, borrowing when there will not be sufficient income in the future to repay debt is a serious problem. If higher federal debt and debt service squeeze other spending, then the federal government will be able to deliver less for a given level of taxation, perhaps leading more people to conclude that they are getting too little benefit for their taxes.

Political incentives for additional borrowing could change quickly if financial markets began to penalize the United States for failing to put its fiscal house in order. And because the recent economic downturn has been worldwide, all interest rates have trended down, while investors have favored U.S. Treasury securities as a perceived safer haven for their money than other countries' debt. This situation has reduced the government's debt service cost. Moreover, because the United States borrows in its own currency, it need not worry, as other nations do, that it may be punished by having to repay in a currency that has become stronger relative to its own.

However, if investors become less certain of full repayment or believe that the country is pursuing an inflationary course that would allow it to repay the debt with devalued dollars, they could begin to charge a "risk premium" on U.S. Treasury securities. That could happen suddenly in a confidence crisis and ensuing financial shock. The United States would be acutely vulnerable to such a crisis because it has to continually refinance its current debt. (The United States rolls over more than one-third of its marketable debt every year before raising a new dollar of borrowing; see U.S. Department of the Treasury, 2009; also see Table F-5 in Appendix F.)

There is precedent for a financial disruption first contributing to large, chronic deficits and then in some cases contributing to the loss of investor confidence and even to a default on a nation's debt (Reinhart and Rogoff, 2009). The unique position of the United States—because of its economic dominance and the dominant role of the dollar internationally—make it difficult to extrapolate from the experience of other nations in estimating the risk or timing of a financial crisis arising from failure to address the projected U.S. fiscal imbalance. However, as many analysts have observed, there is a risk that the nation's status as a world "reserve currency" could be damaged by deterioration of its economic performance arising from a chronic fiscal imbalance (Auerbach and Gale, 2009; Friedman, 1988).

Given the lack of precedent for such a trajectory for a country like the United States, one might get better information on possible effects if Japan or a major European country had a crisis first, but waiting for that to happen is neither reasonable nor practical. A provocative paper even before the current downturn asked whether the country was bankrupt (Kotlikoff,

2006). The paper's answer was "yes" because all governments must satisfy a long-run budget constraint and the United States has made promises that it cannot keep. Its "creditors" (defined broadly as those who work and pay taxes, not just bondholders), will eventually balk—by refusing to lend money, refusing to work, or even emigrating. At that point, the government would have either to cut back from its promises, raise taxes, or renege on its debt. It could do this outright or by stealth, that is, through inflation that reduces the real value of debt principal.

It is impossible to determine or forecast, based on history or the specifics of the fiscal challenge, at what level of debt financial markets will decide that there is an increased risk that debt will not be fully repaid (or repaid in greatly inflated dollars) and react by demanding higher interest rates. Although the credit crisis that began in August 2007 and became a worldwide downturn in 2008 has not yet increased interest rates on U.S. Treasury securities, it serves as a sobering reminder that confidence is a fragile thing (Rubin et al., 2004). Auerbach and Gale (2009) note that a bleaker fiscal outlook already is affecting market assessments of U.S. government debt. By one measure, the implied probability of default rose from under 1 percent before September 2008 to almost 8 percent in early 2009 before declining again. Such a fluctuation illustrates how quickly financial markets could react in the future, triggering a possible spiral of rising federal interest spending and pressures to either reduce noninterest spending or increase revenues, possibly at a time when economic conditions would make these choices even more difficult than under "ordinary" circumstances.

Increased debt decreases U.S. wealth both by depressing the growth of the nation's capital stock and increasing its liability to foreigners. Although the ability of the U.S. government to draw on foreign saving reduces any immediate negative effects of deficits on GDP growth, it also means that more of the income generated by that growth must be transferred abroad in the form of interest and dividends. Bergsten (2009b) notes the contribution that larger budget deficits are making to a projected rise in the broader measure of debt (both public and private borrowings) that the United States owes to investors abroad. He cites as credible a projection that by 2030 the United States would be "transferring a full seven percent ($2.5 trillion) of its entire economic output to foreigners every year in order to service its external debt" (Cline, 2009). Bergsten (2009b) also projects that large budget deficits by 2030 will drive long-term interest rates up by 2.5 percentage points. Even if investors at home and abroad remain confident about buying and holding U.S. Treasury debt, large deficits and debt can have a corrosive effect. And even without a crisis of confidence in the ability of the United States to manage its fiscal problem, chronic large deficits erode the growth of future living standards by reducing national savings, thereby slowing the accumulation of wealth (see Congressional Budget Office, 2005b).

Because economic models are bounded by historical experience, they struggle to illustrate the consequences of deficits and debts that are "off the charts." However, one such exercise vividly demonstrates what the nation is facing. In response to a special request, the Congressional Budget Office (2008g) attempted to gauge what might happen to the economy if federal debt continued to climb. Answering the question meant departing from CBO's (and other organizations') standard practice of using mainstream, "sustainable" economic assumptions in order to analyze inherently unsustainable policies. The CBO analysis concluded that debt would drain funds from the nation's pool of savings, reduce investment in the domestic capital stock and in foreign assets, and cause real interest rates to rise. CBO gauged effects on the economy using gross national product (GNP) per person, which averaged about $45,000 in 2007.[7] The results suggested that rising deficits would cause real GNP per person to stop growing in the late 2040s, sinking from a peak of nearly $70,000 (in 2007 dollars) to about $55,000 in 2060. That is, the United States would begin to become a markedly less wealthy country. The CBO projections ended after 2060 because the model simply could not continue to compute such deterioration. Of course, a financial crisis might come well before that date. CBO noted that simply hiking income tax rates to cover projected spending would not forestall this deterioration because extremely high income tax rates would seriously distort work incentives and hobble economic growth.[8]

Can the country grow its way out of the problem? Some people have suggested that future increases in wealth will allow the United States to meet growing public needs and still have enough left for increased private consumption. A sober analysis of recent fiscal history offers little basis for that view. One reason is that labor force growth, a major driver of GDP, has slowed and will continue to slow. The annual rate of growth in the labor force decreased from an average of about 2.1 percent during the 1970s and 1980s to about 1.1 percent from 1990 to 2008. The 2009 report of the Social Security Trustees (Social Security Administration, 2009d:98) projects further slowing of labor force growth, resulting from slower growth in the working-age population as the baby-boom generation reaches retirement and the succeeding smaller cohorts reach working age. Under the Trustees' intermediate assumptions, the U.S. labor force is projected to increase by about 0.7 percent per year, on average, through 2018. Thereafter, it is projected to increase still more slowly, at an average of 0.5 percent a year, from 2018 to 2050, and 0.4 percent over the remainder of the 75-year projection period. Wages subject to Social Security taxes are projected to fall from 38.5 percent of GDP in 2008 to 33.1 percent in 2083, in part because of a projected increase of nontaxable employer-provided benefits as a share of total compensation (Congressional Budget Office, 2009e; Lavery, 2009). With a smaller part of the population working and paying taxes, even if productivity were to increase at roughly the same rate it has in the past 40 years, real GDP growth—which averaged 3 percent annually from 1967 to 2007—would slow. Under the Trustees' intermediate assumptions, real GDP is projected to grow 2.4 percent annually through 2018, and more slowly thereafter, reflecting slower labor force growth (Social Security Administration, 2009d:100). Personal income and federal revenue growth also would slow as a direct result.

Some people have argued that an increase in immigration can be a solution. Because labor force growth is a major driver of GDP, one way to increase both is to admit more of those seeking to live and work here. U.S. immigration—roughly 1 million a year—has been high in comparison with most European countries and Japan. This immigration has helped keep the U.S. working-age population proportionately higher than in those countries, where high proportions of elderly people must count on a declining fraction of the population of working age to pay for services. In the future, larger numbers of immigrants—especially skilled workers—could boost the working portion of the U.S. population, helping to pay for benefits to the elderly. However, immigrants grow old, too, so it would be a temporary "solution." In fact, to offset slowing labor force growth, immigration rates would have to rise substantially. In the past, immigration has been found to have a small net positive impact on U.S. economic activity, but the effect is so modest that even if immigration doubled or tripled from the current rate, it would make only a small long-term contribution to incomes and therefore to federal revenues (see Congressional Budget Office, 2005a:3; Council of Economic Advisers, 2007; National Research Council, 1997).[9]

Not only is there no easy way out of the nation's fiscal problems, but the challenge now facing the United States is arguably worse than standard analyses suggest. Even as questions are raised about the sustainability of federal retirement and medical insurance programs, many people are concerned about the adequacy of those commitments. The 2009 debate over health reform legislation has highlighted the number of people who risk financial disaster because they lack adequate health insurance. The downturn has highlighted the exposure of many households to financial risk. Many baby boomers have not provided adequately for their own retirement, and recent drops in home and stock values have wiped out part of what they had saved (Lusardi and Mitchell, 2007). Private savings, which equaled 10.4 percent of national income in 1984, had become negative by 2006, even before the downturn (Conley, 2009): The decline in U.S. private savings has been partly offset by foreign purchases of U.S. debt.

A decline in private savings means that many households have a smaller savings cushion against loss of income or unexpected expenses, and therefore are potentially more dependent on government or private charities for financial help in these circumstances. Thus, even as questions are raised

about the sustainability of federal retirement and medical insurance programs, many are pressing to supplement or expand those commitments.

There is no escape from the arithmetic of the long-term fiscal challenge. No one can estimate with any accuracy the risk of any crisis in the
financing of the federal government, nor when any such crisis might occur.
The committee considers it unlikely the federal government would default
outright on its debt. Nor does it believe it likely that the United States
would pursue a policy of deliberately inflating its currency to reduce the
real cost of repaying debt. Such a policy, in any case, would not be sufficient
by itself to escape the debt obligation, partly because much of the debt is
short term or indexed for inflation and partly because benefits of the three
biggest entitlement programs rise in tandem with inflation. The greater risk
of a sudden government fiscal crisis caused by rising interest rates is that the
nation would be forced to respond precipitously. A rushed, ill-considered
budget response to the threat of a debt crisis might deprive people of needed
public services or hobble the economy for many years. The damage to the
country's residents would be immediate, but the damage to the nation's
credibility and ability to manage its finances could be profound and long
lasting. Even if the United States is able to avoid a full-blown financial crisis, it would increasingly find its options narrowed as it juggled competing
demands. Policy makers would lose flexibility to cope with such events as
recession, natural disaster, war, or terrorist attack.

THE OPPORTUNITY TO ACT

Setting aside other priorities to address a seemingly distant, abstract
fiscal challenge is asking a great deal of both leaders and the public. Both
groups already must deal with many urgent matters. Yet the costs of inac-
tion are potentially enormous. In a sense, all of the other goals that people
value and pursue through government already are hostage to finding a
politically feasible way to address the looming fiscal challenge.

The committee believes that this report will be helpful to both the
public and the nation's leaders in addressing the fiscal challenge through a
distinctive approach:

- *We present a range of possible paths rather than a single solution.* Because current policies cannot be sustained, Americans
  and their leaders must find a way to construct a sustainable budget. People hold many views on critical policy issues that reflect
  sharp differences in values and interests: These must be considered
  and balanced before the nation can find such a sustainable way.
  The committee's paths can be a starting point for dialogue and
  compromise.

- *We present a clear set of standards that anyone can apply to assess how close any given set of budget proposals comes to achieving sustainability.* All of the paths to sustainability involve tough choices—most likely requiring new limits on what the government will pay for and possibly requiring new ways to pay for programs that stay in the budget. By presenting some of the major building blocks of a sustainable budget and estimates of their budget effects, the report provides a starting point for practical choices.
- *We recognize that deeply held (and at times, conflicting) values are the lenses through which different people will study and choose among the alternatives.* Because it is so difficult to achieve and maintain a sustainable budget, the committee believes that any effort that hopes to succeed must be rooted in the values of fairness, economic opportunity, and personal and family security that people hold dear.
- *The committee recognizes that prospects for addressing the U.S. fiscal challenge are intertwined with those of other nations around the globe.* The many economic and financial ties between the United States and the rest of the world are now reinforced by increased dependence on foreign investors to fund the nation's growing national debt. The same demographic trends and environmental challenges that contribute to budget pressures in the United States are affecting many other countries and may require cooperative solutions.

The economic downturn has complicated the fiscal challenge. Right now the nation faces an extraordinary clash between demands for expanded government and the inconvenient reality that commitments already made are expected to consume all the available revenues and then some. Reconciling those demands for more with the need to deliver less will require political creativity and compromise. However, the committee believes that reasonable options are still available if action is taken forcefully and soon.

It would be wise to take painful steps now to avoid more painful ones later on. These steps should distribute the required sacrifices fairly and give people affected by benefit changes ample notice so they can adjust their financial plans accordingly. The remainder of this report attempts to spell out some ways that this can be done.

NOTES

1. The cumulative effect of the larger near-term deficits implied by CBO's August revision to its 10-year baseline would be to increase the estimate of debt-to-GDP ratio in 2019 by about 7 percentage points relative to that resulting from the baseline estimates used

in the study. Throughout the report, dollars are nominal rather than adjusted for inflation, budget amounts expressed as percentages of GDP are relative to estimates of GDP in the year referenced, and years refer to federal fiscal years (ending September 30 of the calendar year) unless otherwise noted.

2. Because of its effect relative to tax provisions, lower inflation reduces tax collections in real terms. This effect is partially offset, however, because lower inflation reduces automatic cost-of-living adjustments in some federal spending programs, such as Social Security.

3. The federal government's annual borrowing needs do not exactly match the deficit or surplus in the same year. In fiscal 2008, for example, the government borrowed $768 billion in 2008 although the deficit was just $455 billion. Of the seeming discrepancy of $313 billion, $300 billion went to a special "Supplementary Asset Program" designed to soak up excess liquidity at the Federal Reserve System in extraordinary circumstances. Most of the rest went to the financing accounts established to extend direct loans, chiefly student loans. For details, see U.S. Department of the Treasury (2008:Table 6). The special interventions associated with the downturn, including assistance to Fannie Mae and Freddie Mac in conservatorship and some transactions of the Treasury Asset Relief Program (TARP) in 2009 and beyond, including cash repayments that reduce borrowing needs, will create even larger temporary differences between net borrowing and the deficits recorded in the same years.

4. The effect on revenues of extending the 2001 and 2003 tax cuts (along with indexation after 2009 of the Alternative Minimum Tax and the extension of other, much smaller expiring provisions) beyond their current legal expiration has been calculated by the Congressional Budget Office (2009e:6; Table 2-1) by comparing revenue estimates for 2020 and other selected years to 2080. In 2020, CBO estimates, revenues would be reduced from $20.3 trillion to $18.6 trillion.

5. Over the past century or so, industrial societies have dedicated a growing share of their growing wealth to social protection of vulnerable populations. Affluent governments now spend more on social programs than at any time in history (Organisation for Economic Co-operation and Development, 2008a). Public commitments to provide minimum financial support and services to the most vulnerable people in a country, sometimes termed the "social safety net," supplement or in some cases replace traditional family and community responsibilities, which have been weakened with changes in family structure related to economic modernization and other social changes. Some conservatives argue that, by substituting for personal responsibility, programs aimed at helping the poorest families have sometimes weakened family structure.

6. The exclusion of employer contributions to health premiums and care for their employees is now the single largest tax expenditure, as measured by the revenue that would be collected if this provision were ignored in calculating employer taxes. It is estimated to have reduced federal income tax revenue in 2008 by at least $117 billion (Joint Committee on Taxation, 2008a).

7. For these analyses, GNP is more useful than GDP, because GNP measures net income of residents in the United States after deducting payments to foreigners.

8. For details of the CBO analysis, including estimates of what would happen by offsetting this spending growth entirely through cuts in other programs, see Congressional Budget Office (2008g).

9. Similarly, a sensitivity analysis for the Social Security Trustees shows that if immigration were one-third higher in the future than in their standard projection, the projected negative balance of the trust fund after 75 years would be reduced from −2.00 to −1.81 percent of taxable payroll (Social Security Administration, 2009d).

2

Framing the Choices

Having recognized the magnitude of the long-term fiscal challenge, how can one sort through alternatives for constructing a sustainable federal budget? A sustainable budget, as noted in Chapter 1, must align revenues and spending over a long time horizon. To guide one's thinking about how to put today's federal budget on a sustainable path, this chapter presents a framework for the inevitable hard choices. The right framework—although it cannot by itself resolve fundamental differences—can be a basis for informed deliberation and decision making.

CONNECTING BUDGETS AND VALUES

A budget is a plan to use part of the nation's current and future economic resources to produce public benefits. Among other things, government spending produces goods and services whose benefits are widely shared and not easily divided—what economists call "public goods" or "collective goods" (Samuelson, 1954). National defense spending is a good example. Its benefits are shared by all and not divisible. Budgets also use taxation and spending to transfer resources from some groups to others. Examples are the use of revenues to support low-income families or to compensate wounded veterans. In political terms, the federal budget represents decisions about the use of national resources for public benefits and social objectives and decisions on how to collect the revenues to finance the planned spending. Even more broadly, a budget reflects how the proposed use of resources is expected to yield certain desirable outcomes—improvements in society and in people's lives. The essence—and difficulty—of budgeting is to trade off many desirable social goals against each other when resources are not unlimited. A "good" budget shows clearly whether there is a match between plans to spend and plans to pay for spending and whether the spending implied by current and proposed policies is sustainable.

In this report we insist that it is critical in assessing a budget to take the long view—to be concerned about future generations' opportunities and well-being. Because current policies as projected are not sustainable, either spending must be reduced or revenues must increase. Budgets quantify the priority given to every public objective, from the oldest and most basic, such as national security, to newer ones, such as environmental protection. Federal government responsibilities have expanded gradually over many years. The oldest federal functions included building interstate transportation networks and securing the nation's borders. For example, George Washington's administration built the lighthouse at Montauk Point in New York. The newest functions include protecting endangered species, reducing greenhouse gas emissions, and expanding broadband access.

Public priorities change over time. Although federal spending as a proportion of the nation's gross domestic product (GDP) was relatively stable from 1962 to 2008—increasing from about 19 percent to 20.5 percent—the distribution of spending by function changed dramatically. Social Security and health benefits, mainly to the poor and elderly, roughly tripled as a proportion of total spending, while the share going to defense and veterans fell from about one-half of the total to about one-fourth; see Figure 2-1.

Budget debates reflect fundamental differences: in people's values, interests, and beliefs; about questions of budget priorities or tradeoffs concerning the best allocation of resources among public goals; and on practical questions about the best way to use resources to advance agreed-on priorities.

People hold sharply differing views of what they want or need from government, what they believe government can deliver, and what role they believe government should have in the economy and other aspects of life. In general, people favor policies that they believe will benefit themselves, their families, others like themselves, and the society as a whole—whether "benefit" is seen largely in material or in other terms.

Logically and appropriately, differences in values, interests, and beliefs about government's role will lead people to widely different positions about what the budget should support and how. Differences in values, interests, and beliefs need to be recognized and at least partly reconciled in order to make long-range budget decisions. Fortunately, people who differ in their values and beliefs can and do often find common ground when it comes to practical solutions. In the next section we discuss the values that are most often reflected in budget debates. In the last section we consider practical concerns about how value preferences relate to budget choices.

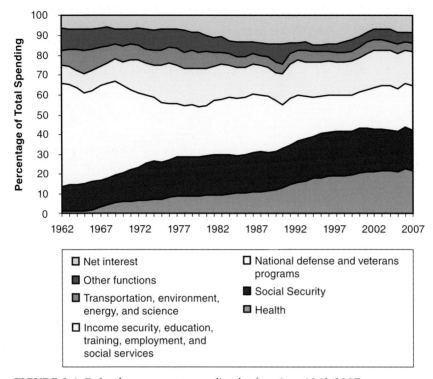

FIGURE 2-1 Federal government spending by function, 1962-2007.

VALUES AND BUDGET DECISIONS

The list of values that are applicable to assessing budgets is potentially long (see, e.g., Yankelovich, 1994). We consider five that have been most prominent in recent budget debates: (1) equity or fairness, (2) economic growth, (3) efficiency, (4) physical security, and (5) the size of government.

Fairness

For many people, the distribution of public burdens and benefits is a principal measure of social justice (see, e.g., Penner, 2004; Rawls, 2001). Of course, people disagree sharply on what is fair and, looking at the same budget, will disagree in their assessments of its fairness.

Budgets affect the distribution of private income and wealth. At various times in the nation's history and again in the past decade, many people have expressed concern about increases in U.S. income inequality and a lack of progress in reducing poverty (see, e.g., Piketty and Saez, 2004; Sherman et al., 2009; Smeeding, 2005). Budgets can affect the distribution of income in two ways: directly, by specifying how revenues will be collected from one income group and distributed to another; and indirectly, by incorporating policies that affect economic opportunities. Over time, for example, budgets that provide education and other basic services to economically disadvantaged people can increase their chances for solid jobs and productive lives and thereby reduce income inequality.

People do not agree on the extent to which governments should aid or tax different groups differently or act to increase opportunities for particular groups. Most people argue that, as a matter of fairness, the government should support people who are unable to support themselves, including the indigent elderly and children of poor families; however, people differ on what degree or scope of support is appropriate.

In their attitudes toward social spending—including programs such as Social Security, Medicare, and Medicaid—Americans have tried to reconcile conflicting concepts of fairness: one based on what people need and another based on what people deserve.[1] In trying to reconcile these two concepts, many people embrace a principle of "reciprocity," which says that people should not get something for nothing, but should get something if they "play by the rules" (Yankelovich, 1994).

Another dimension of fairness concerns the distribution of public burdens and benefits across generations. It is difficult to measure how budgets redistribute costs and benefits from one generation to another. Many have argued, however, that the current federal budget—by failing to pay for current and expected obligations from current revenues—unfairly burdens future generations.[2]

Economic Growth

A budget should sustain and assist in expanding the nation's economy, the ultimate base of resources that are available both for personal consumption and investment and to fund public goods and services. Yet there is no consensus—among either economists or policy makers—about the best policies to advance this goal under any given set of economic circumstances.

Budget choices can have large influence on future economic growth. In principle, well-targeted public investments that accelerate development and the application of new technologies or that increase education levels lead to economic growth and higher incomes on average (Romer, 1986). However, governments may have difficulty determining in advance which investments will stimulate growth and which will not. On the revenue side, many people favor tax reductions as a policy to stimulate private investment and growth; others argue for a tax structure that encourages savings and rewards productive private investments; and still others would use higher revenues to reduce government deficits and increase national savings. In practice, the growth effects of different tax policies, like those of public investments, are uncertain and often in dispute.

The task of determining the differing implications for future growth of alternative revenue and spending policies raises a theoretical problem implicit in many budget debates. Some level of savings and investment (both public and private) is needed to ensure that the next generation is at least as well off as the present one. But the optimal balance of consumption and savings is unknown. A common view is that the United States needs a higher rate of savings and investment, both by governments and by private businesses and households, than has been the case in recent years.

Given how hard it is to estimate the effects of any given policy on economic growth, and therefore on the future income base for government revenues, most analysts recommend against simple or mechanical estimation (see, e.g., Kobes and Rohaly, 2002). The committee has followed this advice in its study. That is, we have neither adjusted our projections of future economic growth nor estimated future budget effects of changes in growth on the basis of changes in the mix of spending or the structure of revenues over time, even though modeling such relationships would be part of the ideal development of budget policy.

Efficiency

Although governments do not have a monopoly on inefficiency, many people believe that a good part of what government spends yields too little benefit to justify taking private resources for public purposes.[3] Government leaders and managers are always looking for ways to identify and eliminate waste and to replace ineffective programs with more effective ones; however, there is no line in the federal budget for "waste, fraud, and abuse." Instead, the task of improving government's effectiveness requires collecting information about alternative uses of funds and the results they yield, and shifting efforts to the most effective uses.

Although evidence on the relative efficacy of alternative policies and programs can help reduce some budget disagreements, such evidence is often lacking or, at best, limited. When even experts are uncertain about the relative effectiveness of different policies or programs, the best approach to budgeting and making other policy choices is to be flexible, to continually test policies against experience, and to remain open to new information about their efficacy. Rigorously evaluating what works can contribute to more efficient use of the public's dollars if the findings are applied to future budget choices and program reforms.

The federal government has historically used only a small fraction of its budget to evaluate the effectiveness of its programs, although in recent years agencies have invested more effort in finding better ways to measure their performance. Thus, information about program effectiveness is slowly improving. The Government Performance and Results Act of 1993 (GPRA) provided federal agencies with the legal framework for this strategic approach, the Obama Administration's 2010 budget calls for "establishing a comprehensive program and performance measurement system that shows how Federal programs link to agency and Government-wide goals" (U.S. Office of Management and Budget, 2009a:9).

In principle, this approach can lead to improved results. In practice, the goal of a performance-driven budget process remains elusive. The intense budget pressures of the looming deficits and debt are likely to put a premium on more efficient use of the public's resources. Possible reforms to reinforce a performance-driven budgeting approach are discussed in Chapter 10.

Security and Risk

Ensuring physical safety, including security from external attacks and internal disorder, is perhaps the oldest and most fundamental objective of national governments. People must be safe before they can pursue other values. The value of security often focuses attention on government's efforts to provide for national security and fight crime; but, viewed broadly, security can be a product of many policy choices, including those to provide the basic means of survival to people who cannot provide them for themselves. In the modern era, the most common view of government's responsibility for security has expanded to include responsibility to provide a minimum level of economic security to all. Even as the budget constraints have increased, many people and policy makers seek to expand health insurance coverage or other federal programs that protect households against financial shocks or economic losses—policy changes that would increase spending but provide greater income security to many people.

Size of Government

Debates about the size of government reflect both a basic value question and a practical one. They have been shorthand for disagreements about whether or not government can be a positive instrument to promote values of equality, freedom, and security (Madrick, 2009). However, government actions can either expand or limit freedom and choice, and the relationship between government's size and these values is quite complicated. Debates about the proper size or scope of government have also been shorthand for disagreements about government power and intrusiveness. On a practical level, size is also a question of how much spending the society is able or willing to pay for through current taxes or by borrowing.

The government's size is commonly measured by comparing the levels of federal government spending and taxes with the size of the economy, that is, as a percentage of GDP. By this measure, government (including state and local governments) is smaller in the United States than other affluent countries; see Figure 2-2. However, as discussed below, this is only a crude measure of government's reach and influence on society and the economy. For one thing, the U.S. federal government makes more use than many other countries of special provisions in the tax code (tax expenditures) that reduce revenues and do not add to spending but do enlarge the role of government, increase deficits, and may distort private choices (Minarik, 2010); this aspect of the budget is discussed more fully in Chapter 8.

As detailed in Chapter 1, the federal government is currently spending much more than it has in the past: even if substantial and difficult reductions are made in the rate of spending growth, spending will rise. A bigger federal government will have major implications for individuals, businesses, and state and local levels of government. This development will renew and intensify old debates about the proper size and reach of the federal government.

The government can also affect individual and business behavior outside of the budget in many ways—for example, through policies that protect personal privacy or regulate the operations of financial institutions. Such laws and mandates have the effect of increasing the role of the federal government, but without increasing federal revenues and spending. Health policy illustrates how similar objectives can be pursued either through or

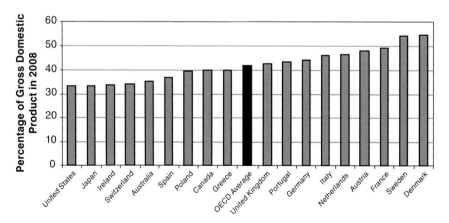

FIGURE 2-2 General government total tax and nontax receipts as a percentage of nominal GDP in 2008.

outside the budget: the two approaches may yield similar public benefits but with widely different effects on spending and revenues; see Box 2-1. Disagreements about which approach to take are not differences about the value of health or about providing access to better care, but about the best way to do so.

People who believe that equity or fairness gives people first claim on the money they earn (or inherit) often favor smaller government: they therefore require that a strong case be made before the government takes money, usually through taxes, for public goods and purposes. Although they may believe it is appropriate for government to help people who have no or limited capacity to take care of themselves, they may demand a high level of proof of need. People with a strong view of individual claims also often see social benefit in asking people to exercise more personal responsibility. This view leads them to argue for relatively less spending on many social programs. They also are likely to believe that high marginal tax rates discourage private investment and work effort. They stress the inefficiency

---

BOX 2-1
Health: An Example of Values and Choices

For some people, health policy is about basic value choices: the extent of government's responsibility for individuals' physical well-being and what constitutes fairness in treating people of different means who face similar health problems. However, most health policy debates focus on more practical questions, such as:

- How should the costs of health care be divided among individuals, their employers, and the government?
- How should essential treatment or care be defined and paid for?
- How should health care delivery be organized to reduce medical errors and save money?

Knowing how a person values health does not necessarily indicate that person's stand on specific policy questions, such as whether the government should spend more or less on health care relative to other goals, or how to pay for it.

If the choice is to increase spending for health, it can be done in various ways. Larger subsidies for health can be added to the budget and paid for by increased revenues or increased borrowing. Or tax subsidies can be provided to employees by allowing their employers to exclude health insurance coverage for them from their business's income, thus lowering their tax obligations. This is the equivalent of adding subsidies on the spending side of the budget, but it has the effect of reducing income tax revenues instead. Or the government may simply mandate that employers pay for their employees' health care, without offering a subsidy. All these options may have the same effect on health care access and health, but only the first would increase the government's direct spending on health.

and ineffectiveness of many spending programs. Moreover, they often argue that government programs impose a burden on the economy by increasing the cost of private investment and perhaps diverting resources to uses that do not contribute to growth. Therefore, in evaluating government spending proposals, they look for evidence that those programs produce benefits that at least exceed their direct costs (see Trenchard and Gordon, 1995).

On the other side are people who believe the government has a basic responsibility both to help individuals with limited capacities or opportunities and to foster a variety of public benefits, including building a society where more people can achieve their dreams. From this perspective, they tend to support government interventions to expand opportunity for personal economic and social achievement, as well as to shield people from events that can negate their efforts. This leads them, often, to support a larger and more robust government than those with different views. In defining a role for government social spending and regulation of private economic activity, they are more likely to emphasize flaws in the way markets function, leading perhaps to highly unequal incomes or to underproduction of public goods, such as training and basic research, needed for optimal growth. They view taxes as a worthwhile price to pay for increased collective benefits, including the opportunity to live in a just society (see Rawls, 2001).[4]

With regard to many federal responsibilities, people with relatively little confidence in the government's ability to spend or invest wisely favor reducing the government's role, as far as possible, to the basics—chiefly, defense and homeland security and environmental and public health protection when clearly justified. In contrast, people with more confidence in government's capacity to use resources wisely often argue that there are economic justifications and unfulfilled demands for public programs that cannot be met either privately or at a community level. They often believe that government is underinvesting in certain areas—notably education, basic research, and infrastructure—that they expect to have large future payoffs that will benefit both society broadly and many individuals.

Views of the proper size of government also affect views on revenue policy. People who believe taxes are a drag on the economy's efficiency or on individual and business incentives to work and invest generally favor low marginal tax rates and lower overall levels of taxation. Economists have tried to assess this contention. A recent analysis of many empirical studies finds no clear relationship and offers a variety of possible explanations; see Box 2-2. In contrast, people who put more emphasis on the tax system as a means to overcome some of the inequalities of wealth and unequal opportunity favor a progressive tax structure, that is, one with high marginal rates for upper-bracket incomes. They also tend to support a relatively higher overall level of taxes to finance the government programs they believe are appropriate.

BOX 2-2
Government Size and Economic Growth

The government's share of the economy varies widely, even among affluent nations. It has been widely assumed that if taxes are high and used to finance increased social spending, economic growth will slow. Economic theory generally posits that taxes impose a "dead weight" loss on the economy by discouraging productive effort and that the transfer of resources to poor and elderly people prevents their use for more productive purposes. The countervailing view is that government investments in education, infrastructure, and research and development will contribute to future economic growth.

Because levels of taxation and social spending vary widely from country to country, it is possible to empirically test the two views. In such a study, controlling statistically for other factors—such as the proportion of the population of working age—that might explain international variations in growth rates, Lindert (2003) found no clear relationship. In recent years, GDP grew as fast in countries with high tax-based social spending as in others.

Lindert also tried to determine why countries that tax and transfer one-third of national GDP have grown no more slowly than countries that devote only one-seventh of GDP to social transfers. He concluded that the keys to this puzzle include the following:

- High-budget welfare states choose a mix of taxes that are more pro-growth than the mix chosen in the United States and other relatively private-market countries of the Organisation for Economic Co-operation and Development (OECD).
- Universalist welfare states have adopted several policies that create strong incentives for young adults to work and obtain training.
- Government subsidies to early retirement bring only a tiny reduction in GDP, partly because the more expensive early retirement systems are designed to encourage the least productive employees to retire.
- Similarly, larger unemployment compensation programs have little effect on GDP because although they lower employment they also may get the least productive workers out of their jobs.
- Social spending, including education spending, often has a positive effect on GDP, even after weighing the effects of the taxes used to finance it.

Whatever the explanation, it appears that merely increasing the size of government through higher taxes and increased social spending does not necessarily reduce economic growth. Much depends on specific policy choices, such as the structure of the tax system and how social programs are designed.

In most cases, the larger size of other Organisation for Economic Co-operation and Development (OECD) country governments (as a percentage of GDP) reflects more comprehensive systems of publicly financed pension and health insurance programs. The apparently smaller public sector in the United States than in almost all other affluent countries, as measured by revenues, is consistent with its strong traditional preference for limited government. However, it also reflects a U.S. decision to support many public purposes by means of tax expenditures, which reduce revenues while extending government's reach.

VALUES AND PRACTICAL CHOICES

The intellectual journey from values, interests, and beliefs to budget choices can be winding and complicated. For example, some policies, if used effectively, can advance multiple goals: examples are education, health care, and the development of new technologies. Education programs have contributed to economic growth while also increasing opportunities for individual advancement. Near-universal public education has added significantly to U.S. economic growth, boosted incomes, and lowered inequality (Goldin and Katz, 2008). Increased access to good health care and public health programs that lead to communitywide improvements in health can have similarly broad effects (Bloom et al., 2001). Public investment that accelerates the development of new technologies that provide a high economic return can boost growth while advancing other important public goals. For example, investments in environmental technologies that seed new industries can provide future job growth while improving energy efficiency and reducing carbon emissions, two other policy objectives. But imprudent or wasteful public investments divert resources from more productive uses; and, quite often, it is uncertain in advance whether a particular investment will be productive or wasteful.

Revenue policies can similarly be analyzed for their likely effects on growth, equity and opportunity, and other values. Such analyses need to consider both the total tax burden for each income group and the extent to which tax provisions favor certain uses of income over others. Many people believe the federal government raises revenues in ways that unnecessarily burden the economy. For example, tax provisions that favor investments in some activities over others may distort private decisions from that which would be financially optimal. If the tax code favors more spending on housing, some people will buy more housing than they would without the tax incentive, perhaps diverting capital from more productive uses. Or if the income directed to savings is taxed at the same or a higher rate than income that is consumed, savings and investment will be lower than otherwise, leading to slower growth (see Chapter 8).

The number of goals people would like to see the government pursue, or pursue more vigorously, is long and seems always to be growing: helping end poverty; improving the justice system; providing more people with better education; fostering new technologies; exploring the universe; expanding access to high-quality health care; strengthening financial regulation; preparing for and responding to natural and human-caused disasters; fostering development abroad; and many more.

In many societies over recent decades, priorities have shifted from an emphasis on economic and physical security to subjective well-being, self-expression, and the quality of life. The wealth accumulated by advanced societies allows an unprecedented share of the population to grow up taking survival for granted. Using public opinion data, Yankelovich (1994) describes how affluence has changed people's priorities, a complicated evolution as Americans have tried to take advantage of the expanded choices that affluence brought them and find a balance with their continuing need for enduring commitments, such as family and community.

People who share common values may disagree on what role government should play in advancing those values. Conversely, because broad values do not dictate specific policy choices, people who have fundamental differences may sometimes agree on specific policies or programs. Still other differences—whether framed as value choices or not—may be driven by financial or other self-interest.

Many people are not comfortable with framing much of the policy debate about budgets as a choice between big and small government. The public's view tends to be pragmatic: Intervention in the economy is warranted when it works, otherwise not (Yankelovich, 1994). Notably, President Obama, in his inaugural address (2009), expressed this more pragmatic view: "The question we ask today is not whether our government is too big or too small, but whether it works—whether it helps families find jobs at a decent wage, care they can afford, a retirement that is dignified." Many people look at questions of the size of government and government programs in this practical way.

The committee proposes, in the same spirit, that people now give priority to finding practical ways to put the budget on a sustainable course. This does not mean that deeply held values and beliefs need be set aside, only that everyone recognize that agreement on prompt, prudent corrective action is needed soon to avoid an outcome that could harm everyone.

NOTES

1. Debates about social insurance programs are also about such practical questions as whether government or individuals are better managers of financial risk. Such questions illustrate the blending of value and practical questions in budget and policy debates.
2. One attempt to measure intergenerational fairness, known as generational budget accounting, is especially relevant to any long-term analysis of the federal budget, but it is methodologically and conceptually challenging. A seminal work by Auerbach et al. (1991) presented this approach to analyzing budgets (see also Gokhale and Smetters, 2003). The Congressional Budget Office (1995) has cautioned that generational accounting requires many debatable assumptions. One central technical challenge of generational

accounting is the rate that is assumed for discounting future costs and benefits (see Nordhaus, 2009:Ch. 9): the higher the assumed discount rate, the less important are the effects of today's spending and borrowing for future generations.

3. Government policies also can have a major influence on the efficiency with which private resources are used. A major example is discussed in Chapter 5: one goal of health care reform is to improve the use of resources in the broader health care system. However, this aspect of efficiency is not a major focus here.

4. Opinions on whether government's role should be bigger or smaller often vary with personal circumstances. For example, a 2009 survey measuring attitudes about risk found that those who had experienced a financial shock or had relatively few assets not only expressed more financial insecurity but were much more likely to believe that their financial well-being depended on events mostly out of their control rather than on their own actions. Not surprisingly, they also were more disposed toward collective, government-sponsored interventions to provide financial security (Allstate/*National Journal* Heartland Monitor, reported in Brownstein, 2009).

3

Fiscal Prudence

Whatever people's values and choices about government and the budget, in the long run many widely shared policy goals that require federal spending will be unattainable if the budget is not on a sustainable path. It will be difficult to simply continue the programs that people have come to expect, let alone allow sufficient flexibility for future generations to develop new policies for a changing world. In this chapter we offer a first step toward dealing with the country's fiscal challenge by specifying concrete and usable tests that any proposed budget must meet to move toward sustainability in a prudent manner.

The committee's members embody a range of disciplinary perspectives and practical experience in dealing with the federal budget. We hold quite varied views of the nation's priorities and how best to achieve them, including the proper size and role of government. We do not necessarily agree, for example, about the extent to which the federal budget ought to aim at expanding individual responsibility and choice or at promoting economic security; whether the nation should limit the use of carbon fuels or eschew such limits to facilitate economic growth; or how much to emphasize national security concerns versus expanding education and other programs that may promote equality of economic and social opportunity. What the committee members do agree on is the need for a set of straightforward criteria that anyone can use to assess the fiscal responsibility of any budget proposal for the overall federal budget from a long-term perspective.

In its work, the committee sought to apply these criteria to the development of an illustrative set of policy and budget scenarios that demonstrate several possible paths to sustainability. These scenarios are detailed in

Chapter 9. The criteria also can be applied to the President's budget or any alternative set of budget proposals, as discussed in Chapter 11.

LIMITING THE GROWTH OF FEDERAL DEBT

In consequence of our concerns about the current trajectory of the federal budget, the committee believes the overriding goal of long-term budget policy should be to slow the rate of future accumulation of the federal public debt—through some combination of revenue increases and spending restraints—so that such debt first ceases to grow faster than the economy and then subsequently returns to a prudent proportion of gross domestic product (GDP) within a reasonable period of time. The choice of a particular path for deficit reduction will ultimately be made by elected leaders, in light of the information available to them when they make budget decisions. But the committee believes that the projected level of federal government debt relative to GDP is an appropriate benchmark for assessing the prudence of long-term budget policy, and that aiming for a level of 60 percent within a decade of initiating policy actions that could begin as soon as fiscal year 2012 is prudent under current circumstances.

The remainder of this section explains our rationale for these views. The trajectory of a nation's level of debt relative to its GDP has been widely used by U.S. government agencies, international organizations, and other countries as a benchmark for assessing a nation's fiscal condition (see Peterson-Pew Commission on Budget Reform, 2009; also see Appendix G). The three major federal agencies that regularly make long-term projections each highlight the debt as a percentage of GDP as a principal measure of the budget outlook: (1) the Congressional Budget Office (2009c), (2) the General Accountability Office (2009), and (3) the U.S. Office of Management and Budget (2009a:Ch. 13).

The most recent assessment of the state of public finances in advanced economies and emerging markets by the International Monetary Fund (IMF) (2009b) uses the ratio of total public debt to GDP as the basis for international comparisons (International Monetary Fund, 2009b). The IMF also used simulations to project the evolution of public debt as a percentage of GDP as a way of judging which countries are most vulnerable to an adverse debt dynamic following the current downturn. Those simulations noted, for example, that "[projected] increases are particularly large in absolute terms for the United Kingdom and the United States, where debt levels rise sharply" (International Monetary Fund, 2009b:18). Similarly, the Center for Budget and Policy Priorities has estimated that "driven primarily by health care costs, rapidly growing deficits will push the debt held by the public up to roughly 300 percent of gross domestic product by 2050, or nearly *three times* as large as the record level reached at the end of World War II" (Cox et al., 2009:1).

The Congressional Budget Office (2009e) and others (e.g., Auerbach, 1994) have calculated another measure that is useful in assessing the long-term fiscal outlook, termed the "fiscal gap." It is the amount that spending has to be reduced or revenues increased as a percentage of GDP so that the debt is the same at the end of a specified projection period as today, expressed as a percentage of today's GDP. It is similar to our measure in that the debt is eventually stabilized relative to GDP, but it is more stringent in that it depends on stabilizing the debt ratio at *today's* level. Because the stimulus plan, financial bailouts, and the lingering effects of the recession have the debt ratio on a strong upward course, the committee believes that the total elimination of the fiscal gap would require an overly painful change in tax and spending policies.[1]

Yet another alternative fiscal yardstick would be the size of the annual budget deficit. A different target and an even more stringent goal than ours for budget policy in the long term would be a return to the easily grasped idea that budgets should be balanced—either year-by-year or on average—and as expeditiously as possible. Because the government's debt in dollar terms would be constant if budgets were balanced, the economy's growth would gradually reduce the federal debt as a percentage of GDP. A balanced budget, although not consistently achieved, was the norm over most of U.S. history (Schick, 2007). Adopting this more stringent approach would, over time, provide a widening margin for error in case projections are overly optimistic or adverse developments ensue. However, the committee concluded that such a goal is unnecessarily restrictive: It would both be extraordinarily difficult to achieve in the foreseeable future—and goes well beyond what prudent fiscal policy requires for sustainability over a long period. Moreover, many would argue that running modest deficits to finance wise public investments that will benefit future generations is appropriate (see also the discussion in Box 3-1 of the relationship between deficits and GDP growth).

Having selected the ratio of debt to GDP as a reasonable (albeit not the only possible) indicator of fiscal prudence, the committee then considered possible targets for it and on what time line the target should be reached. Within certain bounds, the choice of a target for debt is a matter of judgment, but that does not mean that it is arbitrary.[2] The federal government could eventually stabilize its debt at a substantially higher percentage of GDP than our chosen level of 60 and could run larger deficits in the meantime (which would in part accommodate the resulting additional debt service). Or, it could stabilize debt at a smaller percentage of GDP, requiring larger policy adjustments to reach the goal in a given period of time.[3] Box 3-1 provides illustrations of the relationship among interest rates, the primary budget balance, growth in incomes and GDP, and the debt-to-GDP ratio.

There is no magic number either for the debt target as a percentage of

BOX 3-1
The Arithmetic of the Debt

Suppose borrowing were used only to finance the interest portion of spending, that is, revenues were always sufficient to cover noninterest ("primary") spending. And suppose that the interest rate on the debt equals the growth rate of incomes (or GDP, given that incomes and GDP grow at nearly the same rate). Under those conditions, the debt will grow at the same rate as incomes, and the debt-to-GDP ratio will remain constant. For example, if the interest rate on the debt is 5 percent and the U.S. Treasury borrows just enough to cover it, the debt will grow 5 percent annually. If GDP also were to grow at 5 percent, the debt-to-GDP ratio would remain constant. At 60 percent of GDP, which is the target ratio the committee proposes, debt service at an interest rate of 5 percent would be 3 percent of GDP (0.6×5). If all spending totaled about 20 percent of GDP, interest on the debt would be 15 percent of all spending. With revenues at 17 percent of GDP, the budget would be balanced except for interest on the debt. The annual budget deficit—equal to the additional borrowing or growth of debt—would be 3 percent of GDP and the debt would grow by that amount or at a rate of 5 percent (3/60). If GDP grew 4 percent in one year, then debt at the end of the year would be 60.6 percent of GDP.[a] If budgeters wanted to prevent the debt from growing, they could either raise revenues or reduce primary spending as a percentage of GDP. This "solution" might not be practical for long, however, given that the study's baseline projects primary spending to grow faster than GDP if no changes in policy are made. In that case, it would become increasingly difficult to either limit or offset spending growth in order to keep debt stable.

The simple relationship between growth rate of the economy and the federal debt is summarized by the following equation (adapted from von Furstenberg, 1991):

$$R_t = P_t + (r - n)D_{t-.5} - [D_t - D_{t-1}],$$

where **R** is revenues, **P** is noninterest spending, and $D_{t-.5}$ is the average publicly held federal debt during the year, all expressed as percents of GDP. The average interest rate on debt is represented by **r**, **n** is the growth rate of GDP, and **t** is the fiscal year. When **r − n** is zero, revenues can equal primary spending plus the change in the debt resulting from borrowing the amount needed that year for interest on the debt paid that year. If **r − n** is negative, either revenues can be lowered or spending increased without increasing the debt. Conversely, in a year when **r − n** is positive, the debt will grow unless revenues are increased or spending reduced as a percentage of GDP. As the debt grows, so does the burden of interest on that debt.

Even if **r − n** were always zero, if **P** is on a rising path, as this study's baseline projects, then to keep the debt from increasing relative to GDP, **R** must rise by the same amount. Or, to keep **R** constant as **P** rises, **D** must fall instead. However, **r − n** can be (and often has been) positive, as in the example above. Although **n** can be (and often has been) greater than **r**, it is precisely when the opposite is true that the nation can least afford to run primary surpluses, so these circumstances deserve special attention (Bohn, 1995). The most recent downturn serves as an example. In 2008 and 2009, **n** turned negative while **r** fell slowly, **P** rose as a result of additional spending demands and efforts to stimulate recovery, and **R** fell with the drop in employment, incomes, and profits: the result was a rapid rise in federal debt, **D**.

The following example illustrates how quickly **D** can rise as a percentage of GDP in and following a less severe downturn than the one we have experienced. Assume that at the recession's onset D_t = .60 and **r** = **n**. The primary deficit, $P_{t+1} - R_{t+1}$, suddenly equals .08, and **n** falls to −.05 while **r** = .05. Rearranging the budget constraint,

$$D_{t+1} = P_{t+1} - R_{t+1} + (r - n)D_t + D_t$$

Then, substituting the assumed numbers, we have

$$D_{t+1} = .08 + (.055 \times .6) + .6 = .713$$

The recession has raised **D** by 11.3 percentage points. Now assume a partial recovery next year. The primary deficit improves to .02, **n** = .02, and **r** remains at .05.

$$D_{t+2} = .02 + (.03 \times .713) + .713 = .754$$

The debt has risen by over 15 percent of GDP in only 2 years. This exercise illustrates how fast **D** can rise in a recession and its aftermath.

Suppose that interest rates on the debt doubled in the future while annual GDP growth continued to average 4 percent. In that case, debt service would more than double in a few years as the debt grew relative to GDP and as maturing debt rolled over and was replaced by new debt carrying higher rates. If annual interest payments on the debt doubled from 3 to 6 percent of GDP, for example, then one of three things would have to happen: the additional interest spending would be covered by borrowing and the debt would grow by that amount; noninterest spending would be reduced by about 18 percent (equal to 3 percent of GDP, assuming total spending is 20 percent of GDP); or revenues would be increased by 3 percent of GDP. The first option would put the budget on an unsustainable path. The other two options would be very painful but perhaps barely manageable. If the debt reaches much more than 60 percent of GDP, an interest rate doubling might be too difficult to manage.

Suppose instead that the debt is stabilized at 80 percent rather than 60 percent of GDP. With the interest rate at 5 percent, the interest bill would be 4 percent of GDP (0.8 × 5), that is, interest spending would be one-third higher than at a 60 percent debt ratio. Even if GDP growth matches interest rates, absent a decision to increase revenues by 1 percent or to reduce noninterest spending by 1 percent, the deficit would increase from 3 to 4 percent of GDP because of the additional interest spending. Not only would annual interest payments be higher on this larger debt, but the margin for future spending and revenue increases would be reduced.

In the budget baseline used for this study, the publicly held debt is projected to increase by more than 40 percentage points of GDP from 2008 to 2021. Suppose that after some years the United States faced one or a series of economic or other emergencies of magnitude comparable to the 2008-2009 financial crisis and downturn, contributing to a comparable increase in borrowing, which would put the debt at 120 percent of GDP. At that level, even with no increase in borrowing rates, annual interest payments would be 6 percent of GDP, requiring a decision about whether to borrow, raise revenues, or lower spending to cover the higher interest payments. If revenues are not increased or noninterest spending reduced in this case, the debt would begin to grow as a percentage of GDP. If interest rates doubled, debt service would consume 12 percent of GDP; if other spending were maintained at 17 percent of GDP, spending would equal 29 percent of GDP, and interest would be 41 percent of total spending.

continued

BOX 3-1
Continued

These calculations assume that the debt level or changes in the debt level do not have their own effect on future interest rates. However, if investors in federal debt demand higher interest rates when debt is high or rising because they perceive an increase in risk, then interest costs will rise, increasing the probability that **r** in a given year would exceed **n**. There is no scientifically established nor expert consensus on the relationship between debt levels and interest rates; one estimate is that an increase in **D** of 1 percentage point of GDP would increase the long-term real interest rate by .03 percentage points (Engen and Hubbard, 2004; Foster, 2008). Another estimate is that long-term rates rise by .05 percentage points for each 1 percentage point increase in government debt (International Monetary Fund, 2009b). Using the smaller of these estimates, a decision to stabilize the debt at 80 percent rather than 60 percent of GDP would increase **r** by a further 0.3 percent over a long period. If this relationship between debt level and interest rates held, stabilizing the debt at 120 percent of GDP would increase **r** by 0.9 percentage points relative to the proposed target. An equal increase in **R** or equal decrease in **P** would be required each year to keep **D** constant.

---

[a]CBO's latest forecast is for GDP growth averaging just over 4 percent following the economic recovery, i.e., from 2014 through 2019, and for the Treasury's borrowing rate to average around 5 percent. The intermediate assumptions of the Social Security Administration (2009d) have GDP growing in the long run at an annual rate of about 4.5 percent. The Trustees' intermediate assumption is that nominal interest rates over the projection period after 2010 (on the fund's holdings of special Treasury securities) will range between 5 and 6 percent.

---

the GDP or for the number of years until the target is reached. These choices must follow from the underlying purpose of adopting such a standard. The federal budget will be sustainable if investors around the world (including the United States) are willing to lend to the Treasury at affordable interest rates. Maintaining that willingness to lend now and in the future requires, in our view, a credible public commitment to responsible fiscal behavior.

The choice of the target and the time line are important. A target or a schedule that is too stringent risks failure because it imposes such painful policy choices. A failure to achieve a publicized goal could shake the confidence of domestic and international financial markets. An excessively rigorous standard might require either what would be viewed as excessive taxation or forgoing government services that most people believe are essential.

The higher the level of debt, the closer the nation would be at any time to a major problem as the result of any adverse events—such as an economic downturn or a national security crisis—that can drive revenues down and increase spending needs. In fact, the IMF (2009b:21) found that the size of the fiscal stimulus during 2008-2010 was inversely related in large countries to the initial level of public debt. Presumably, those with higher debt burdens were more constrained either politically or economically than others. Furthermore, the larger the debt and the government's interest obligations, the more the budget would be vulnerable to any upward spike in interest rates.

Both theory and evidence suggest that higher debt itself will tend to increase the long-term interest rate on government debt (Engen and Hubbard, 2004; International Monetary Fund, 2009b). The observed effects are even larger "for countries that start from high debt ratios or deficit levels, or that confront faster population aging" (International Monetary Fund, 2009b:21-22). With interest payments as a larger share of spending, the task of maintaining debt at a given percentage of GDP in the face of an interest rate rise becomes harder. There is a danger of a debt spiral. The tax increases or spending cuts necessary to finance a growing interest bill become more difficult politically as they become larger. Legislators may lag in enacting them. The deficit grows, and interest pressures become more severe. Faced with such pressures, many countries throughout history have simply given up and decided to finance deficits by creating money (Reinhart and Rogoff, 2009). The hyperinflation that follows destroys personal wealth and government programs. It is often said that cannot happen here, but the prospect is so terrible that we must be extremely vigilant in avoiding even the smallest probability of such an outcome.

It can also be argued that an "easy" standard would result in a government that many people would believe is too large. The larger the debt, all else equal, the more the government must spend on interest payments before it can spend to meet any of the nation's needs. Larger government borrowing competes with other uses of capital, including productive business investment, and can increase interest costs for other borrowers. To the extent that productive investment is crowded out or the United States must rely on borrowing from abroad, either wage growth is slowed or a higher portion of our income must be devoted to paying interest and dividends to foreigners.

The committee believes that some combination of revenue increases and spending restraints should be implemented soon to constrain the growth of federal debt as a percentage of GDP within a decade to a level that provides an appropriate balance between the risks associated with a higher ratio and the additional difficulties of implementing policies that would be consistent with a lower ratio. The committee judged that a debt of 60 percent of GDP reflects an appropriate balance and is an achievable target within a decade—and is therefore useful to guide policy choices that will ultimately be made by elected leaders. This is a different ratio than the committee would have likely proposed under different circumstances. Indeed, it will surely be seen by some as too high and by others as too low.

But the committee believes it is the lowest ratio that is practical given the fiscal outlook and reflects the best balancing of practicality and risk, taking into account a range of concerns.

In establishing a debt target, the nation needs a standard that balances risk—maintaining credibility, but not excessively constraining public services or raising taxes—through either too low a constraint on debt or too high a level of debt service. Maintaining credibility will require a debt target that is within a reasonable range, based on the nation's economic history. Although the U.S. economy survived a debt in excess of its GDP in the years immediately following World War II, those were extraordinary—probably unique—times. There was enormous pent-up demand for domestic goods and services as a result of war-time rationing, the labor force grew enormously with the return of the troops, and the federal government had not yet made sizeable commitments for retirement and health care that would later cause spending to automatically rise much faster than revenues. As a result, the debt-to-GDP ratio fell rapidly as the GDP grew quickly, and the budget remained close to balance from 1947 through 1960. Today, this favorable situation is almost completely reversed, as the post-World War II baby boom generation is just beginning to retire, both slowing the potential growth of the labor force and the economy and (along with rising health care costs) putting severe pressures on the budget.

Our target of stabilizing the ratio of debt to GDP at 60 percent still would leave the public debt relative to the size of its economy at its highest point since 1952. Assuming as a rough rule of thumb that the average interest rate on the debt is 5 percent, that would leave the government's net interest cost at 3 percent of GDP—which would be higher than in any years other than the period of high deficits and elevated interest rates of 1985 through 1997.[4]

With the future spending and higher debt relative to GDP implicit in the nation's promises to the elderly both larger than at any time in the past, the credibility of a target debt level of 60 percent of GDP is not a foregone conclusion. However, a 60 percent target would have institutional confirmation in the financial world. The European Monetary Union (EMU) set as its standard for membership the achievement and maintenance of a debt-to-GDP ratio of 60 percent.[5] Of course, just as the U.S. debt has increased in the current economic and financial crisis, so have the debts of EMU members. However, should the United States articulate and pursue a target for the public debt of 60 percent of GDP, there is a strong probability that the financial credibility of the nation in world financial markets will be maintained.

In considering feasibility, we concluded on the basis of the analysis in this report that a debt target of 60 percent of GDP could be reached consistent with appropriate levels of spending and taxation. In fact, there are many plausible policy combinations that would produce this result if action is taken in our proposed time frame. We note again that the members of the committee would choose different levels of taxation and of spending in different categories of the budget. Those decisions ultimately must be made by the citizens of the nation, through their elected representatives. Our findings demonstrate that many reasonable choices are available to meet the standard that we have chosen.

Apart from the numerical target for the debt as a percentage of GDP, there are further specific questions about how quickly it should be reached. We selected fiscal 2012 (which begins October 1, 2011) as a reasonable time to start—to first slow the rapid increase of the debt relative to the economy and then, over several years, to reduce it to a more prudent level. We expect the economy to find its feet by that date. The longer the time taken to change course, the longer the debt will continue to rise relative to GDP and the higher the level before it begins to be stabilized or reduced, raising all of the concerns about excessive debt. However, given the situation as the committee writes its report—and with an economy that is still fragile and in a slow recovery—sharply and quickly raising revenues or reducing spending quickly could be a mistake, even with a debt-to-GDP ratio above 50 percent and rising rapidly as it currently is in the United States. Withdrawing purchasing power from the economy while the recovery is fragile could return the economy to a recession. The committee is aware both of the many spending demands that the federal government must meet in the immediate future and the dangers of quickly raising revenues or reducing spending relative to their current paths. We believe that articulating an extended adjustment path from the outset would help to cushion the impact on the economy, reducing the risk of extending the recent slowdown. We note that once a 60 percent debt-to-GDP ratio is reached, the government can run annual deficits (after 2022) that average between 2 and 3 percent of GDP at the projected rate of interest on the debt without causing the debt to grow in proportion to the economy.[6]

A target or schedule that is delayed too long could itself lose the nation's credibility with investors by failing to assure that the nation's debt-servicing obligations will be met. In fact, we believe that the reassurance of financial markets that would come from the national determination to meet a clear fiscal standard would help keep interest rates lower than they otherwise would be, facilitating the economic recovery and ultimate expansion. We then believe that 10 years would prove to be a sufficient time horizon to achieve the necessary savings in a nondisruptive manner.

The choice of the starting date and time line, as with the level of the target will ultimately be a decision of elected leaders, taking into account the best information available to them when they must make budget choices. However, we judge that waiting longer to begin changing course or enacting a less stringent target (thereby allowing the debt to GDP ratio to rise even further before its rise is arrested and reduced to the proposed target) will only add to the ultimate budgetary cost—and the economic risk. This, in turn, will add to the political difficulty and pain of reaching the 60 percent target. The budget costs of such delays are highlighted by an analysis, presented in Chapter 9, showing the budget effects of waiting 5 or 10 years longer before beginning to introduce similar policy changes.

As the discussion of illustrative policy options in the following chapters makes clear, achieving the committee's proposed stabilization of the debt-to-GDP ratio by 2022 would require the adoption of painful policies. The fact that the goal is so politically challenging to reach is an indication of the depth of the nation's fiscal hole. The committee would prefer a more ambitious goal for the very long run, but believes that it is unrealistic to aim for a significantly lower debt ratio within the next 20 to 25 years. Thus, we selected a 60 percent debt-to-GDP target as reasonable and reachable within this time frame—particularly since a higher target or longer glide path would leave the nation at too much risk of being unable to cope with unforeseeable shocks that require a vigorous federal response. Chapters 4 through 9 present first an overview of, and then describe, specific sets of, policy options and possible combinations that would put the U.S. budget on a path to achieve this target federal debt-to-GDP ratio by 2022. The committee's different scenarios are intended as an illustrative, but by no means, definitive or exhaustive, set of trajectories toward a sustainable fiscal future.

Reasonable people may differ with our views about what target and time path to choose, and there should be a full and rich debate about those decisions. However, the committee urges those who differ significantly on these choices—especially those who would choose a less ambitious target or a slower time path—to consider seriously the benefits in terms of credibility from formally setting *some* target and *some* schedule to reach it. We believe that such a public commitment would be beneficial even if the target and schedule chosen were different from ours.

TESTS FOR FISCAL PRUDENCE

Having set a long-term target for sustainability, the committee suggests that people apply to any comprehensive set of budget proposals three primary fiscal prudence tests, on the debt target and on the long-term relationship between revenues and spending. We also offer secondary fiscal prudence tests on the deficit, age-related programs, cost-effectiveness and growth, and effects on states.

Primary Tests for Fiscal Prudence

A budget must be judged primarily by the extent to which it moves from the current unsustainable path to one that is sustainable for the foreseeable future. The committee proposes three primary tests to assess whether it puts the country on a path of economic sustainability.

1. Does the proposed federal budget include policy actions that start to reduce the deficit in the near future in order to reduce short-term borrowing and long-term interest costs?

The budget should include proposals that begin to close the gap between revenues and spending, first slowing the growth of the debt and then gradually reversing its growth. This cannot be done overnight, but it can be done gradually and steadily over a decade or more. It is important to minimize near-term annual deficits that add to the future size of the federal debt and the costs of servicing that debt, in part because many policy changes to entitlement programs will take a long time to yield substantial budget savings, even if enacted soon.

2. Does the proposed budget put the government on a path to reduce the federal debt within a decade to a sustainable percentage of GDP?

Given the fiscal outlook and the committee's analysis of the many factors that affect economic outcomes, the committee believes that the lowest ratio of debt to GDP that is economically manageable within a decade, as well as practical and politically feasible, is 60 percent. If the budget is put on a path beginning in 2012 to reach that target, savings from interest payments that are avoided by reducing borrowing requirements would accumulate slowly at first, but would equal nearly $800 billion in the first 10 years (2012 through 2021), exceeding $5.7 trillion by 2031 and multiplying quickly thereafter: see Figure 3-1. These estimates are derived from the scenarios developed and analyzed in Chapters 4 through 9.

In addition to contributing directly to deficit reduction, less borrowing in this period would contribute to creditors' confidence in the United States' ability to manage its affairs and thereby reduce the risks of a disruptive financial crisis that could harm the economy, as well as greatly illustrative complicate efforts to achieve budget sustainability.

3. Does the proposed budget align revenues and spending closely over the long term?

Projections of the long-term path (75 years or beyond) implied by a proposed or enacted budget should show revenues and spending that are roughly aligned and parallel and appear likely to remain so beyond the end of the projection period. The size and timing of changes that affect the budget's path matter a great deal. It may be too much politically to ask

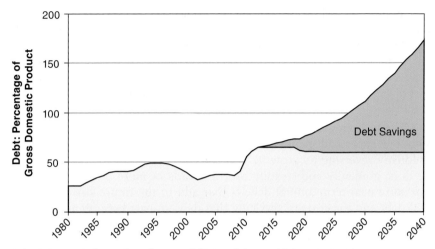

FIGURE 3-1 Debt savings from stabilizing debt-to-GDP ratio in 12 years.

leaders to provide specific policies in a single year's budget sufficient to accomplish the entire, large task of aligning spending and revenues. However, each year's budget should demonstrate a credible commitment to policy changes that substantially move toward sustainability, with an explicit commitment to the longer-term goal of aligning revenues and spending over the long term.

Secondary Tests for Fiscal Prudence

The standards of fiscal prudence proposed above address the overall long-term balance between revenues and spending. The additional criteria discussed in this section can help people assess whether budgets are moving in the right direction. Most analysts are likely to agree on these in principle, although they may disagree on how to apply them in practice. The three secondary criteria offered below are applicable to any budget, but they are particularly important given the current path of the U.S. budget.

4. Does the proposed budget restrain health care cost growth and introduce changes now in the major entitlement programs and in other spending and tax policies that will have cumulative beneficial fiscal effects over time?

For entitlement programs, peoples' reasonable expectations about current benefits will be honored. Changes will be easier to manage if spending restraints or revenue increases are introduced soon, but applied in a way that minimizes their effects on current beneficiaries. This means that even budget savings from changes introduced immediately would take effect slowly—so the sooner the effort is started the better.

If programs can be designed that truly yield productivity gains by restructuring major sectors of the economy or the budget (or both), investments in these may increase spending in the short run but yield permanent gains from more productive use of resources. Proposed investments in information technology for health and investments in new forms of energy, if they yield hoped-for gains in productive capacity and other social benefits, fall into this category.

For both sets of policies, it may take many years after major policy changes are made before they achieve results of the magnitude required to help bring revenues and spending into stable alignment. For this reason, if policy changes are deemed necessary to yield large long-term changes in levels of spending or revenues relative to the baseline, they should be introduced as soon as possible. The costs of waiting—in forgone budget savings and accumulated additional borrowing to finance deficits—are high.

5. Does the budget include spending and revenue policies that are cost-effective and promote more efficient use of resources in both the public and private sectors?

A budget should include those investments—perhaps in education, preventive health, infrastructure, and scientific research—that can be shown to yield high returns. A budget should raise revenues in ways that do not create undue distortions and inefficiency in private-sector decisions about the best use of resources, which slow growth. And a budget should eliminate or curtail programs that have proven ineffective or inefficient and use information about performance to redirect public resources to more effective programs addressing the most important national objectives.

6. Does the federal budget reflect a realistic assessment of the fiscal problems facing state and local governments?

It would be easy for the federal government to improve its books by simply dumping its burdens onto state and local governments. Because cutting federal transfers to states and localities adds to *their* fiscal burdens, applying this test requires consideration of the fiscal stresses that are facing state and local governments. In the medium and longer term, states will face daunting fiscal pressures from some of the same sources as the federal government, including commitments for health and retirement. Their freedom of action is more limited than that of the federal government because in most cases they have, at most, limited borrowing capacity to finance these commitments. Shifts of responsibilities to state and local governments should be predicated on evidence that these will improve overall government efficiency and responsibility to local circumstances. However, arguments for devolving to states some functions traditionally performed at a national level—if these changes are made thoughtfully—are stronger now than in the past. States' governing capacities have increased and become more uniform over time, and state governments are often leaders in both policy innovation and service administration. States can be expected to do more than some years ago partly because of convergence among states in their economies and policies. In particular, many southern states whose economies were so weak they could not easily provide basic services to their residents or have had a history of racial discrimination are today closer to economic parity with other states. However, the principal test for deciding whether to devolve some federal responsibilities to state and local government is whether those government can better take account of local conditions and be more responsive to people's varied demands than the federal government.

In a broad sense, these secondary tests help to ensure that the federal government makes the most efficient possible use of its share of the nation's resources, allowing other governments and private actors to allocate the rest.

APPLYING THE FRAMEWORK

The framework presented in this and the preceding chapter is intended to have immediate practical application. A proper understanding of how values and beliefs shape budget choices provides a starting point for understanding how to approach the difficult choices that face the country. A set of practical tests of fiscal prudence will enable every person to judge how far a proposed or enacted budget goes to meet the looming fiscal challenge and put the budget on a sustainable course. The committee believes that these tests ought to be applied by everyone to all proposed budgets, starting with the budget that the President will present for the next fiscal year.

The tests outlined above do not, of course, help policy makers and others decide what combination of reductions to spending, increases in revenues, or both to choose. If policy makers agree that the nation must reduce the debt and bring spending and revenues into long-term alignment, then some combination of the following must occur soon: some objectives must be abandoned or pursued by means other than federal spending, government spending must yield much more for each dollar, or government spending will take a larger share of the economy's resources and must be financed by higher revenues. If the majority decision is to continue to pursue the federal government's long and growing list of responsibilities with the same vigor, and perhaps to take on new challenges, either such efficiencies must be achieved or more revenue will have to be raised. If the majority decision is to avoid or minimize tax increases, then the rate of spending growth must be slowed even more, and, eventually, quite dramatically.

Several aspects of the relationship between value choices and budget choices are becoming increasingly clear. First, to bring spending and revenues into alignment over the next two decades and then keep them there will require not merely tactical changes but rethinking the way government is used to achieve the goals Americans consider most important. Explicit and deep debate over these questions is needed to inform choices. If political leaders are to act responsibly without being punished at the polls, the culture and character of the nation's politics—typically dominated by organized clienteles lobbying to protect or expand narrow benefits—may need to change to represent better the more diffuse public benefits and the lower but perhaps more concentrated costs of a prudent fiscal policy.

Second, unless revenues are raised to a level consistent with spending over the long term, some federal responsibilities on which people place great value eventually will have to be sacrificed or significantly reduced. This change can be achieved in part by shifting resource decisions to state and local governments or to the private sector or by mandating specific use of private resources through federal regulation.

Third, if the nation fails to bring spending and revenues into closer alignment over the long term, then all of the values that are now reflected in federal programs and fiscal policy will be threatened by a financial meltdown. If the nation fails, *everyone's* ox may be gored.

Fortunately, perhaps, values do not translate directly or consistently into positions on particular policies, as discussed above. People with similar values may arrive at different positions on questions of policy. And conversely, those with sharply different values may be able to agree or compromise on a particular policy. A proper framing of the problem can help. The hard fiscal choices facing everyone in the country put a premium on rational discussion. There is no magic formula for resolving value and other differences and reaching the consensus and accommodation that are necessary. In Chapter 10 we suggest some process changes that can help. In a democratic society, different values and interests, and differing views of how to pursue them, are eventually compromised or reconciled through healthy argument and bargaining. Ultimately, the nation will have to rely on democratic politics, shaped by responsible leaders, to set a new course.

NOTES

1. The fiscal gap represents the government's long-term projected flows of revenues and spending by a single number, which is the present value of future payments to and from the Treasury, discounted for the time value of money to make them comparable with payments today; see Appendix A. The fiscal gap would be zero if it was expected that

over a long period the debt would remain the same proportion of GDP. Although the committee might have constructed such a measure and set a target on this basis, the debt target is more easily understood and communicated.

2. In December 1991 the Maastricht Treaty of the European Union (EU) set future targets for deficits and debt that were to be used as conditions for membership in the European Monetary Union. The debt criterion was that publicly held debt may not exceed 60 percent of GDP. However, several EU member nations currently do not meet this standard. An official of the International Monetary Fund noted in a conference call in July 2009 that there is no "magic number" for debt-to-GDP (International Monetary Fund, 2009c). Buiter (2006) has written about the nature of the 1991 EU debt and deficit targets and the subsequent failure to enforce them, either as originally defined or with modifications.

3. Stabilizing the ratio of debt to GDP implies and is equivalent to stabilizing deficits at a constant percentage of GDP (or deficits minus debt service, the so-called primary deficit, as a percentage of GDP). The target could as easily be expressed in these terms. As discussed below, stabilizing the budget at a higher debt-to-GDP ratio would permit the government to run larger annual deficits.

4. With a 1-year respite in 1994, when debt service was 2.9 percent of GDP.

5. The IMF has used a target of 60 percent by 2030 as the basis for measuring "the aggregate adjustment required to restore advanced economy ratios to safer levels" (2009b:23).

6. The projections assume that inflation is generally well behaved during the projection period. A higher inflation rate allows a higher deficit, because the real value of past debt is being eroded. But the effect is limited in the United States because so much of its debt is short term and the average interest rate on the debt will adjust upward quickly.

4

Choices for a Sustainable Budget

Given the fiscal arithmetic, changing the nation's economic course will almost certainly require an early dramatic adjustment in the level and mix of government spending and/or higher revenues. As discussed in Chapter 2, if people want to continue all the federal government programs at levels consistent with current policies, given the growing elderly population and rising health care costs, spending will have to greatly increase as a percentage of gross domestic product (GDP). This higher spending will require commensurately higher revenues. Also, as is discussed in Chapter 8, given the inefficiency of the present tax structure, it will almost certainly also be necessary to change *how* revenue is collected. If, instead, people prefer to keep government's share of the economy's resources about what it has been in recent years, the government will have to do much less in the future than implied by current policies, and choices will have to be made about what social goals to pursue less vigorously or what programs to give up. And it is important to stress that there are many possible paths between these two that would both reduce spending growth and raise revenue levels.

Chapters 5-8 present major policy options for three major categories of spending and for revenues. Options for the three major entitlement programs are treated first: Medicare and Medicaid in Chapter 5 and Social Security in Chapter 6. Spending options for defense and domestic programs other than the three big entitlements are treated in Chapter 7. Each combination of options to create a future spending path implies a roughly parallel revenue path needed to ensure fiscal sustainability. Chapter 8 describes alternative approaches to raising the necessary revenues, including structural changes to the tax system that would be required for the higher revenue levels. Chapter 9 then puts the spending and revenue pieces together to illustrate different ways to reach fiscal sustainability.

This chapter serves as the broad introduction to the detailed analyses in Chapters 5-9. It also outlines how the options can be assembled to produce an illustrative set of budget "paths" (or "scenarios). The purpose of presenting a set of options and paths is not to argue for a particular set of policies, but to highlight the range and magnitude of the choices that the nation has to confront in seeking a sustainable course for the budget. All of the options to adjust spending and revenues are changes relative to the study baseline, which is the path of the budget projected by the continuation of current policies; see Box 1-3 in Chapter 1.

SPENDING OPTIONS

Options for Medicare and Medicaid

The health care policy problem is extraordinarily difficult. From a budget standpoint, one of the greatest difficulties is the inability to estimate with any confidence how most of the widely discussed reform options, or combinations of them, will affect the future trajectory of health spending.

Although spending increases for federal health programs are driven in part by the same demographic forces as Social Security (i.e., the aging of the U.S. population), for other reasons health spending has grown and is likely to continue growing at a faster rate than the economy.

Any plan to change the health care system is likely to be highly complex. There is little agreement on an overall approach or even on incremental steps to limit spending. The budget savings from any single option or a combination of options are highly uncertain. In addition, if savings can be realized, there will be strong pressures to use the savings for improvements in health and to extend federal support to people who would not otherwise have adequate insurance or care.

Given the uncertainties about savings and recognizing the pressures for spending, the committee's approach is to present an array of options that could, collectively, reduce cost growth; but we do not attribute savings to any particular option or strategy for Medicare and Medicaid. The resulting paths for health spending are essentially a range of guesses as to the potential effectiveness of any change. As described in Chapter 5, at least in the short run, achieving any significant savings in Medicare and Medicaid with some measure of certainty will most likely require strong measures that directly control their costs in order to slow their rate of spending growth. Such measures could take several forms. The high cost of health care in the United States compared with other industrialized countries certainly suggests that the nation can provide care more efficiently than it currently does. However, imposing direct limits on Medicare and Medicaid spending runs the risk of reducing either access to care or the quality of care, with potentially negative consequences for some people's health. For the Medicare and Medicaid programs, there is a limit to how much cost containment can be achieved, without doing harm, and without reorganizing the nation's overall health care system. In the medium term, major reforms that change incentives for providers and consumers, provide better information to both about costs and benefits, and reorganize health care delivery can both improve care and yield budget savings. Such reforms will ease the pain imposed by—and eventually perhaps obviate the need for—an overall budget limit for health spending.

Options for Social Security

The committee's options for Social Security are among many that have received wide discussion. Unlike the options for health, it is possible to estimate their budgetary effects with a good deal of confidence. Absent policy changes, future spending for Social Security benefits and future payroll tax revenues are relatively predictable from data on population aging, work and retirement patterns, immigration, and trends in wages.

The range of options for Social Security is wide, and a set of frequently discussed and relatively incremental reforms can put the program on a financially self-sustaining trajectory. Moreover, there is precedent from the early 1980s for agreement on significant changes, although the adjustments required now to bring Social Security revenues and benefits into alignment over the long run would be larger than those adopted earlier.

The options the committee presents would eliminate the now-projected Social Security shortfall in different ways, showing how it is possible to preserve benefits scheduled under current law by increasing payroll taxes or what adjustments to the rate of the growth of benefits would be needed to avoid payroll tax increases. The committee's options illustrate the broad range of choices available to keep Social Security solvent without changing the fundamental nature of the program. Restoring Social Security to solvency is not a prerequisite for putting the entire budget on a sustainable path, but it is desirable in itself and can make an important contribution to the broader goal of budget sustainability.

Options for Defense and Other Domestic Spending

In 2008, 56 percent of all spending (excluding interest on the national debt) was for programs other than Medicare, Medicaid, and Social Security.[1] The hundreds of programs in this broad category address a wide range of goals pursued by the federal government: for national and homeland security, veterans, education, the environment, transportation, and many other functions. This diverse category of domestic and defense spending rose sharply in 2009, if temporarily, as the government addressed the major economic downturn and its consequences.

People have widely differing views of the value of some of the programs in this category, and some arguably are sustained more by the power of their political constituencies than by evidence of their effectiveness. The options for limiting this range of spending are similarly numerous. For this category, the committee broadly illustrates in Chapter 7 how priorities for spending cuts might be set and what the likely implications are of different levels and mixes of spending.

Four options are presented for defense. All assume that costs for the wars and Iraq and Afghanistan are reduced over time, as in the study baseline. On the high end of the committee's options, defense spending would remain nearly at its current level as a percentage of GDP, although lower than in the Cold War period. At the low end of the committee's options, defense spending would be a smaller share of GDP than in any recent period, though it would be higher than the combined amount spent by U.S. allies in the North Atlantic Treaty Organization (NATO).

Four options are presented for other domestic spending. At the lowest spending level, this broad category of programs would be reduced by 2019 to a level 15 percent below the study baseline. At somewhat higher spending levels, two broad strategies for other domestic spending are illustrated. One intermediate option would allow other domestic programs to grow to a level 10 percent higher than the baseline. This growth would allow for substantial new investments intended to enhance the economy's future growth, as well as benefiting people directly. These kinds of investments might be viewed as favoring younger age cohorts, because they will have more years to enjoy the future returns. The other intermediate option would reduce other domestic spending to a level 6 percent below the baseline, leaving no room for new investments unless offset by other program cuts. A fourth option for other domestic spending suggests what could be done if spending were to grow to a level 14 percent above the study baseline.

REVENUE OPTIONS

Options for federal revenues depend in part on whether the nation pursues a path to sustainability that keeps spending and revenues close to their recent historical levels, as a percentage of the economy, or pursues a path with higher spending, which would require higher revenues. If revenues need to increase substantially, then there are severe limits on how much can be collected efficiently by simply raising rates within the current income and payroll tax structure. Reform of the tax structure would be needed, probably including (in the higher-spending scenarios) new forms of taxation. An alternative to the present tax structure that is simpler and treats various sources of income more uniformly is described in Chapter 8, as is the possibility of a value-added tax (VAT) similar to that used in other industrialized countries. The analysis in that chapter of options for collecting additional taxes illustrates the different levels and mixes of taxes and other revenues that could be used to move the budget to a stable relationship between revenues and spending.

BUDGET SCENARIOS

The policy options presented in Chapters 5 through 8 can be combined to produce long-term federal budget scenarios (or paths) that first close the gap between spending and revenues to reduce the debt to no more than 60 percent of GDP and then align spending closely with revenues, to put the budget on a sustainable trajectory. In Chapter 9, four such scenarios are presented, each of which leads to long-term budget sustainability. The four scenarios differ significantly in their composition and in the resulting level of spending and revenues. As a set, they are hardly exhaustive (but, rather, are illustrative) of the wide range of plausible—not necessarily politically feasible—potential policy paths to long-term fiscal stability.

The rest of this section provides an overview of the committee's four scenarios:

1. low spending and revenues
2. intermediate-1 spending and revenues
3. intermediate-2 spending and revenues
4. high spending and revenues

The low path strives to maintain revenues at about their historical share of GDP and tightly limits federal spending to align with that level. In contrast, the high path envisions substantially more robust spending for the federal government (although less robust than under current policies), with correspondingly much higher revenues. The intermediate-1 and intermediate-2 paths lie in between, with the latter committing more resources to elderly oriented entitlement programs and the former more to investments that confer greater benefits on the young and on future generations.

These scenarios—all of which meet the primary tests of fiscal prudence presented in Chapter 3—have differing implications for the values and beliefs that shape budget debates, as discussed in Chapter 2. The lowest spending and revenue path would limit what government can do to provide health care, pensions, and a range of other benefits. Certainly, in that scenario, many people who rely on the federal government for income, health care, or other benefits will suffer, even if some spending reductions are offset by more efficiency in government programs. Much slower spending growth would almost certainly also slow the rate of public investment in future growth—in people, infrastructure, and technology—which would probably limit the opportunities for future generations.

Choosing a path of lower spending and revenues also means that more decisions about spending and savings would be made by private households and businesses, or by state and local governments, rather than by the federal government. People who doubt the national government's ability to make wise spending decisions or fear that too large a government will have too much power are likely to prefer leaving more choices in private or local government hands.

Under scenarios for higher levels of spending, the federal government would be able to do more, although not all, of what it has been doing to aid people and invest in public goods that contribute to future growth. If the government can increase its effectiveness by shifting resources to programs that provide greater return on the public dollar, it can do still more. But a sustainable budget scenario at a higher spending level requires much higher revenues: In at least one scenario the government's claim on the economy's resources would increase to levels unprecedented in U.S. history.

Clearly, it is possible to construct many other scenarios. The committee's four should be viewed as illustrative. Policy makers, analysts, and others can use them as the starting point for constructing other paths that achieve the same long-term sustainability and are more consistent with their personal values and beliefs.

Low Path

The committee's low path will appeal to people who seek to minimize future revenue increases. Even if they would prefer a somewhat different mix of spending options, they can use it to estimate the extent to which spending in each of the three major areas must be constrained. In considering the options for Medicare and Medicaid (see Chapter 5), for example, one can assess the realism of enacting and maintaining policies that would hold the growth of per capita health spending to no more than the growth rate of incomes over a long period. And one can consider which combination of options discussed for Medicare and Medicaid are sufficient to achieve this result.

The low path also helps one assess whether it is both feasible and desirable to constrain the growth of Social Security benefits in the future to what can be financed with payroll taxes under current law and perhaps ask whether the options proposed or some other set are the best available to do so. For defense and other domestic spending, people can decide whether the program cuts suggested to reduce spending by 20 percent from the study baseline are the best available and whether such reductions are feasible and consistent with their values and view of the role of the federal government. Apart from changes to existing spending programs, it is also important to consider easy-to-imagine but hard-to-specify future demands for federal spending that could be difficult to accommodate within such a constrained budget.

Intermediate Paths

People who believe that the reductions from the baseline rate of spending required to hold revenues near current levels are either infeasible or unacceptable will find other scenarios more appealing. However, these scenarios will all require substantially higher federal revenues in the future than have been historically acceptable in the United States. By some time in the next decade, on these intermediate paths, government's share of the economy would need to be 4 or 5 percentage points higher than in the three decades prior to the recent downturn (when spending temporarily soared and revenues sagged as a proportion of the economy) and would continue to grow faster than the economy for many years thereafter. Although such proportions are within the experience of most wealthy countries, they would represent a change in government's share of the nation's resources that some people may find unacceptable. The two intermediate scenarios also illustrate the broad choice between spending that makes more room for the growth of benefits to an aging population and spending that represents investments in future growth, including education. And within the context of that broad tradeoff, there are many possible variations in the specific mix of policies that put spending and revenues on a higher long-term path consistent with a sustainable budget.

Government can do more with more revenues, but it is important to recognize that both of the intermediate scenarios (and the high revenue and spending scenario discussed below) represent reductions in the baseline rate of growth in spending implied by current policies. As noted above, collecting more revenue efficiently probably would require broadening the base of the income tax and perhaps adding a new form of taxation.

High Path

People who are most concerned about the effects of reductions in the rate of projected spending growth may prefer the committee's high path. The current tax structure cannot be used to achieve the high levels of revenue, so a more efficient structure with new sources of revenue would be required. This scenario would permit health spending to grow faster than the economy for a few more decades, although eventually at a rate slower than in the baseline. Under this scenario, Social Security benefits and retirement ages would continue as they are scheduled under current law. And spending for all other programs would grow at the same rate as the economy. Budget savings from any reductions due to efficiencies or changing needs in this category could be used to pay for new initiatives or to respond to emergencies and other unanticipated events or needs.

The result would be a federal government that spends and taxes at rates far higher than in the past—possibly one-third higher as a percent of GDP within two decades and even higher thereafter. The implications of a much larger government for the economy's performance and for individuals are important considerations in constructing a sustainable budget. It is also important to reiterate that even this scenario would represent a major reduction in spending for health relative to the baseline projection of current policies.

CONCLUSION

Although some people will see raising revenues—especially other people's taxes—as the best way to address anticipated higher spending, other people will argue just as strongly against this path. Given the pressures for higher spending for an aging population and rising health care costs, holding revenues near recent historical levels would force large changes to limit spending growth. Such a limitation would probably require drastic restructuring of the nation's entire health care system, and it would certainly require caps on health spending, reductions in rate of growth of benefits for future Social Security recipients, and abandonment or curtailment of federal support for many other purposes. But if revenues are increased to permit faster spending growth, the federal government's claim on national resources will be far larger than ever in the nation's history, necessarily reducing the resources available for private purposes.

Taken together, the various policy options discussed in the following four chapters and the four scenarios that are presented in more detail in Chapter 9 illustrate the very wide range of available policy choices and plausible fiscal strategies that can be pursued to achieve a sustainable budget. They are the building blocks of a prudent fiscal policy consistent with the principles proposed in Chapter 3.

As noted above, the committee is not recommending any one of these paths to sustainability. Our task was to identify how to put the federal budget on a sustainable path, and in this report we present many ways to do so. The decisions that will be made will reflect the diversity of values and preferences of the nation's population. The best choices consistent with a sustainable budget are matters for the public and the nation's leaders to debate and decide. We stress, however, that finding compromises around some set of options that leads to a sustainable budget is a must. Doing nothing is not a viable option.

NOTE

1. Because this category of domestic and defense spending rose sharply, if temporarily, as the government addressed the downturn and its consequences, 2008 may be a better benchmark for many historical and future comparisons.

5

Options for Medicare and Medicaid

Rising health care costs are projected to increasingly dominate the federal budget, as noted in Chapter 1, and they threaten to squeeze out other public needs and priorities. This chapter presents illustrative options for limiting growth in the federal Medicare and Medicaid programs—the largest of the government's health programs.[1]

THE CURRENT CONTEXT

As the committee was completing this report, the nation was debating systemwide health care reform: see Box 5-1. The proposed legislation, if enacted in a form similar to one of its most recent versions, would cover a majority of people who now lack health insurance, and it would raise revenues and increase spending without increasing the deficit over the next 10 years (Congressional Budget Office, 2009f). Although the proposed legislation includes provisions that have the potential to reduce the long-term growth of both federal and private-sector health spending, most of the provisions are to be implemented as demonstrations or experiments rather than systemwide:[2] their effects are uncertain and, at best, will be modest.[3] Thus, even with health reform as currently considered, the major fiscal challenge of rising health care costs has yet to be faced head-on.

The growth rate of federal health spending has been higher than the growth rate of the economy for more than three decades. At the same time, health care costs are projected to rise in the private sector, burdening households and businesses. Because the charge of this committee is the future of the federal budget, the options presented in this chapter focus on the pub-

BOX 5-1
2009 Health Care Reform Legislation

As this report went to press, the House of Representatives had passed the Affordable Health Care for America Act, and the Senate had passed the Patient Protection and Affordable Care Act. (For details on the House bill, see Committee for a Responsible Federal Budget, 2009; Congressional Budget Office, 2009d, 2009f. For details on the Senate bill, see Congressional Budget Office, 2009i, 2009j.)

In order to expand access to health care, the proposed health care bills would, among other things:

- establish an individual mandate for the purchase of health insurance;
- create "insurance exchanges" through which individuals would be able, within a subsidized and regulated framework, to choose among plans offering differing levels of coverage;
- impose coverage requirements on larger employers;
- provide tax credits to certain small employers who offer health insurance; and
- expand eligibility for Medicaid.

Under the two bills, 94-96 percent of the nonelderly U.S. population (who are legal residents) would have insurance coverage by 2019—an increase in the number of insured people of 31-36 million (Congressional Budget Office, 2009d, 2009j).

The Congressional Budget Office (2009d, 2009i) projects that the proposed expansions in insurance coverage would increase net costs by $614-$891 billion over the next 10 years. That increase would be offset by increases in federal revenues of $264-$574 billion and a combination of spending changes that would save $427-$483 billion: the result would be a net reduction in federal deficits of $109-$132 billion. The largest savings would come from changes in the Medicare Advantage payment rates ($118-$170 billion) and reductions in annual updates to Medicare payment rates for most services in the fee-for-service sector other than physicians' services ($186-$228 billion).

One or both bills include a number of other measures designed to slow the growth of systemwide health care costs: payment reforms to discourage unnecessary hospital readmissions; pilot programs to help hospitals and physicians better manage and coordinate care (through "accountable care organizations") and deliver more cost-efficient care (through payment "bundling"); increased payments to primary care providers and the promotion of medical homes designed to coordinate care; funding of new comparative effectiveness research and the development of new quality measures; measures to encourage greater price transparency; and measures to promote preventive services and wellness programs (Committee for a Responsible Federal Budget, 2009:5). According to an analysis that relies heavily on the Congressional Budget Office, the 10-year savings associated with these measures in the House bill are quite modest—in the neighborhood of $5 billion (Committee for a Responsible Federal Budget, 2009:5).

In the second decade, the Congressional Budget Office (2009f, 2009i) expects the spending and revenue provisions of the House and Senate bills to slightly reduce federal budget deficits (relative to those projected under current law), by between zero and 0.5 percent of GDP. The effects of the spending provisions alone would be even more modest.

lic programs (and tax expenditures) that have direct effects on the federal budget. However, public-sector health care costs cannot be considered in isolation from private-sector costs. The services paid for by Medicare and Medicaid (and other federal health programs) are similar to those delivered in the private health care system by the same providers (doctors, hospitals, imaging facilities, nursing homes, etc.). Some analysts have pointed out that changes in government programs can have considerable influence and leverage over the health system as a whole (see, e.g., Finkelstein, 2007; White, 2007:160). Medicare policy, in particular, can have such effects because virtually every health care provider is affected; and private insurers often adopt Medicare payment schedules and coverage policies, with adjustments reflecting their own market conditions. Other analysts (see, e.g., Aaron, 2007) are skeptical about the possibility of practices spreading from Medicare to the private health care sector: they argue that it is more likely that providers will try to recover from private payers whatever income they lose from Medicare. Instead, they emphasize that the health care cost growth curve must be bent downward for the entire system in order to avoid major cost shifts from the federal budget to all other payers.

The nation's health care system is complex and multifaceted, and it includes many expensive and long-lived investments in structures, equipment, and skills. Accordingly, many reforms that promise to limit cost growth through efficiencies, better practices, and organizational changes cannot be counted on to produce significant savings in the near term. Indeed, some ideas for cost savings may even require some up-front increases in spending. Furthermore, the ultimate effects of changes in such a complex system are inevitably difficult to quantify.

Given the history and structure of the broader health care system and the uncertainties just noted, the committee believes that achieving any significant near-term savings in Medicare and Medicaid spending (relative to the baseline) with some measure of certainty will most likely require taking strong measures that directly impact their costs. Such limits could take several forms, which could be adopted singly or in various combinations. For example, provider reimbursement rates could be cut, Medicare beneficiary cost-sharing could be increased, or federal cost-sharing for Medicaid could be reduced. In a more far-reaching step, Medicare coverage could be converted to a defined contribution that could be used to purchase private insurance. Essentially, each of these steps could provide estimable amounts of budget savings to keep the total budget within prescribed limits.

However, such near-term reductions in Medicare and Medicaid spending growth would not obviate the need for systemwide changes to the nation's health care market to relieve the underlying pressures that spur spending growth. At best, they might help generate longer-term systemwide improvements by providing incentives for administrators and payers to search for major increased efficiencies, but most likely they will contain the cost pressure rather than prevent it. The committee does not support terminating the entitlement status of Medicare and Medicaid. Rather, the savings from such reductions are intended to be a "bridge" to savings from fundamental and systemic reform.

FOUR TRAJECTORIES

Given the uncertainty about the long-term budgetary savings that could accrue from the many possible combinations of health reforms described later in this chapter, the committee has sketched four health care spending trajectories that vary in their assumptions about the stringency of direct spending reductions in the near term, while leaving open the possibility that slower-acting redirection of incentives and improvements in information (among other things) may eventually achieve savings that will reduce or eliminate the need for direct reductions. Figure 5-1 shows the baseline and the committee's four trajectories (see Appendix F for details). The lower the spending trajectory, the tighter the necessary limits (at least in the near term). We also discuss a range of illustrative reform approaches and options below, but uncertainties as to the effects of some of the options make it

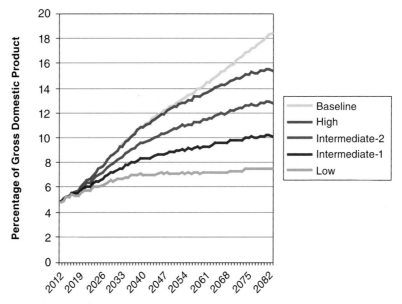

FIGURE 5-1 Federal health spending under four sustainable budget trajectories and in the baseline.

impossible to map specific combinations of reforms onto particular long-term spending trajectories.

The lowest trajectory assumes that there will be zero percent "excess cost growth" starting in 2012, a sharp decrease from recent historical averages (see below). Zero percent excess cost growth means that per capita federal spending on health care will grow no faster than the gross domestic product (GDP) per capita.[4] This low-spending trajectory makes the extremely ambitious assumption that a major slowdown occurs almost immediately and can be sustained through the entire projection period.

Spending for Medicare and Medicaid, which equaled 4.1 percent of GDP in 2008, would still increase to 6.8 percent by 2035 (3.1 percentage points below the baseline level of 9.9 percent) because of projected changes in both the number and average age of beneficiaries. By 2083, it would be at 7.5 percent of GDP, 10.9 percentage points below the study baseline. This steep, sustained slowdown of spending growth is possible only under a regime of tough cost controls in at least the near and medium term. Many analysts would consider this trajectory to be politically unrealistic. It also may be regarded as implausible to the extent that competing policy objectives of expanding access to care and improving quality are taken seriously. Nevertheless, this is the only one of the four trajectories for Medicare and Medicaid that would not require significant increases in federal revenues (as a share of GDP) above their recent historical level even when combined with stringent policy changes in other areas of federal spending.

The high health spending trajectory does far less to slow the growth of health costs.[5] In fact, on this trajectory, spending is assumed to track the study baseline until 2030. However, even this trajectory assumes that the rate of excess cost growth will gradually fall to zero by 2083, leaving program spending at 15.4 percent of GDP by 2083 (3 percentage points below the baseline).

The two intermediate trajectories have federal Medicare and Medicaid spending increasing from 4.1 percent of GDP in 2008 to 7.8 percent (intermediate-1) and 8.8 percent (intermediate-2) in 2035 (2.1 and 1.1 percentage points below the baseline, respectively) and 10.2 percent (intermediate-1) and 12.8 percent (intermediate-2) in 2083 (8.1 and 5.5 percentage points below the baseline, respectively). The intermediate-1 health spending trajectory is set at the midpoint between the low and intermediate-2 trajectories, and the intermediate-2 trajectory is set at the midpoint between the intermediate-1 and high trajectories. Both intermediate trajectories are considerably more restrictive than the study baseline and would likely have to rely, to different degrees, on direct spending reductions for quite a few years. We assume that the intermediate-1, intermediate-2, and high spending trajectories would raise the Medicare payroll tax, now at 2.9 percent, to 3.6 percent in 2012 and 5.8 percent by 2025.

HEALTH SPENDING

As noted throughout this report, the health care sector of the economy is large and growing rapidly. Total health spending is projected to reach almost $2.8 trillion, or 17.9 percent of GDP, in 2011 (Centers for Medicare and Medicaid Services, 2009b). This amount represents more than a doubling of spending as a percentage of GDP over the past three decades, from 8.1 percent in 1975.[6] The Congressional Budget Office (2009c) projects that if current price trends continue and with known demographic developments, these expenditures will grow to 46 percent of GDP by 2080.

Federal outlays for Medicare and Medicaid have gone from about 1.5 percent of GDP to 4 percent over the past three decades (Congressional Budget Office, 2008b:20). Medicare and Medicaid costs per beneficiary have historically risen at about the same rate as that for private insurance (Centers for Medicare and Medicaid Services, 2009c:Table 13; Congressional Budget Office, 2007c:8). Figure 5-2 displays the historical averages for excess cost growth in Medicare and Medicaid. The rate of excess cost growth was slower in the 1990-2005 period than in the 1975-1990 one. It is difficult to determine whether this difference reflects one-time changes (such as the spread of managed care) or if the underlying trend has changed (Congressional Budget Office, 2009e:27).[7]

In 2008, Medicare and Medicaid accounted for about 20 percent of all federal spending (Congressional Budget Office, 2009c). According to the same analysis, nominal spending for Medicare and Medicaid will grow at an average rate of around 6 percent a year in the decade after 2009, significantly faster than the economy (which is expected to grow at an

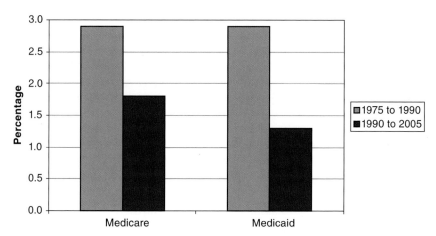

FIGURE 5-2 Average excess cost growth in Medicare and Medicaid.

average annual nominal rate closer to 4 percent over the same period). Given the size and projected growth of Medicare and Medicaid, achieving slower spending growth for this part of the federal budget is likely to be central to any strategy to make the budget sustainable over the long term. The rapid growth of health spending has also put increasing pressure on the budgets of consumers, employers, and state and local governments: for example, premiums for health insurance offered through employers have doubled since 1999, as has the cost paid directly by workers (Kaiser Family Foundation and Health Research and Educational Trust, 2008). Choosing between health care and other priorities will become increasingly difficult even in good economic times unless the nation takes steps to improve the health system's performance and to slow spending growth.

Reasons for Increasing Spending

The causes of the rapid growth of public and private health care spending in the United States are multifaceted and complex. Improvements in medical technology, broadly defined, are clearly important (Congressional Budget Office, 2008h). New ways of diagnosing and treating disease typically depend on expensive new equipment and devices, drugs, and the skills of increasingly specialized physicians with advanced training. Even when a medical advance reduces the cost of treating an individual patient, the benefits of the advance (such as clinical response, reduced discomfort, and shorter time for recuperation) often lead more patients to seek the new treatment, which can result in higher total health spending. Looking to the future, technological change may increasingly raise difficult decisions.

Yet it is difficult to separate the effects of technology from other contributing developments. The way the nation and its residents pay for health care has interacted with technology to fuel the growth of spending.[8] Indeed, some analysts argue that the lack of cost consciousness on the part of providers and consumers is a key cause of rising health spending in both the public and private sectors (see, e.g., Committee for Economic Development, 2007). In one respect, demand is fed by health insurance, which reduces the costs paid directly by patients and thus removes a possible constraint on the use of services; health insurers generally support volume-driven high-cost medicine so long as they can cover the costs through higher premiums. There has been a significant increase in insurance coverage in the past four decades: more than 50 percent of the cost of health care in 1965, but only about 13.5 percent in 2008, was paid for directly by patients (Centers for Medicare and Medicaid Services, 2009a). The drop in direct, out-of-pocket payments occurred partly because employer contributions to health insurance premiums are exempt from taxes; this encourages more generous and expensive coverage, including coverage of relatively small, predictable health costs. Demand for services has also grown because as incomes rise, people consume more health care services (Hall and Jones, 2007).

Another factor promoting the use of health care is the dominance of fee-for-service medicine, under which health care providers are compensated for the services they deliver. Fee-for-service medicine encourages the delivery of more services and dulls market incentives to adopt cost-saving technologies and conservative practice styles (Congressional Budget Office 2008f; Eddy, 1997). The result is an inefficient delivery system that promotes the use of medical services, discourages economizing behavior, and encourages the use of increasingly expensive and complex technology. Thus, spending in the health care system rises faster than incomes in the economy at large, and neither consumers nor providers have incentives to stop the spiral.

The ability to treat disease has expanded greatly over the past few decades, but so has the need for health care as the older population has grown rapidly. In 2000, one of six adults was age 65 or older; by 2030, the number will be one of four adults (Census Bureau, 2002; Council of Economic Advisers, 2009). An aging population uses more care, and a high proportion of that spending is financed through Medicare and Medicaid. The Congressional Budget Office (CBO) has calculated that aging by itself accounts for 37 percent of the projected growth in federal Medicare and Medicaid spending through 2035 and 21 percent through 2080 (Congressional Budget Office, 2009c). The prevalence of chronic diseases is also rising, based in part on the spread of obesity; excessive weight is associated with diabetes, heart disease, and other serious illnesses. About 34 percent of adults were obese in 2004, an increase from 23 percent in 1988 (Congressional Budget Office, 2008f). The treatment of the rising prevalence of chronic diseases also contributes to increasing health spending: the fee-for-service medical system is more likely to pay for expensive treatment of symptoms than for the maintenance of health through control of the underlying condition.

Health Spending and the Federal Budget

The federal budget is directly affected by the rising cost of health care in two major ways: Medicare and Medicaid outlays increase as the population ages and as the standard of medical practice expands to encompass the use of more, and more-advanced, interventions; and tax subsidies for health care increase as the cost of employer-sponsored insurance rises. In 2008, Medicare and federal Medicaid spending totaled approximately $671 billion (U.S. Office of Management and Budget, 2009c); see Box 5-2 for program details.

Medicare and Medicaid are entitlements, essentially guaranteeing a level of health benefits that is not bound by any spending limit (which are

---

BOX 5-2
Medicare and Medicaid

In 2008, Medicare spent about $468 billion and helped pay for hospital care, doctor visits, and outpatient care, and prescription drugs for 37 million elderly over the age of 65, as well as 7 million disabled beneficiaries under age 65 (Boards of Trustees, 2009). The Medicare program has four components:

1. "Part A" helps pay for hospital, home health, skilled nursing facility, and hospice care. Funded primarily by a 2.9 percent payroll tax, it represented about half of total Medicare expenditures in 2008.

2. "Part B" helps pay for doctor visits and outpatient care (as well as home health services) and represented about 40 percent of total Medicare expenditures in 2008. Part B services are funded by a combination of general revenues and beneficiary premiums (set by law to cover 25 percent of total spending under Part B).

3. "Part C," or "Medicare Advantage" (MA), is an alternative to traditional Medicare services offered under Parts A and B. It allows beneficiaries to receive care from private health insurance plans that contract with Medicare. Federal payments to MA plans are drawn from the trust fund accounts for Parts A and B.

4. "Part D" covers outpatient prescription drugs through privately administered insurance plans and is funded by a combination of premiums and general revenues (set by law to cover 25 percent of total spending under Part D). It constituted about 10 percent of total Medicare spending in 2008.

About 22 percent of Medicare beneficiaries were enrolled in Medicare Advantage plans in 2008, and the rest were enrolled in traditional Medicare. In addition, about 70 percent of Medicare enrollees had prescription drug coverage under Part D (Boards of Trustees, 2009).

Medicaid covers the cost of acute and long-term care services for about 50 million low-income individuals, including children and parents in working families, children and adults with severe disabilities, and low-income Medicare beneficiaries. Although the elderly and disabled comprise only about one-third of Medicaid beneficiaries, they account for two-thirds of the program's expenses (Council of Economic Advisers, 2009).[9] The Medicaid program is financed jointly by federal and state governments, with the federal share varying according to state per capita income. On average, the federal government has paid about 57 percent of program costs (Congressional Budget Office, 2009h). The federal government spent about $201 billion on Medicaid in 2008 (U.S. Office of Management and Budget, 2009b).

---

imposed on most other programs by the appropriations process). As noted in Chapter 1, if current policies remain unchanged and health spending grows as projected, outlays for Medicare and Medicaid as a share of GDP would more than double over the next quarter century, rising from 4.1 percent of GDP in 2008 to 9.9 percent in 2035, and they would continue to increase at a somewhat slower pace thereafter (consuming about 12.6 percent of GDP by 2050).

Separate from Medicare and Medicaid, the federal government subsidizes health care through tax expenditures—large subsidies that are provided through tax provisions that support the purchase of health care in general and private health insurance in particular. The largest subsidy is the exclusion of employer contributions to health insurance premiums from employees' taxable income, which reduced income tax collections by at least $117 billion in 2008 (Joint Committee on Taxation, 2008a).[10] And as noted above, this tax subsidy, which undergirds the employment-based system of private health insurance, encourages the use of high-cost care and drives up systemwide costs (Burman, 2006; Steuerle, 2006).

The committee estimates that financing the projected growth of Medicare and Medicaid spending alone would require an increase in total federal revenues (from the recent historical average of about 18.5 percent of GDP) of about 25 percent by 2030 and about 45 percent by 2050. Without such tax increases or an explosion in borrowing, rising federal health outlays would reduce the funds available for spending on virtually all other national priorities, such as education, housing, energy, and transportation.

REFORM ISSUES

Competing Reform Objectives

Slowing the growth of federal health spending seems essential to any strategy to put the federal budget on a sustainable path, but that fiscal goal must be balanced against other health policy objectives. Indeed, one of the reasons that ever-higher levels of health spending are problematic is that the nation does not appear to be getting its money's worth for the additional dollars being spent "at the margin." For example, between 44,000 and 98,000 preventable deaths annually are associated with hospital care (Institute of Medicine, 2000). Conversely, by one estimate only about 55 percent of the care called for under generally accepted standards of medical practice is actually delivered (McGlynn et al., 2003). The substantial variation in per-capita health care spending across the country—with no evidence that regions with higher spending experience better health outcomes—is also often regarded as an indicator of inefficiency in the U.S. health care system (Congressional Budget Office, 2008d; Fisher et al., 2009a, 2009b).

Although federal budget savings are the primary focus of this report, health reform should also aim to improve the value that people receive for health spending. Given the evidence of waste and poor-quality care in the system, there is wide agreement that the nation needs comprehensive health reform—that is, fundamental changes in system organization and service delivery. In addition to slowing the growth of total health spending, truly successful reform would increase the efficiency of the health system, expand access to health insurance, widen the availability of essential health services, allow choice and control by individuals over their own health insurance plans and care, encourage medical innovation, and, ultimately and perhaps most importantly, produce better health outcomes. Inevitably, those policy goals are partly in conflict, which forces policy makers to consider tradeoffs and priorities. Policies intended to reduce federal health outlays could reduce insurance coverage and the quality of care, disproportionately affecting the poorest and sickest people in the country. Measures that discourage the provision of services believed to be of limited value to a patient's health may also squeeze out services beneficial to some patients. The challenge for reformers is to balance cost containment with other policy objectives.

Reforms of Medicare and Medicaid that shift costs to individuals (e.g., increasing the eligibility age for Medicare) or states (e.g., converting federal subsidies for Medicaid to block grants) should be distinguished from those that improve efficiency and might be emulated by private insurance companies (e.g., devising incentives that reduce hospital readmissions or improving the way Medicare pays for services). Other policies—such as a mandate on employers to pay for health coverage for their employees—may not increase federal outlays even though they require additional health spending by the private sector. Shifting responsibility for policy goals through regulation would not create an entry in the federal budget even if the effects would be equivalent to imposing a tax and expanding a federal subsidy or program. Such policies might improve the federal government's narrowly construed fiscal position and yet worsen the health spending burden on the rest of the economy.

Uncertainty About What Works

In contrast to the policy options for Social Security (discussed in the next chapter), there is little certainty about the magnitude of budget savings that could be realized from the many possible reforms in Medicare and Medicaid. Social Security makes cash payments to a known population of beneficiaries, but health programs pay for the use of medical services for which the total cost depends on many factors—such as how many people are diagnosed with particular illnesses, the severity of those illnesses, and how those illnesses are treated according to prevailing and emerging medical practices in different parts of the country.

The savings that can be expected from Medicare and Medicaid options that make adjustments to existing payment levels or otherwise work within current institutional settings are somewhat predictable, at least over a short time span. However, the budget effects of policies that depart from current practices or that rely on significant changes in the practice of medicine or the business of health care are much more difficult to predict, particularly over a long period of time. Options such as expanding the use of health information technology or expanded funding for research comparing the effectiveness of alternative treatments may have the potential to achieve significant reductions in health system costs, particularly over a horizon of several decades. However, existing evidence on the performance of such major changes in the delivery of health care also suggests that near-term savings would be quite modest and longer-term savings highly uncertain.

Poor incentives, inadequate information, and structural impediments to more cost-effective practice have defeated many efforts to limit costs throughout the health care system. Successful reform will require many building blocks, including changes that would transform private insurance, public programs, individual behavior, and the culture and practice of medicine. It will be an ongoing learning process, not a one-time event. Thus, the extent to which any proposal can achieve that goal is an open question. There is a great deal that is not known about the potential effects of specific policies, and policies will have to be adjusted to take advantage of successes and to learn from failures.

BROAD REFORM APPROACHES

The debate over the best general strategy for reform raises fundamental questions about the system and people's values. Should the system rely on the competitive market and consumer choice to establish appropriate incentives for greater efficiency? Or should it rely on strong government regulation to manage health delivery, control costs directly, and protect individuals from financial risks that they should not have to bear? Without attempting to answer these questions definitively, this section presents some of the very broadest classes of alternative health care cost-control strategies. Some of these broad alternatives would change the entire health care system and could encompass Medicare and Medicaid as part of a major reform. Still others would bend the cost curve in the non-federal market and thereby help Medicare and Medicaid to achieve similar savings. Each alternative has a set of enthusiastic advocates and a set of strong-voiced opponents. The discussion begins with those options that entail the strongest government intervention in the health care system and end with the most market-driven policies.

A Single-Payer Health Insurance System

The most interventionist broad policy option would probably be a government-run single-payer health insurance system. Under this approach, the federal government would establish an insurance entity to offer health insurance and would prohibit private health insurance, except perhaps as a supplement to the publicly provided insurance. The government insurance entity could operate in different ways. For example, it could run the entire health care system, as is the case in the United Kingdom. Alternatively, like Medicare, it could set payment rates and contract its operations to private companies (which is handled differently under traditional Medicare, as one model, and Medicare Advantage, as another). There are many other possible options.

Government would dictate the terms of coverage, and it could also become much more closely involved in deciding how medicine is practiced. Advocates (see, e.g., Krugman, 2005; Krugman and Wells, 2006) argue that government as insurer would end the worst practices ascribed to private insurers, notably including denying coverage because of individuals' medical conditions. Because it would set prices, government could slow the growth of costs by fiat. With only one insurer, administrative costs (now driven in part by multiple paperwork requirements of different insurers) would decline. The government insurer would be free to innovate, perhaps along the lines of the arguably successful Veterans Health Administration (Longman, 2007). Furthermore, such a system would relieve businesses of the burden of managing health insurance for their employees.

Opponents (see, e.g., Committee for Economic Development, 2007; Goodman, 2005) reply that any monopoly in health care would slow or end innovation and that a government monopoly would be the worst of all. Government price setting, they say, inevitably would lead to significant misallocation of resources. The Medicare program has failed to overcome political constraints to drive innovation in the practice of medicine, and it remains largely stuck in fee-for-service medicine with only a costly flawed and partial attempt at managed care (now known as Medicare Advantage) as an alternative. In this view, a single-payer system would fail to achieve innovation for the same reason. Opponents also argue that Medicare's administrative costs are low only because the program is underadministered, as evidenced by what they say are frequent revelations of provider fraud. Simpler paperwork systems could be created with far less intrusion. Government price setting in Medicare has not been successful in limiting total cost growth, at least in part because providers have found ways to bill for more and more expensive diagnoses and treatments to recover some of the income they lost when government cut the prices of individual services.

In answer to some of these arguments, it should be noted that single-payer systems can vary greatly in generosity and costs by, for example, varying deductibles and copayments. They can be operated with a budget cap, as in Canada, or as an open-ended system.

A "Robust Public Option"

Short of a single-payer system, a so-called "robust public option" would set up a government insurance company to compete with private insurers. The public insurer would have authority to compel doctors, hospitals, and other providers to work for it at rates dictated by government, usually specified as Medicare rates (which are estimated to be below provider cost for at least some services and institutions). Advocates (see, e.g., Hacker, 2009) claim that such a public insurer would use its pricing power to lower the prices of private insurers by competition and would raise the standards of the insurance industry by its example, such as by offering coverage to individuals regardless of their medical condition.

Opponents (see, e.g., Cannon, 2009a; Minarik, 2009a, 2009b) counter that a government insurer's power to dictate prices, its absence of a need to earn a profit, its lower cost of capital, and the implicit guarantee of a bailout would be sufficient to drive private firms out of the market or out of business, even if they were more efficient. With private insurers gone, the robust public option would quickly become a single-payer system, with all the problems that entails. And until private insurers were driven out of business, they would be squeezed by providers' attempts to recover their losses in the public plan with higher charges in the private sector.

A "Non-Robust Public Option"

For want of a better term, a "non-robust public option" would create a government insurance company that competes on the proverbial "level playing field"—without the power to compel providers to work with below-cost compensation, without access to Treasury Department financing, and without a government guarantee. Advocates (see, e.g., Committee on Ways and Means et al., 2009) believe that such a public insurer would attract customers through ethical practices, including covering individuals without reference to health conditions. It would inject competition into the marketplace, especially in markets, such as those in less populous or rural areas, that are now dominated by a single private insurer.

Opponents (see, e.g., Cannon, 2009a; Minarik, 2009a, 2009b) reply that there already are many private insurance companies and that one more company competing on a truly level playing field would not change the competitive nature of the marketplace. Rural markets are uncompetitive in large part because of the small number of insured consumers (because of sparse populations and also because of the large percentages of uninsured individuals in those areas) and limited health care purchasing power; with a reform that extended coverage to all, those problems would solve themselves to the extent feasible. Opponents also question whether a truly level playing field is attainable: the implicit guarantee that any government enterprise would enjoy, even with a legal disclaimer (noting the recent experience of Fannie Mae and Freddie Mac, for example) would inhibit private competitors and thereby reduce the degree of competition in the marketplace. It is also possible that sicker consumers would be drawn to a public plan and would thereby make its risk pool less viable. These factors would not exactly or completely counterbalance the possible market advantages of such a public plan, but they would make the management of the plan even more difficult and its effects more problematic.

Price Controls

At another level of intervention, government could impose price controls in health care (see, e.g., Oberlander and White, 2009; White, 2009a, 2009b). At a stroke, advocates say, this would end the unsustainable growth of health care costs and the alleged unconscionable profits and incomes in the health care industry. Evidence that health spending varies substantially across the country suggests that there are excesses that could be eliminated without effects on health care.

Opponents (see, e.g., Butler, 1998; Coulam et al., 2009) respond that the controlled prices across thousands of different health products and services would inevitably be wrong and would lead to massive resource misallocations. They point to examples of price reductions in Medicare: one result was that providers partly offset reduced prices for individual services by making more aggressive diagnoses and ordering more and different services. The variation in spending across the country arises more because of differences in the volume of services delivered than on variation in price, suggesting that price controls are not a simple way to cut spending. Finally, opponents doubt that either political and administrative processes or economic science would allow cutting only those prices that are excessive, in only the geographic areas where they are excessive, by precisely (or even nearly) the amount of the excess. Rather, the political process would gravitate toward equal across-the-board cuts, which would reduce reimbursements of both efficient and inefficient treatments and providers.

Individual, Cost-Conscious Choice of Insurance Plans

A less interventionist and more market-oriented approach would be to have individuals use a fixed-dollar contribution to choose from the available private insurance plans (see, e.g., Committee for Economic Development, 2007). A fixed-dollar contribution means that an individual saves money by choosing a less expensive plan. A similar system, known as the Federal Employees Health Benefits Plan, is available to members of Congress and all federal employees. Under it, the central market-maker (the U.S. Office of Personnel Management) sets rules for insurers and acts as a broker or "exchange" for individuals. This system prohibits consideration of preexisting conditions for enrollment (or re-enrollment). Advocates argue that such a system, if extended nationwide, would subject all private insurers to competition and give providers a reason to try to deliver quality care at the lowest possible price. As under the regulated Federal Employees plan, insurers would not be able to select their customers and so could not profit from selecting lower-risk individuals. Instead, they would direct their energies toward attracting and satisfying customers. In sum, market forces would drive both providers and insurers to pursue efficiency and innovation.

Opponents (see, e.g., Berenson, 2005) argue that private insurers behave badly under the current system and will not change their ways, or that penny-pinching competition is not the health care that the country needs. They also doubt that competition would in fact help to reduce costs in health care, given that the "market" that now exists has not done so. Large employers and labor unions oppose this approach because they believe that the current system delivers quality health care today, and because they are advantaged by their ability to provide better health care than smaller employers with small risk pools that are unattractive to insurers.

Eliminating Group Health Insurance

An even more market-oriented approach than one like the Federal Employees Health Benefits Plan would eliminate group health insurance so that there would be only an individual insurance market (see, e.g., Cannon, 2009b). It would establish a large—perhaps income-related—tax credit for all individuals to buy health insurance and replace the current tax exclusion for employers who provide group insurance. This approach could reduce existing regulation, so that people could choose health insurance plans that do not meet current state regulations or could allow people to purchase insurance across state lines. Advocates claim that individuals would shop for cheaper health insurance and drive market prices down. Under that pressure, and especially if empowered by loosening of state regulation, insurers would offer relatively inexpensive plans stripped of mandated coverages (such as mental health) that are required by many current regulators and that increase costs. Plans would be expected to move toward high deductibles with medical savings accounts, and individuals would respond by forgoing unnecessary care.

Opponents (see, e.g., Barry et al., 2008; McDevitt et al., 2010) counter that insurers in an individual insurance market will always have an incentive to avoid bad risks and that a stronger market organizer in a competitive large-group system (like the Federal Employees plan) is essential. They also characterize the supposed competition among less regulated insurers as a "race to the bottom," in which insurers drop coverages that are necessary for people with expensive medical conditions, thereby beginning a zero-sum competition on the basis of risk selection. Furthermore, opponents argue, the omission of such coverages may be accepted by people while they are healthy and enjoy lower premiums, but, ultimately, the absence of those coverages will cause medical expense crises when people are older or contract serious illnesses. Opponents also believe that high-deductible plans do not focus on the real health cost problem, because most money is spent on expensive cases whose costs are far more than feasible deductibles; thus, individual patients have little incentive to forgo unnecessary care. In addition, opponents argue, individuals lack the technical knowledge to make complex medical decisions.

Summary of Broad Reform Approaches

Advocates of these various broad reform approaches believe that they would induce the health care industry to find ways to deliver quality care more efficiently and that those improved methods would be applied in serving Medicare and Medicaid patients as well. In some options (including use of the individual market or of individual choice as in the Federal Employees plan), individuals could have the option of keeping the cost-efficient plans that they choose over their working lives, thereby "growing into" an alternative to the Medicare program gradually over time. Through those mechanisms, the federal government would share in the savings from systemwide reform.

SPECIFIC REFORM OPTIONS

The rest of this chapter presents some of the most widely discussed specific reform options that depend (in various combinations) on market incentives and on government regulation to slow spending and improve health outcomes and the quality of care. This list of options is meant to be representative rather than exhaustive; it would be impossible to describe all of the major proposals for reforming health care and limiting federal health spending.

Although a number of these ideas have the potential to slow the growth of spending, their success is not assured. Some options require extensive further development and experimentation before they can be implemented widely, and it would likely take a long time for them to yield systemwide savings. At least in the near term (for three out of the four health spending trajectories laid out by the committee), the "strong medicine" of mandated limits on Medicare and Medicaid spending may be the only reasonably certain way (politics aside) to slow federal health spending as much and as soon as necessary. Such restrictions are hardly without problems, not the least of which is that they can be blunt instruments that could limit access or deny some necessary or beneficial care. In addition, experience with various limits to date shows that they may fail to be enforced even if they are legislated.[11] Nevertheless, if political barriers can be surmounted, direct controls (imposed gradually) offer the most certain short-term route to slowing the growth of federal health spending until longer-term improvements can take effect. And although it cannot be predicted, such spending constraints may spur stakeholders to seek out system improvements and efficiencies in ways that they would not otherwise. However, spending caps should not be confused with true reform. This section discusses two variants of caps on federal health spending: absolute limits on government payments to providers and capped-amount vouchers in place of open-ended entitlement. (A separate cap on the largest tax expenditure for health is also discussed below and presented as an element of a simplified tax option in Chapter 8.)

Other system reforms and improvements fall into two categories: those with relatively direct implications for slowing spending growth and those whose effects are less direct. Examples of system reforms that are focused on reducing federal spending include capping the tax exclusion for employer-sponsored coverage, reforming Medicare payment systems (through the use of bundled payments, accountable care organizations, pay-for-performance measures, improved fee-for-service pricing, and lower payments to private Medicare Advantage plans), restricting Medicare eligibility, restructuring Medicare premiums and cost-sharing requirements, and limiting malpractice awards. Examples of system reforms that are primarily concerned with care quality and health outcomes rather than cost, but which may also have indirect implications for slowing spending growth, include comparative effectiveness research, health information technology, disease management, and health promotion. These options merely illustrate some of the plausible approaches and are by no means a comprehensive list of possible reforms.

The estimated savings from most individual reform options are small in comparison with the total savings that will be needed to slow Medicare and Medicaid spending growth to a rate closer to that of GDP growth. The savings that could be achieved through a combination of options may be more or less than the sum of the savings estimates for individual options, depending on whether they reinforce or reduce each other's effectiveness and the degree to which they overlap in achieving particular savings. It also should be kept in mind that these cost estimates were generated within the context of a financing and delivery system that is frequently characterized as fragmented and misaligned (see, e.g., Cebul et al., 2008); many of these options may very well produce different results under a reformed, better organized payment and delivery system.

Imposing Caps on Federal Health Spending

As noted above, because savings from restructuring the large and complex health care industry take time to achieve and are very difficult to estimate, achieving overall federal fiscal stability may require near-term savings through more direct and potentially more painful methods, as unattractive as that course would be (although the pain of such caps would be mitigated to the extent that they lead to improvement in the efficacy and efficiency of the health system). It will be a challenge to set payment limits in ways that fully account for the health needs of the beneficiary population, minimize the financial hardships for low-income people, and take account of the difficulties that the elderly and low-income populations might have in navigating complex health coverage choices on their own. Congress also would have to adhere to any budget limits it sets for itself, and experiences to date have been disappointing. (See Chapter 10 for a discussion of ways to encourage greater congressional budget discipline.)

One way to impose a spending cap on Medicare is to set an absolute limit on federal payments to providers, placing pressure on them to manage their patient loads and trim nonessential services. However, establishing such caps in a fashion that would minimize dislocations would be quite difficult, and patients would ultimately bear the effects of the limitations. Alternatively, public insurance programs could be converted from defined benefits with open-ended subsidies to fixed-value vouchers, whose aggregate cost to the government could be controlled. This approach would be more transparent in transferring the risk of high-care spending from the government to patients, who would use vouchers to shop for private insurance. However, given the limited and expensive nature of coverage in the individual insurance market, reforms that make competitive group rates available to uninsured individuals would be necessary. For either approach to be successful, the traditional Medicare program would have to become fully and irrevocably accountable for its spending. (The law currently provides that shortfalls in Parts B and D of Medicare are automatically covered by general revenues, which means Medicare does not now face a binding budget constraint.) After-the-fact bailouts would have to be prevented.

For Medicaid, vouchers also could be used to help individuals pay the cost of private health insurance instead of paying directly for health services for the low-income population.[12] However, the potential for significant savings would be limited because Medicaid already costs less than private insurance for comparable beneficiaries (Hadley and Holahan, 2003; Ku and Broaddus, 2008). Another way to cap Medicaid spending would be to convert federal matching payments into a block grant, eliminating the open-ended payments to states for services delivered under the program and making states fully responsible for the fiscal consequences of program management and fluctuations in caseloads. States already have experience with managing such hard budget constraints, given the annual struggles of many states to comply with balanced budget requirements—which often centrally involve Medicaid costs. Yet given the importance of Medicaid costs as a component of state budgets, it likely would be very difficult to meet still tighter targets.

In the study baseline, nominal spending for Medicare and Medicaid is projected to grow at an annual average rate of 7.5 percent in the decade after 2012 (with nominal GDP growing at an annual average rate of 4.1 percent over that period).[13] If federal spending caps were to do all the work of slowing the rate of federal health spending growth during that decade, they would have to reduce the growth rate (as a share of GDP) by an average of 1.1 percentage points per year for the most constrained spending trajectory (see Figure 5-1, above), and they would have to do so by an average of 0.8 and 0.4 percentage points per year for the two intermediate trajectories. (The high spending trajectory, as has been noted, follows the study baseline until 2030.)

It is difficult to predict how the health care industry would respond to a federal spending cap (and also how the health industry would react to state government responses to a federal cap) and what the ultimate consequences would be. The outcomes will depend in part on the extent of institutional bottlenecks to achieving efficiency (administrators who can only imperfectly control the behavior of physicians, a shortage of nurses, etc.) and whether or not the "shock" of imposing dollar constraints would be sufficient to force changes in long-standing arrangements. Similarly, wage reductions and service cuts may or may not have an effect on quality, depending on whether (for example) health professionals behave as monopolistic actors who obtain extra income through their market power and whether the services that are cut are really necessary or not. Geographic factors will also be relevant: genuine savings may be easier to achieve (all else equal) in regions of the country that are now less efficient, but fewer gains may be possible in the regions that are already relatively more efficient. Savings in Medicaid, if not achieved through efficiencies, would burden the states through their share of the cost of the program. Reductions in Medicare growth could be passed on to patients and employers in the private sector.

System Reforms with Direct Implications for Slowing Federal Health Spending Growth

Cap the Tax Exclusion for Employer-Sponsored Coverage

Health-related tax expenditures are open ended and have been growing at a rate not much slower than that of Medicare and Medicaid spending (and health costs in general). The current tax code excludes from workers' taxable incomes the contributions made by employers to health insurance premiums, without any limit. That exclusion has fueled the growth of employer-sponsored coverage, but it has also contributed to the escalation of health care spending in ways that are inefficient and inequitable. As noted above, there is substantial evidence that the tax preference increases the volume and price of health care, although there is also considerable uncertainty regarding the true size of this effect (Newhouse, 1996, as cited in Joint Committee on Taxation, 2008b). The value of the tax exclusion also increases with income, so that people with more income receive larger tax savings.[14]

Capping the value of the exclusion would increase awareness of the costs of health care by beneficiaries and is likely to promote the offering and purchase of lower-premium health coverage with more efficient networks of providers, possibly with higher deductibles and copayments. Such a cap also would increase revenues and is one element of the simplified income tax structure option described in Chapter 8. A cap could be designed in many ways, with estimated savings varying accordingly. The Commonwealth Fund, for example, estimates that a cap on the deductibility of premiums set at 110 percent of the value of the median employer-sponsored plan could generate an additional $130 billion in tax revenues over the next decade (Schoen et al., 2007). The Urban Institute has estimated that policy options capping the exclusion at the 75th percentile of premiums would generate $62 billion in tax revenues over the next 10 years if indexed by the rate of growth of medical expenses, and it would generate $224 billion if indexed by the rate of growth of GDP (Clemans-Cope et al., 2009).

Reform Medicare Payment Systems

Medicare outlays could be reduced by improving the program's efficiency through at least five different payment system reforms (which imperfectly approximate the incentives from capitated prepayment as practiced in the private sector).

First, Medicare could restructure payments to cover more of a patient's episode of care, such as including certain preadmission and post-discharge services in the same "bundled payment." Providers, who would be at risk for costs in excess of the bundle amount, would have an incentive to avoid unnecessary care and might be motivated to reduce the chance of having an avoidable complication or preventable readmission. However, there is reason to be concerned that providers might be penalized for unanticipated spending that is outside of their control and that inaccurate payment rates could distort incentives to provide needed care. Evidence regarding cost savings is also mixed.[15]

Second, Medicare could promote "accountable care organizations" in conjunction with a cap on reimbursements. The members of such organizations, which would include hospitals, primary care and specialist physicians, and other providers, would agree to be held accountable for their performance in terms of cost and quality of care. The organization would not function as a traditional managed care plan; rather, it would be paid on a fee-for-service basis. Any savings from more efficient delivery of care would be shared between the organization and the federal government (see Fisher et al., 2009c). Although accountable care organizations have the laudable goal of promoting more efficient and integrated care, the extent to which participating providers would actually change their behaviors is unknown.

Third, rather than continuing to pay for services without regard to their effects on patients, Medicare could incorporate measures of performance in fee-for-service payment formulas. Program expenditures would fall if the average payment rate was lowered as performance-based pricing was introduced. Implementing a pay-for-performance approach is not necessarily simple or straightforward, however, and system errors may adversely affect health care quality and access (Cannon, 2006).

Fourth, the accuracy of fee-for-service prices could be improved. Some analysts have argued that formula-based pricing for health services is likely to overpay some services relative to the market and underpay others (Ginsburg and Grossman, 2005; Hayes et al., 2007). These inaccuracies distort the provision of care, leading providers to oversupply care when reimbursement levels exceed actual costs, and undersupply care when reimbursement is lower than actual costs. Market-based reforms, such as competitive bidding methods, might improve payment accuracy and reduce program spending. Competitive bidding has been proposed to set payments for durable medical equipment and clinical laboratory services. However, there is a risk that prices might go up and services to beneficiaries might be reduced as smaller suppliers go out of business (Antos and Rivlin, 2007b).

Fifth, the payment differential between Medicare Advantage private plans and traditional Medicare could be reduced. In 2008, payment "benchmarks" for the Medicare Advantage program were, on average, 17 percent higher than projected per capita spending in traditional Medicare (Congressional Budget Office, 2008b:106). Much of this benefit accrues to private plan participants in the form of supplemental benefits or lower premiums (Congressional Budget Office, 2007d:7). The Congressional Budget Office (2008b) estimates that setting the benchmark for Medicare Advantage private plans at the same level as local per capita spending in traditional Medicare would yield approximately $157 billion in savings over the next 10 years.

Restrict Medicare Eligibility

The federal government could gradually increase the Medicare eligibility age from 65 to 67, as was done for the age of retirement with full benefits in the Social Security program. That would reduce program spending and increase revenue from payroll taxes somewhat as at least some people delayed their retirement. The resulting Medicare savings would be modest, because the youngest elderly as a group are healthier and use less expensive medical services than those who are still older. The Congressional Budget Office (2008b) estimates that raising the Medicare eligibility age by 2 months annually starting in 2014 until the eligibility age reached 67 in 2025 would reduce Medicare spending by $85.6 billion over the next decade. It is also estimated that an additional $6.8 billion would be saved in Social Security payments in that period because some people would delay their retirement to retain employer-sponsored health benefits.

Although increasing the eligibility age might keep older workers on the job longer and raise their retirement income, it would also expose employers to higher payroll and benefit costs. Moreover, Davidoff and Johnson (2003) estimate that increasing the Medicare eligibility age to 67 would cause 9 percent of 65- and 66-year-olds (amounting to approximately 356,000 people) to become uninsured.

Restructure Medicare Cost-Sharing Requirements

Fee-for-service Medicare has a complex benefit structure, largely because of historical and political factors (Oberlander, 2003; Patashnik, 2000). There are separate deductibles for hospital and outpatient care, and copayments vary among covered services. This structure is confusing to beneficiaries and fails to provide consistent and effective financial incentives for prudent use of services. The program could be restructured with a single deductible and copayment requirement for all services, with the levels set to reduce federal outlays. The Congressional Budget Office (2008b) estimates that Medicare could save $26.4 billion over the next decade through one such restructuring.

Several changes to Medicare premiums also could generate savings. For example, raising the Medicare premium for physicians' and other outpatient services (Part B) from the current 25 percent to 35 percent of the program's costs would generate $217 billion in savings over the next 10 years. For the prescription drug part of the program (Part D), the Congressional Budget Office (2008b) estimates that changing it to conform to the current Part B premiums (25 percent of the program's cost for beneficiaries with annual incomes of up to $85,000, gradually increasing to 80 percent of costs for couples with annual incomes of more than $426,000 in 2009) would increase program savings by $7.8 billion over the next decade.

An alternative to higher premiums would be to raise the payroll tax rate for Medicare. Premiums are essentially user fees that force those who directly benefit from the program to pay part of the cost, unlike payroll taxes, which shift the cost of current beneficiaries to younger generations.[16] A 1 percentage point increase in the tax rate would generate $592 billion over 10 years. If the Medicare tax rate was increased only on earnings above $150,000, the revenue gain would be $77 billion (Congressional Budget Office, 2008b).

Limit Malpractice Awards

It has been argued that legal liability fears cause providers to engage in the practice of "defensive medicine," administering treatments that do not have worthwhile medical benefits (Kessler and McClellan, 1996). However, the effect of defensive medicine on health spending is unclear (Congressional Budget Office, 2006b), and the budgetary effects of limiting awards from medical malpractice torts may be relatively modest. The Congressional Budget Office (2008b) estimates that limiting awards from medical malpractice torts would lower federal health spending by $4.4 billion and increase federal revenue by $1.3 billion over the next 10 years. These figures may understate the potential savings if litigation fears have suppressed (in ways overlooked by conventional cost estimates) physicians' efforts to pursue cost and quality improvements in medical care settings. Opponents of limits on tort awards argue that such limits might cause health care providers to exercise less caution and make it more difficult for victims to obtain appropriate compensation for their injuries (Congressional Budget Office, 2008b:22).

System Reforms with Indirect Implications for Slowing Federal Health Spending Growth

Systematic, comprehensive reform must also concern itself with care quality and health outcomes. A number of health reform options speak to these issues: comparative effectiveness research, health information technology, disease management, health promotion, and better primary care.

Comparative Effectiveness Research

Comparative effectiveness research assesses how well a health care technology or treatment for a specific disease works in comparison with other options. Such research can, ideally, provide a scientific basis for using treatments that provide the highest-quality care at the lowest possible price. A government role in financing and promoting the research will be unavoidable, since there are few incentives for private-sector entities to invest in comparative effectiveness research.

Randomized clinical trials can cost tens of millions of dollars (National Institutes of Health, 2007) and take years to complete. Analyzing data on medical claims or synthesizing existing studies would be less expensive than clinical trials, but might yield less definitive results. Even when the research is completed, there is no mechanism for ensuring that providers use the information in their practices. Historically, disseminating practice guidelines has seldom had significant effects on providers' actions, although practices might change if the health industry became more market oriented.[17] A more effective but controversial approach, given the limitations and complexities of comparative effectiveness research (Gottlieb, 2009), would require Medicare to base its coverage decisions on such research. Alternatively, Medicare might increase payments to providers who adhere to guidelines derived from such research. State Medicaid programs might adopt similar policies. Currently, neither the federal nor state programs use cost-effectiveness information to make coverage and reimbursement decisions (Gold et al., 2007). The Congressional Budget Office (2008b) estimates that an increase of $1.1 billion over the next decade in federal funding for comparative effectiveness research would modestly reduce health spending, resulting in an increase in net federal spending of about $860 million. The American Recovery and Reinvestment Act of 2009 appropriated $1.1 billion for such research.

Health Information Technology

Health information technology refers to a variety of electronic tools used to manage health care information. It has the potential to save money and improve quality by reducing the need to maintain paper files, eliminating duplicative tests, encouraging more-accurate and efficient drug prescription, improving hospital patient flow, and reducing demands on hospital nursing staff. Like comparative effectiveness research, health information technology is generally recognized as a form of public good in which the private sector will underinvest. To date, information on the cost and quality effects of such technology is limited to a relatively small number of studies. It is not clear whether these findings can be broadly generalized (see Shekelle et al., 2006). The Congressional Budget Office (2008b) predicts that, by requiring all Medicare providers to adopt health information technology by 2015, the federal government could save $34 billion during the next decade.[18] The American Recovery and Reinvestment Act of 2009 provided approximately $19 billion in payment incentives to encourage Medicare and Medicaid providers to adopt health information technology.

Disease Management

Disease management programs are designed to reduce avoidable complications associated with chronic disease by assisting patients in managing their conditions. Programs vary, but components include patient outreach to encourage adherence to medication regimens, fastidious monitoring of weight or other key features, behavior modification programs, and an emphasis on preventive care. Studies have shown that disease management is associated with improved adherence to evidence-based guidelines and better disease control (Mattke et al., 2007), but the evidence on cost savings is inconclusive. Early results from a disease management trial in Medicare suggest the program is unlikely to achieve savings and may actually increase spending (McCall et al., 2007). Some people have argued that the savings potential of the Medicare demonstration project was hindered by implementation challenges (Wilson, 2007), but previous trials in Medicare also failed to produce significant savings (Bott et al., 2009).

Health Promotion

Unhealthful behaviors—including poor diet, lack of exercise, smoking, and excessive alcohol consumption—contribute both to poor health outcomes and increased health spending. Public policies aimed at smoking cessation, including cigarette taxes and workplace smoking bans, have been shown to reduce smoking rates (Carpenter, 2007; Carpenter and Cook, 2008; DeCicca and McCleod, 2008; DeCicca et al., 2008; Evans et al., 1999). Similarly, studies have shown that alcohol consumption falls in response to higher taxes and other policies, such as Sunday sales bans (Baltagi and Goel, 1990; Baltagi and Griffin, 1995; Cook and Tauchen, 1982; Dhaval and Saffer, 2007; Stehr, 2007). The effects of policies to reduce obesity are less certain.[19] Small school- and community-based obesity programs have been effective at reducing body mass indices (Economos and Irish-Hauser, 2007; Gortmaker et al., 1999), and some workplace interventions have been associated with modest health improvements (Goetzel et al., 2009; Haines et al., 2007; Proper et al., 2003). If an effective clinical method of preventing obesity could be found, it would probably result in lower lifetime medical spending (Goldman et al., 2009). However, evidence is lacking as to whether such programs are cost-effective in practice (Cawley, 2007).

Better Primary Care

Better primary care could improve health-care quality and contribute to lower health-care costs by keeping people out of emergency rooms, doing a better job managing chronic diseases, and reducing reliance on medical specialists. One proposal, sometimes referred to as a patient-centered medical home, would reimburse primary-care providers at a higher rate for improvements such as facilitating better disease management, extending office hours, or adopting health information technology. A medical home demonstration project in the North Carolina Medicaid program reported savings of 11 percent per member per month (Mercer Human Resources Consulting, 2007), and preliminary findings from a trial in the Geisinger Health System indicate that medical homes led to a 7 percent savings (Paulus et al., 2008). However, it is uncertain whether similar savings could be achieved if medical homes were widely adopted by public programs, such as Medicare. Medical homes also do not address the larger issue of the growing deficiency in the number of primary-care physicians.

Caveats Regarding Savings from Reform

A major objective of health system reform is the more efficient use of resources—but efficient use might not yield federal budget savings. Policies that increase the efficiency of health care delivery might promote the wider use of more effective but more expensive treatments, improving health outcomes without reducing spending. For example, the identification of better treatments through comparative effectiveness research might result in an increase in the number of patients treated—and, therefore, in higher costs.[20] Any savings that result from comparative effectiveness research, moreover, would occur well after the research was funded because of the long lead time required to produce treatment recommendations and for the medical community to put those recommendations into practice.

In a similar vein, better health information technology may increase health spending by identifying people who need treatment but are not currently receiving it. Substantial savings through various applications of technology are possible only if medical practice becomes dramatically more efficient. Health information technology might promote such a change (albeit with attendant adjustment costs for providers), but by itself would not necessarily create such savings.

Preventive medical care (which includes things such as immunizations and screening tests) also may not be the most promising place to look for significant systemwide cost savings. Most preventive medical care improves health outcomes but increases costs (Cohen et al., 2008; Russell, 2007, 2009). Typically, preventive care must be offered to a relatively large group of people of whom only a small fraction will directly benefit through an averted illness (Cohen et al., 2008).

CONCLUSION

The difficulty of establishing a fiscally sustainable long-term growth curve for federal health spending can hardly be overstated. The reform challenge is complicated by the need to balance cost containment with other important objectives. Virtually any plan to expand access will require additional federal spending. Similarly, reforms aimed at improving health care quality are likely to increase spending, at least in the near term. Delivery system changes—such as the expansion of health information technology and better primary care—may require considerable up-front investment, with cost savings not being realized until well in the future. Other popular ideas, including prevention and wellness initiatives, may add value to the health system but are unlikely to reduce spending.

Better payment approaches also cannot, by themselves, ensure that the resulting trends in federal health spending will be sustainable, and there is considerable uncertainty about the total budgetary savings that would accrue over the long term from the many possible combinations of health system reforms. At least in the near term, some form of health spending cap is more likely to reduce federal spending than any particular reform or combination of reforms. Although a cap would have the undesirable effect of shifting costs to nongovernment payers, it also has the potential to contribute to longer-term system improvements as fiscal constraints spur administrators and payers to seek efficiencies; given the complexities and uncertainties at issue, the response cannot be predicted. At any rate, the committee does not intend to imply that spending caps could be a long-term substitute for fundamental and systemic reform.

Health spending on its current trend is unsustainable, yet the nation has structured its health system and policy-making process as if there were few resource constraints. An essential prerequisite for change is full acceptance by the public that difficult steps need to be taken. We do not minimize the nature of the challenges that lie ahead. Reorganizing and rationalizing the ways in which health benefits and services are delivered are essential to ensure the fiscal sustainability that is vital to the nation's future.

The four Medicare and Medicaid spending trajectories described above illustrate a range of potential reductions in the rate of growth for health spending, without specifying which combination of reform options would achieve those reductions. These illustrative options reflect an appropriate modesty about what will lower costs, especially in the near term. They also highlight the very difficult decisions of how much stringency to apply to this sector of the federal budget and national economy. The amount of federal health spending growth reduction achieved over the next several decades will determine the range of choices in other areas of the budget, on both the spending and revenue side, for putting the federal government on a fiscally sustainable course.

NOTES

1.   The federal government also finances several smaller programs, including the Children's Health Insurance Program, the military's TRICARE program, health care for veterans, and the Indian Health Service.

2. Pilot projects are more likely than demonstrations to yield large-scale improvements because pilot projects, if they prove successful, can be implemented nationwide without congressional action.

3. Moreover, CBO's scoring of the Affordable Health Care for America Act (see Box 5-1) assumes that major spending provisions (such as constraints on Medicare payment rates) "are enacted and remain unchanged throughout the next two decades, which is often not the case for major legislation" (Congressional Budget Office 2009f:13).

4. For this purpose, health care spending has to be adjusted for changes in the age and gender composition of the population. Thus, for example, even with effective discipline on costs, spending will grow faster as the population becomes older on average.

5. See Burman (2008) for a discussion of using the value-added tax as a financing source for health care. (See Chapter 8 for a discussion of the value-added tax as a general revenue source.)

6. The rate of growth of health spending in the United States is nearly the same as that of European countries. Between 1997 and 2003, for example, the 15 original members of the European Union (EU) experienced a 4.2 percent increase in health spending, compared with an average GDP growth of 2.4 percent. Over the same period, U.S. health spending grew 4.3 percent, while GDP grew 1.9 percent (Antos and Rivlin, 2007a).

7. The Congressional Budget Office (2009c:27) also notes that Medicare began paying hospitals a predetermined rate for each admission under a "prospective payment system" in 1983.

8. For example, see Smith et al. (2009) for a discussion of the interrelationship between technology and health insurance and the possibility that insurance coverage may not continue to stimulate technological change to the extent that it has in the past.

9. Medicaid pays for cost sharing, premiums, and some treatments and services that Medicare does not cover, but it is a secondary insurer for this group.

10. An alternative approach to calculating the cost of this tax expenditure (Joint Committee on Taxation, 2009) goes beyond conventional estimates by looking at the impact of the employer-sponsored health care exclusion on payroll taxes and assuming certain behavioral responses by taxpayers. This analysis puts income and payroll tax revenue losses in 2008 at $133 billion and $94 billion, respectively.

11. The sustainable growth rate formula stands as an example of a budget cap that has not worked. Created by Congress to limit the growth of Medicare payments for physician services, the formula ties physician payments to economic growth. Since Medicare physician spending has been growing significantly faster than the economy, the formula consistently calls for cuts in physicians' fees. The magnitude of these reductions has proven to be politically untenable, however, and Congress has repeatedly used its authority to override the sustainable growth rate formula.

12. With vouchers, private plans would have a relatively fixed budget and have to manage care as efficiently as possible. The financial risk is borne by the plans: if there are insufficient funds available, beneficiaries might get less care or poorer quality care.

13. This discussion refers to rates of growth of aggregate spending, rather than the excess cost growth measure used at the beginning of this chapter.

14. For example, people in the lower tax brackets receive cash savings from the exclusion valued at between $600 and $3,000 per year, while people with annual incomes of more than $100,000 obtain average cash savings of between $4,000 and $5,000 (Joint Committee on Taxation, 2008b:5).

15. The Medicare Participating Heart Bypass Center demonstration project found that bundled payment was associated with a 10 percent reduction in spending among Medicare bypass patients (Cromwell et al., 1998). However, another bundled payment trial implemented in the Medicare system found no effect on costs for patients undergoing cataract surgery (Abt Associates, 1997).

16. Using payroll taxes is also somewhat progressive, because although health expenses can be expected to be roughly equal for each person, people with higher incomes from work pay higher payroll taxes.

17. For an example, see Mathews (2005), who describes how Kaiser Permanente reviews clinical trials and provides guidance to its practitioners.

18. A study by RAND predicted that, if implemented effectively, fully operational health information technology systems could reduce U.S. health spending by as much as $77 billion annually (Hillestad et al., 2005). However, the RAND study came under criticism by the Congressional Budget Office (2008c) and others for using overly optimistic assumptions.

19. Food taxes are less straightforward to implement than cigarette and alcohol taxes because food is a necessity, there are few externalities associated with overeating (compared to, for example, drunk driving), and even healthy people at low risk for obesity-related problems consume junk food on occasion. A federal excise tax of 3 cents per 12 ounces of "sugar sweetened" beverages (which include a variety of carbonated and noncarbonated drinks) would generate $50.4 billion in additional revenue over the next decade (Congressional Budget Office, 2008b).

20. A comparative effectiveness research center in the United Kingdom has not produced significant savings, and some have argued it has increased spending by giving a "stamp of approval" to expensive but cost-effective treatments (Pearson and Littlejohns, 2007).

6

Options for Social Security

Social Security is today the largest and perhaps best-known federal government program. As of the end of 2008, the program had paid $9 trillion in retirement benefits for elderly and disabled people and their dependents and survivors since its inception. About 52 million people, one of every 6 Americans, currently receive monthly Social Security benefit checks: 33 million retired workers, 2.4 million spouses, 6.4 million survivors of deceased workers, and 9.5 million disabled workers and their dependents (Social Security Administration, 2009a).

Although Social Security is currently running annual surpluses, it is projected to be in substantial deficit over the long run. In the near term, Social Security's benefit payments will rise rapidly as the baby boomers retire, while its revenues will grow more slowly. In less than three decades the program's reserves will be depleted; from that time forward its sources of revenues will be sufficient to pay only about three-quarters of currently scheduled benefits. However, the program's financial course is correctable, and corrective action would contribute to making the entire federal budget sustainable.[1]

The Social Security part of the federal government's overall fiscal challenge is less complex than that posed by Medicare and Medicaid, the range of potential changes to the program available to address it are much better defined, and their consequences are easier to quantify. In the last section of this chapter we present four possible sets of program changes to make Social Security fiscally sustainable, drawn from a much larger set of potential changes that have been proposed and extensively analyzed elsewhere. (See below, "Options to Restore Solvency.") Each set—or reform option—varies in the extent to which it will reduce the future growth of benefits or increase revenues or both, and each achieves the goal of restoring Social Security to long-term solvency without altering the program's familiar and widely popular basic design.

The committee's options are illustrative: many other packages of program changes (some of them frequently advanced) are obviously possible—with similar fiscal effects but differing distributional consequences. Options that would augment or alter the program's basic structure are also possible and have been considered by others; however, the premise of the committee is that these options for structural change are neither necessary nor as politically feasible as the options we offer.

PROGRAM OVERVIEW

Since its enactment in 1935, Social Security has helped protect people against economic insecurity in old age. The basic program structure since its inception has been to assess payroll taxes on current workers and use those revenues to pay benefits to retirees.[2] Virtually all workers—more than 160 million people—pay Social Security taxes. The program's total income in 2008 was $805 billion.

In July 2009, the average monthly benefit paid to retired workers was $1,159 (about $14,000 annually), that for widows and widowers aged 60 and older was $1,118, and that for disabled workers $1,062 (Social Security Administration, 2009a).[3] In the 2008 calendar year (the last year for which complete data are available), the total amount paid in benefits was $615 billion (Social Security Administration, 2009a).

Revenues are credited to the program's trust fund, and benefit payments are made from it. The program was initially designed with the intent that dedicated, payroll tax revenues plus the interest earned on the trust fund reserves would generally cover the payments to current retirees. The balance of revenues not used immediately to pay benefits is retained in the fund,[4] where it is held in the form of special Treasury bonds. Interest earned on those reserves—which are currently in excess of $2 trillion—is also retained until used to pay benefits.

Now, and in the near future, the annual flow of dedicated tax revenues is projected to be sufficient to fully cover the annual cost of currently scheduled benefits. But starting in 2016, Social Security revenue will fall short of benefit spending by a growing amount: when that occurs, first the interest on the reserves and then the reserves themselves will have to be drawn upon. Once the latter are exhausted—now projected to be in 2037—annual Social Security tax income will be sufficient to cover only about 75 percent of the annual benefits currently "scheduled." If nothing is done to remedy the situation in the meanwhile, benefits would have to be reduced for all beneficiaries; those reductions would be about 25 percent from their currently scheduled levels.[5]

The financial outlook for Social Security has also been problematic in the past. Two circumstances have contributed to the need for periodic fiscal adjustments to maintain the program's solvency. First, legislation has expanded Social Security coverage and increased the level of benefits. Second, the evolution of work, longer average life spans, and other demographic and economic changes have resulted in the need to reestimate how many retirees will be supported in the future by those still working.

When enacted in 1935, Social Security provided only retirement benefits: that is, the program did not cover widows or widowers, children, or disabled workers whose own work experience did not qualify them for retirement benefits. And it was only for workers in commerce and industry, about 60 percent of the workforce.[6] The program (today formally known as Old Age, Survivors, and Disability Insurance or OASDI) was expanded periodically to cover additional categories of people. Benefits for surviving spouses and dependents were added early in the program's history. Later, in the 1950s, coverage was extended to those unable to work due to total and permanent disability (and for their dependents). This part of the program, although it has grown rapidly, is much smaller than the OAS part. The overall OASDI expansion greatly increased the scale of the future commitments to retirees and their dependents and survivors as well as to disabled persons and their families. And these commitments also grew after benefits were indexed for inflation. (Monthly retirement benefits were increased by legislation 10 times before automatic cost-of-living adjustments were enacted in 1972 and then periodically modified.)[7]

By the late 1970s, Social Security had all of the basic features it has today. Thereafter, legislative changes focused primarily on shoring up the program's long-run financial stability. These changes included increases in the payroll tax rate and the maximum earnings subject to the tax, future increases in the age—previously 65—at which retiring workers would be eligible for full benefits, and other minor adjustments to benefits and revenues (for details, see Apfel and Flowers, 2007).

The biggest changes that affected the program's future finances were enacted in 1983 when it appeared that the program's trust fund would soon be depleted and across-the-board benefit cuts were imminent. Payroll tax rates were increased. For certain higher-income beneficiaries, benefits became subject to the income tax, with those proceeds dedicated to the trust fund. Beginning that year, the annual cost-of-living adjustment was delayed from June to December. And the 1983 reforms provided for gradual increases in the age at which a person could retire with what are called full benefits—from 65 to 67.[8] The increased age for full benefits affected only people who were 45 or younger at the time, which allowed workers to plan for the change by increasing savings before retirement or by working longer (Achenbaum, 1986; Light, 1995).

The Social Security program has both a social and an insurance aspect.[9] Its "social" aspect refers to its helping alleviate fear (particularly for low-income workers) of an impoverished retirement, to its compulsory character, and to its progressive benefit structure. Social Security has always replaced more of the former earnings of low-wage workers than of those at upper earning levels.

Figure 6-1 shows how, for illustrative workers with different lifetime earnings paths, lower earnings lead to lower cash benefits (left axis; line with diamonds) but higher replacement rates for those earnings (right axis, line with squares).[10] Elderly retirees with the lowest income from all sources—including pensions, savings, and earnings—are most dependent on Social Security benefits; see Figure 6-2. On the basis of a 2006 survey of families and individuals 65 and older, for the lowest income quintile (with annual income of less than $11,519), Social Security benefits average 93 percent of all income. Even for the fourth quintile (total income between $28,911 and $50,064), program benefits are 50 percent of all income. Only for the top quintile (total income of at least $50,064 annually) are Social Security benefits a small (26 percent) share of all income.[11]

Social Security aims to alleviate economic insecurity in old age and among disabled people. As part of its "social" aspect, Social Security replaces a large proportion of preretirement wages for retirees with relatively low life-time earnings. This replacement is especially important

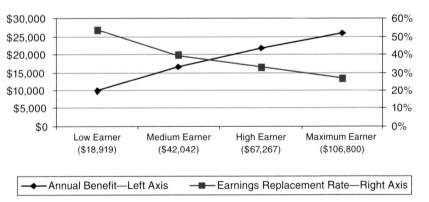

FIGURE 6-1 Annual Social Security benefits and earnings replacement rates, for workers who retire at age 65, scheduled for 2010.

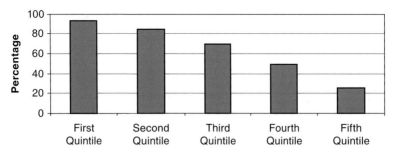

FIGURE 6-2 Social Security benefits as a percentage of total income, for families and individuals aged 65+, by quintile of total income, 2006.
NOTE: Couples are included if at least one is aged 65 or older; see also note 11.
SOURCE: Data from the Current Population Survey (Social Security Administration, 2009b:301).

and provides a safely net for those who cannot (or are not expected to) obtain retirement income on their own through individual savings, pensions, or postretirement earnings.[12] The program also provides benefits to dependents without reducing the primary earner's benefit. For all but the highest-earning 20 percent of older Americans, Social Security is the largest single source of income (Reno and Lavery, 2009). The program, moreover, provides continuing benefits for surviving spouses and dependent children if a worker dies before retirement.

Social Security helps people reduce the risk of having inadequate resources later in life by requiring them to contribute a portion of their earnings in exchange for earned benefits they will receive when not working. Also, in retirement a spouse receives either one-half of the other spouse's monthly benefits (if a nonworker and married to a worker) or her or his own Social Security benefits, whichever is larger.

It is important to keep in mind that currently scheduled benefits rise over time for successive cohorts of new retirees, even though replacement rates for those retiring at the full benefit age remain relatively constant.[13] In order for future cohorts of retirees to have the same percentage of their covered earnings replaced by Social Security as current retirees, initial benefit levels have to rise over time with real wage growth. Wage growth is expected to continue to exceed inflation by about 1 percent a year on average because increases in per capita productivity result in increases in total compensation (i.e., earnings plus benefits). Accordingly, adjusted for inflation, Social Security benefit payments for workers who retire at age 65 would nearly double over the next 75 years (see Table C-3 in Appendix C) if no changes are made to the current benefit formula and if program revenues are adequate.

FINANCIAL PROJECTIONS

It is more than a generation since the major program and financing reforms of 1983, and many of those who were age 45 then are now retired or planning to retire. Americans are now living longer in retirement. A generally declining birthrate and changing work patterns have changed the actual and projected ratios of numbers working and paying into the program's trust fund to those retired and collecting benefits. Within a generation, as the baby boomers retire, the number of people over the age of 65 will rise from about 13 percent of the population (in 2007) to about 20 percent (in 2040) (Census Bureau, 2009). On average, people will spend many more years in retirement—and drawing Social Security benefits—than previous generations.[14] Consequently, the ratio of workers covered by Social Security to program beneficiaries is projected to decrease from its current level of 3.2 to 2.1 in 2035. Thereafter, this ratio is projected to continue to decline, but much more slowly, reaching 1.9 in 2085 (Social Security Administration, 2009d).

Social Security benefits now total 4.8 percent of GDP and they are projected to reach 6.2 percent by 2035. Over the same period, under current law (i.e., without any changes), Social Security revenues will decline from their present level of 5.8 percent to about 4.8 percent of GDP, resulting in a gap of 1.4 percent of GDP. On the basis of such straightforward projections by the Social Security actuaries and others, it is widely agreed that financial reforms are required soon to ensure that the program's implicit promise is kept for the current generation of workers, as well as with future generations.

What will soon become a growing discrepancy between Social Security's benefits and revenues will exhaust the trust fund and so threaten the program's solvency as well as the payment of currently scheduled benefits; see Figures 6-3 and 6-4.[15] Box 6-1 sketches how the projected depletion of the Social Security trust fund relates to other indicators of the program's long-term financial prospects (see Social Security Administration 2009d; see also Appendix C). The program's financial outlook presents a looming problem not just for Social Security, however; given the program's size and pending cash flow deficits that must be somehow financed by the U.S. Treasury, it is a problem for the U.S. budget as a whole.

OPTIONS TO RESTORE SOLVENCY

Overview

The fiscal future of the Social Security program could be assured in various ways, but virtually all experts agree that reform likely will require

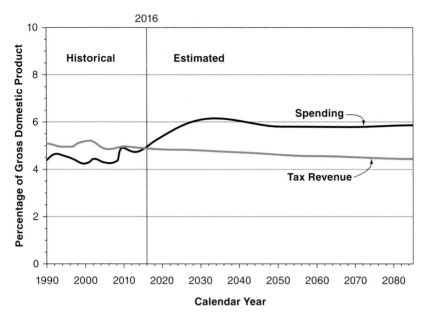

FIGURE 6-3 Social Security scheduled spending and tax revenue as a percentage of GDP.

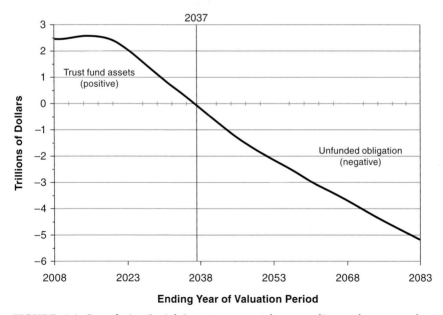

FIGURE 6-4 Cumulative Social Security revenue less spending under current-law tax rates and scheduled benefits.
NOTE: Present value as of January 1, 2009.

BOX 6-1
Sustaining the Social Security Trust Fund

The expected date of the depletion of the Social Security trust fund is only one indicator of the seriousness of the program's problem (see Appendix C). Another important indicator of the program's financial soundness is its actuarial balance, based on the discounted streams of revenues and spending projected over a 75-year period. This indicator does not show the size of the trust fund at the *end* of the 75 years. A major Social Security reform—like that in 1983—might achieve actuarial balance during 75 years but still lead to insolvency *after* that time. However, a low or falling trust fund level (relative to benefits) at the end of the 75-year projection period can signal looming insolvency.

Each reform option discussed in this chapter has been tested against multiple indicators. The estimates show that, under the Social Security trustees' current economic and demographic assumptions, each of our illustrative reform options finances the program's costs through the 75-year projection period and results in a positive or near-positive cash flow into and out of the trust fund at the end of the 75-year period.

---

either a substantial increase in currently scheduled payroll tax revenues, a substantial reduction in currently scheduled lifetime benefits for future retirees, or some combination of the two. Commonly discussed changes to reduce the future growth of benefits include: raising the full-benefit retirement age and the earliest retirement age; reducing the additional benefit percentage for spouses; reducing the postretirement cost-of-living adjustment; increasing the number of years used to compute average earnings; and changing the way initial benefit levels (i.e., at retirement) are calculated so that they grow more slowly than wages for higher earners. Examples of commonly discussed revenue changes include raising additional payroll tax revenue by covering newly hired state and local government workers; increasing the maximum amount of wages subject to payroll taxes; raising the payroll tax rate; and taxing Social Security benefits similarly to private pension income. The options presented are just a few combinations of the many proposed changes within the current program framework that have been made to address the program's projected shortfalls. For detailed descriptions and analysis, see, for example, American Academy of Actuaries (2007), Congressional Budget Office (2009b), Reno and Lavery (2009), Shelton (2008), and Social Security Advisory Board (2005); the list of the Social Security actuary is particularly comprehensive (Social Security Administration, 2009c).

Some observers also note that an increased share of general federal revenues could be designated for the Social Security trust fund, or new revenue sources could be dedicated specifically to Social Security. However, since the use of such revenue sources for the program would simply make the already difficult task of achieving appropriate fiscal balance in the remainder of the federal budget even more difficult, we did not include this approach among our illustrative reform options.[16]

The four illustrative options discussed below entail different combinations of the broader array of possible changes outlined above—thus sustaining the program's finances in the current, long-established framework in which payroll taxes paid by current workers support benefits for current retirees.

- Option 1 would achieve fiscal balance for the program without any revenue increases, relying instead solely on program changes that would generally reduce the rate of growth of currently scheduled benefits for future retirees.[17]
- In contrast, Option 4 would maintain currently scheduled benefits for all future beneficiaries by relying solely on increases in the payroll tax.

Between these two, the other two options combine tax increases and benefit growth reductions in different mixes:

- Option 2 would rely two-thirds on slower growth in benefits for future retirees and one-third on future increases in payroll tax revenues.
- Option 3 is the opposite mix: it would rely two-thirds on future increases in payroll tax revenues and one-third on slower growth in benefits for future retirees.

All four options are designed to have roughly the same overall long-term fiscal impact and to sustain the program's solvency for the next 75 years and beyond (see Box 6-1, above). All four also would phase in benefit and tax changes over many decades, and none would introduce a major change in benefits for people who are close to retirement.

In the rest of this section we describe each option and its "ground-level" consequences for benefits and payroll taxes. Table 6-1 provides a summary comparison of the program changes in the four options (see Appendix C for more detail). Two questions guided our analysis of the options: (1) How does each option affect future benefit levels and the proportion of individual workers' past earnings that benefits replace? and (2) How does each option tend to affect the progressivity of Social Security benefits and taxation?

TABLE 6-1 Four Illustrative Social Security Options: Overview

Question of Effects	Option 1	Option 2	Option 3	Option 4
How is sustainable solvency achieved?	Reductions in the growth of benefits only	2/3 benefit-growth reductions; 1/3 payroll tax increases	1/3 benefit-growth reductions; 2/3 payroll tax increases	Payroll tax increases only
General Reductions in the Growth (under Current Law) of Monthly and Lifetime Benefits				
Does the option increase the future age for retirement with full benefits and for early retirement?	Accelerate by 5 years the scheduled increase in the full-retirement age, to 67, and then increase retirement age with longevity. Similarly for early retirement.	No	No	No
Does the option change the preretirement calculation of monthly benefits?	For the top 70% of wage-earners in the retirement program: reduce the rate at which overall wage increases raise monthly benefits.	For the retirement program: a different form of the change for Option 1.	For the retirement program: a milder form of this change.	No
Does the option change the cost-of-living adjustment to monthly benefits in retirement?	Use a new price index that usually grows somewhat more slowly.	No	No	No

Increases in the Payroll Tax

Does the option raise the dollar cap on wages that are taxed?	No	No	No	Raise tax cap by extra 2% over current formula, starting 2012, until it applies to 90% of earnings; no benefit credit for earnings over current-law cap.
Does the option change the tax rate for earnings under the (possibly raised) tax cap?	No	Raise tax rate for earnings under the current cap formula to 12.6% in 2012 and then in steps to 13.3% in 2060.	Raise tax rate for earnings under the current cap formula to 12.6% in 2012, then in steps to 14.5% in 2075.	Raise the tax rate for earnings under a raised cap formula to 12.7% in 2012 and then in steps to 14.7% in 2080.
Does the option: 1. Add a new tier of payroll tax? 2. Change the tax rate for any earnings above existing tax? 3. Change the benefits for any such tax paid?	No	No	1. Yes. 2. 2% starting 2012, to 3% in 2060. 3. Benefits not increased by second-tier taxes paid.	1. Yes. 2. 2% starting 2012, then in steps to 5.5% in 2060. 3. Benefits not increased by second-tier taxes paid.

Option 1: Benefit Changes Only

In comparison with the current program formulas, this option changes benefits for future retirees. Recognizing that longevity is increasing, Option 1 accelerates the currently scheduled increase in the age for retirement with full benefits, to 67 in 2012, instead of remaining at 66 for several more years. More specifically, the age to retire with full benefits would increase by a projected 1 month every 2 years. The age for the earliest retirement with Social Security retirement benefits would increase the same way.[18]

In addition to changes in retirement age, the other two provisions that affect monthly benefits under Option 1 are "progressive indexing" of the *preretirement* benefit-entitlement formula and a change in the cost-of-living adjustment *during retirement*.[21] First, under the benefit formula in current law, improvements in average wages before a worker's retirement generally increase future benefits for that worker (and all others). Under this illustrative reform option, the current indexing to average wage levels would be reduced by "progressive indexing." For workers with the lowest 30 percent of earnings, the growth rate of benefits would be maintained. For most others, initial benefits would grow more slowly—although, on average, at least as fast as prices. Benefits would grow slowest—keeping pace only with consumer prices—only for workers with steady earnings at the current-law taxable maximum.

Second, the annual cost-of-living adjustment for retirees receiving monthly benefits would be computed from a newer price index that is generally considered more accurate, which usually provides smaller benefit increases.[20] Upward cost-of-living adjustment would continue and so benefit checks would continue to be protected from price inflation during retirement.[21]

Benefit Effects

Figure 6-5 compares monthly benefit levels—adjusted for projected inflation—for new retirees in 2050 under Option 1 with those scheduled under current law for new retirees in 2010 or 2050. (Discussed below, Figure 6-6 presents another aspect of this option.) Benefits are compared for new retirees at age 65, that is, for those taking early Social Security retirement in 2010 and 2050. Because Option 1 accelerates the increase in retirement age, its age-65 benefit as illustrated in Figure 6-5 reflects benefits reduced by what is effectively even earlier retirement. Since Option 1's age for full retirement benefits is later than current law's—68 years and 4 months in 2050—retiring at 65 under Option 1 (in 2050) leads to a bigger reduction in monthly benefits for early retirement than retiring (in 2050) under current law, assuming payment of scheduled benefits.[22] (With a different format and more detail, Tables C-3 through C-5 in Appendix C

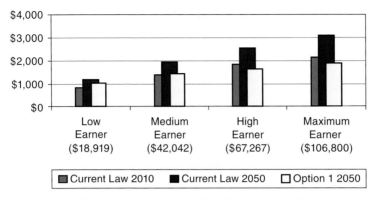

FIGURE 6-5 Monthly Social Security benefits for workers who retire at age 65 under current law and under Option 1 (in 2009 dollars).

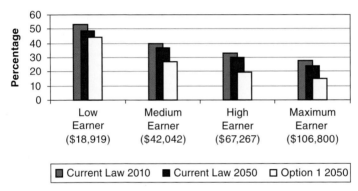

FIGURE 6-6 Social Security benefits as a percentage of past earnings for new retirees at age 65 under current law and under Option 1.

show the option's effects on monthly benefits, the replacement of individual earnings by benefits, and on payroll taxes paid.)

Although it leads to more years of benefits, early retirement makes a big reduction in monthly benefits, under both current law and this option. For example, under current law, retiring in 2050 at 65 rather than at that year's age for full benefits of 67 means 15.4 percent less in scheduled monthly benefits. As a result, Option 1's increase of the retirement age for full benefits markedly contributes to lower monthly benefits. The first triplet of bars in Figure 6-5 represents monthly benefits of illustrative "low earners," people with average lifetime earnings of $18,919 per year, in 2009 dollars.[23] The three bars show that under current law, new retirees categorized as low earners are projected to receive $834 per month in 2010, rising (by 39 percent) to $1,161 per month for the cohort of low earners who retire in 2050.

Under Option 1, benefits in 2050 for low earners would be 25 percent above the 2010 level. Real monthly benefits would grow over time for low earners, but they would grow slower than under current law. In contrast, for the "maximum earners," people who earn at the current taxable maximum of $106,800 per year (in 2009 dollars), real benefits would decline over time. Under existing law, maximum earners are projected to receive $2,156 a month in 2010 and $3,094 in 2050; under Option 1 they would receive only about 60 percent of that amount.

Because Option 1 achieves long-term solvency of Social Security by changing only the benefit formula—with no tax increase—the benefit changes are bigger than with the other options. Through benefit changes, all future retirees would contribute to the program's solvency, with higher earners contributing much more than other workers. Yet there would continue to be growth in real, monthly benefits—though at a reduced rate—for all but about the highest-earning third of workers.

Figure 6-6 illustrates the benefit effects of Option 1 another way, by showing not monthly benefit dollars, but to what extent a worker's Social Security retirement benefits replace her or his preretirement earnings. For all earnings levels, these "earnings replacement rates" for individual wage earners who retire at age 65 are set to be slightly less in 2050 than in 2010 under current law.[24] That is, the real benefits grow, but they grow more slowly than real wages. For example, under this option, Social Security benefits for medium earners in 2050 would replace 27 percent of prior earnings, compared with 40 percent for 2010 under current law (see Table C-4 in Appendix C).

Option 1 is designed so that in 2050 the benefits or the growth rate of benefits of all new retirees are less than those for new retirees in 2010, but they are reduced more for higher earners than for lower earners; see Figure 6-5.

Payroll Tax

Under this option there are no changes in the payroll taxes for Social Security; for illustrations of payroll taxes under this option, see discussion below.

Option 2: Two-Thirds Benefit Growth Reductions, One-Third Payroll Tax Increases

The committee's second option would achieve long-term actuarial balance with smaller cuts in benefit growth and an increase in the payroll tax. One of the same "building blocks" in Option 1 that reduces the growth of benefits—progressive indexing—is applied here, too, though in a different form. A new building block for Option 2 is on the revenue side: an increase in the rate of Social Security payroll taxation. The current tax rate of 12.4 percent—half levied on employees and half on employers—would be raised in stages to 13.9 percent in 2040. Thereafter, reflecting the reduction in the growth of benefits, growth in the economy, and the retirement of the baby boom generation, the now-sufficient tax rate would decline slightly in stages to 13.3 percent in 2060.

Benefit Effects

Option 2 reduces future benefits and benefit growth rates in comparison with those scheduled under current law, but it does so less than Option 1; see Figure 6-7. Medium earners who retire in 2050 would receive 13 percent more in constant dollars than they would receive in 2010 under current law. Under the current benefit formula, they would receive 39 percent more in 2050 than in 2010.

As with Option 1, people with lower earnings fare better with respect to their benefits, in comparison with current law, than higher earners. Monthly benefits for low earners are the same as in current law for all years (see Table C-3 in Appendix C). In contrast, the benefits (in constant dollars) for steady maximum earners who are new retirees would decrease slightly in 2050 in comparison with 2010. Real benefits would continue to grow—but at a reduced rate—for all but about the highest-earning one-fifth of workers.[25]

Reflecting an increase in the payroll tax that would permit higher benefit levels than in Option 1, replacement rates for Option 2 are higher than for Option 1: compare Figure 6-6 with Figure 6-8, which shows replacement rates under Option 2 in comparison with current law. By 2050, the benefits for medium earners would replace 30 percent of preretirement earnings rather than 40 percent in 2010 as under current law. Low earners would receive a higher percentage: 49 percent in 2050, in comparison with 54 percent for that group in 2010. Benefits for high earners would replace less of their prior earnings: 22 percent in 2050, compared with 33 percent in 2010.

Payroll Tax

Unlike current law and Option 1, Option 2 would raise the payroll tax, but would not change its other characteristics. Figure 6-9 depicts the effects for four groups of workers in 2010 and 2050 and for the current law for 2050. (Because Option 1 doesn't change the existing payroll tax for Social Security, there is no comparable figure for it; see, instead, the bars for the current law in Figure 6-9. See Appendix C for definitions of the wage levels of the illustrative groups.)

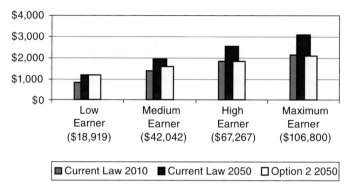

FIGURE 6-7 Monthly Social Security benefits for workers who retire at age 65 under current law and under Option 2 (in 2009 dollars).

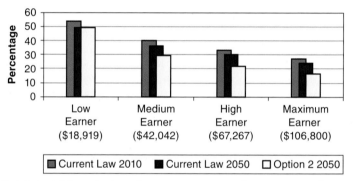

FIGURE 6-8 Social Security benefits as a percentage of past earnings for new retirees at age 65 under current law and under Option 2.

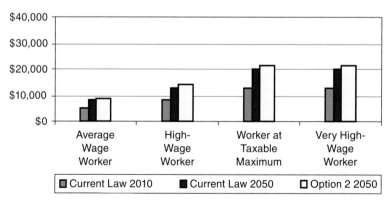

FIGURE 6-9 Annual Social Security payroll tax projected for 2010 and for 2050 under current law and under Option 2 (in 2009 dollars).

Because wages are projected, on average, to continue to grow faster than prices, payroll taxes paid will increase in the future, adjusted for price inflation. The increase of the payroll tax rate under Option 2 means that workers whose wages grow at the rate of price inflation (and with earnings below the taxable maximum) would pay 9 percent more in payroll tax in 2050 than under current law.

Option 3: One-Third Benefit Growth Reductions, Two-Thirds Payroll Tax Increases

The committee's third option restores long-term actuarial balance by cutting benefit-growth rates less and increasing payroll taxes more than under Option 2.

Benefit growth would be slowed by a milder version of progressive indexing than is proposed in Options 1 and 2. Under Option 3 two provisions affect taxes: the current tax rate of 12.4 percent would be raised in stages to 14.5 percent in 2075, and a new, second tier of Social Security payroll taxation would be added to the existing tax. This second tier would tax earnings above the taxable maximum under current law, and—as with the existing Medicare payroll tax—there would be no cap on earnings that are subject to this new tax. The second-tier tax would be imposed at a rate of 2 percent in 2012 (employer and employee combined), and rise to 3 percent in 2060. Unlike the existing Social Security tax, collections under this added tax would not be credited toward a worker's Social Security benefits. The second-tier tax would move the program's financing in a progressive direction.[26]

Benefit Effects

Option 3 would provide higher real benefit levels than Options 1 and 2; see Figure 6-10. In 2050, medium earners would receive an estimated $1,792 monthly under Option 3 (compared with $1,559 under Option 2, for instance). For replacement rates, the pattern under Option 3 is similar to but higher than that under Option 2; see Figure 6-11. They would decrease with earnings and would be lower in 2050 for Option 3 than under current law. For example, in 2050 the replacement rate for medium earners would be 34 percent (compared with 30 percent under Option 2).

Payroll Tax

Under Option 3, all workers would pay higher taxes than under current law or Option 2; see Figure 6-12 (for details, see Appendix C). Because

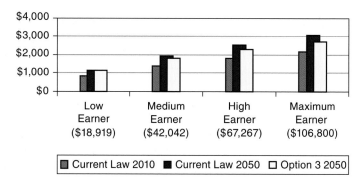

FIGURE 6-10 Monthly Social Security benefits for workers who retire at age 65 under current law and under Option 3 (in 2009 dollars).

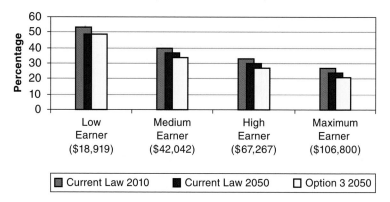

FIGURE 6-11 Social Security benefits as a percentage of past earnings for new retirees at age 65 under current law and under Option 3.

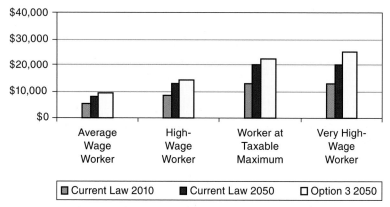

FIGURE 6-12 Annual Social Security payroll tax projected for 2010 and for 2050 under current law and under Option 3 (in 2009 dollars).

Option 3 adds a second-tier tax, very high-wage workers would pay more than those at the first-tier taxable maximum. For very high-wage workers, the total payroll tax of $25,250 in 2050 under Option 3 would be almost twice as much as they would pay in 2010 under current law.

Option 4: Payroll Tax Increases Only

Under this option, the benefit growth rates provided under current law are maintained by introducing three changes to taxes. First, the current Social Security payroll tax would be increased by raising both that tax's cap and its rate. Currently, about 84 percent of all earnings in the economy are subject to the payroll tax; under this option, the cap on wages subject to this tax would be raised to about 90 percent, where it has been in the past.[27] Second, the current payroll tax rate would be increased—on earnings up to its new maximum—rising in stages to a combined 14.7 percent in 2080. Third, this option would add a second-tier tax on covered earnings at all levels, which would begin at 2 percent in 2012 and rise to 5.5 percent in 2060. These changes would move Social Security taxation in a progressive direction.

Benefit Effects

Under this option, there would be no change to the benefit growth rates scheduled under current law. For the benefit levels and earnings replacement rates, see the bars for the current law in the figures above.

Payroll Tax

Sustaining the benefits scheduled under the current law will require substantially higher revenue from payroll taxes; see Figure 6-13. Adding a second-tier tax makes the increase much larger for those at higher earnings levels than at lower earnings levels. For example, for very high-wage workers, annual payments in 2050 would increase 109 percent, from $19,960 under current law to $41,608 under Option 4. These very high-wage workers to date have typically paid Social Security tax on just about one-half of their earnings. Contributions by those at average earning levels would increase far less, however.

CONCLUSION

Changes to make the Social Security program financially solvent are an essential element of a strategy to put the federal budget on a sustainable path. Restoring confidence in the program's future is especially vital

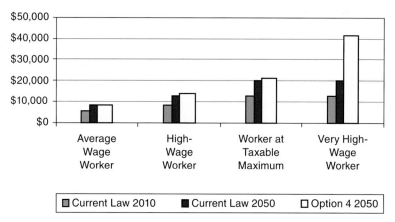

FIGURE 6-13 Annual Social Security payroll tax projected for 2010 and for 2050 under current law and under Option 4 (in 2009 dollars).

now, when other sources of retirement security, such as private savings and housing equity, have been so severely diminished. If changes are enacted soon, it will be possible to close the program's financing gap with relatively modest, incremental tax increases or restraints on the growth of benefits (or both): the longer action is delayed, the larger will be the required changes to restore long term-solvency. Future retirees will confront increasing un-certainty about what they can expect from Social Security in their old age; and low-earning workers, who rely far more than others on Social Security benefits for retirement income, will be particularly vulnerable to sudden or unexpected benefit reductions.

The four illustrative reform options outlined in this chapter would all retain Social Security's familiar program structure, avoid sudden or unex-pected increases in payroll taxes and benefit cuts, and place the program on a solid financial footing for both the standard 75-year projection period and beyond. Their differences lie primarily in the extent to which they rely on benefit reductions or tax increases to restore long-term solvency and in the particular consequences for the level of future taxes paid and benefits received over time by workers at different levels of lifetime earnings.

The macrolevel implications of these differences for the size of government—as measured by levels of spending and revenues—are straight-forward and easy to describe. Option 4, which relies on higher taxes to maintain currently scheduled benefits, would eventually raise revenues by about 1.3 percent of gross domestic product (GDP); in contrast, Option 1 would not increase them at all; and Options 2 and 3 would have intermedi-ate effects in proportion to their reliance on tax increases.

In contrast, the microlevel distributional consequences are more complicated and difficult to characterize. Some sense of them, in terms of taxes paid and for benefits received, can be seen in Figures 6-5 through 6-13, above, and they are detailed in more depth in Appendix C. Developing summary distributional measures that integrate the tax and benefit changes of each option is a complicated undertaking beyond our scope. However, we note that Social Security is now somewhat progressive in its overall consequences (Congressional Budget Office, 2006a): that is, those with higher earnings pay more in taxes in relation to lifetime benefits received than those with lower earnings, and we judge it likely that all four of our options would retain or increase the program's current degree of progressivity.[28]

As we note at the outset of this chapter, other packages of frequently advanced program changes with similar overall fiscal impacts and differing distributional consequences, can be constructed, depending on one's policy preferences. Our four illustrative options are indicative of the range of choices available to put Social Security on a solid financial footing and continue its role as a foundation for economic security in retirement for most working Americans.[29]

NOTES

1. Changes to sustain Social Security finances will contribute to making the entire federal budget sustainable in at least two ways. First, it is now the largest federal program and so changes have a large effect relative to the entire budget. Although Social Security is designed to be self-financing, if its spending exceeds the program's revenues, the difference adds to the federal deficit, and, conversely, if the program spends less than it takes in, this difference reduces the federal deficit. Second, sustaining Social Security finances helps rebuild public confidence that the federal government will finance the benefits it promises and promise only benefits that it can finance.

2. In addition to payroll taxes, which account for most Social Security revenue, small amounts come from the personal income taxes paid by upper-income individuals and families on their Social Security benefits and from interest earned on trust fund reserves.

3. Contrary to popular understanding, the benefits received by a retiree are only loosely related to the amount that retiree paid in payroll taxes because the benefit formula is progressive and because benefits are based on the average of the retiree's highest-earning 35 years.

4. The retirement and the disability programs have separate trust funds and shares of the payroll tax. The former is much larger than the latter. For purposes of explication, the two separate trust funds are usually treated in the text as one. The illustrative options presented below sustain both the retirement and the disability programs. However, projections of trust fund balances combine the two.

5. "Scheduled" benefits are those payable when the trust fund is adequate: in projections, "payable" benefits are what they would be if they had to be reduced because the trust fund was inadequate to cover scheduled benefits. Except as noted otherwise, all benefit levels mentioned are scheduled. Also, except as noted otherwise, the projections for Social Security in this chapter, Appendix C, and in the design of the committee's illustrative

reform options all draw on the intermediate assumptions of the 2009 Social Security Trustees' Report (Social Security Administration, 2009d). For the long term, the less detailed projections of the Congressional Budget Office (2009f) take a generally similar path, although its projections of the gap between spending and revenue are somewhat smaller and, as a result, it projects the exhaustion of the trust fund slightly later. For consistency with the rest of the study, the baseline for the overall budget and the analysis of our paths use the Congressional Budget Office projections for Social Security.

6.   Only the briefest history of the program's finances is presented here: for more detailed histories, see, among others, Aaron and Reischauer (1998) and Diamond and Orszag (2005).

7.   For details on these program changes, see Aaron and Reischauer (2009) and Diamond and Orszag (2005).

8.   Those who start receiving Social Security retirement benefits at an earlier age—62 is the earliest allowable—have their benefits reduced by about 8 percent a year, and those who delay retirement beyond the age at which they can receive full benefits gain about 8 percent in benefits for each year—up to age 70—they delay retirement. These adjustments were intended to equalize lifetime benefits for those who retire at different ages, based on average life expectancies.

9.   Considering the Social Security program as a whole, the program is like private insurance in that it insures against adverse events (such as the risk of an impoverished retirement), yet it is part of a social contract that includes almost all workers and their families.

10. Except for Figure 6-2, this report shows Social Security replacement rates for individual earnings for individual workers—not for families—and does not include other sources of income in retirement. These replacement rates are percentages of individuals' earnings creditable to Social Security. (Illustrations of earning levels are in 2009 dollars.) This definition is widely used, not just currently by the Social Security Administration, but by others (see, e.g., Congressional Budget Office, 2001:20-21). However, it differs markedly from that used in retirement planning; see Appendix C.

11. Noncash income, such as Food Stamps or housing subsidies, are excluded, as are lump-sum pension payments and income from capital gains, such as from the sale of a house or stock. Periodic pension payments are included in the total, however. The quintile "break points" in the distribution of total money income are $11,519, $18,622, $28,911, and $50,064 per year. Percentages graphed are the mean proportion of benefits as a share of all income, within each quintile. Although the total is shown, elderly individuals tend to be more dependent on Social Security benefits than couples.

12. Some analysts argue that the availability of Social Security and Medicare acts to reduce voluntary savings, however.

13. "Remain relatively constant" refers to the illustrations of workers at different positions in the lifetime distribution of earnings covered by Social Security. Individual workers who retire at a given age (such as 65) in the future will generally have somewhat lower earnings replacement rates. These lower replacement rates will occur because, under current law, the retirement age for full benefits, which once was 65, will rise in 2-month increments to reach 67 after 2022.

14. For example, the life expectancy for those turning 65 in 1990 was 15.8 years for men and 19.1 years for women; currently, it is 17.7 years for men and 20.0 years for women; and it is projected to be 20.9 years for men and 23.1 years for women in 2060. In other words, increased longevity means about one-third longer retirement for men and one-fifth longer for women in 2060 in comparison with 1990 (Social Security Administration, 2009d).

15. The "present values" shown in Figure 6-4 use projected interest rates to discount streams of future revenue and spending to a single dollar figure, in this case for January 1, 2009.

16. Appendix C briefly discusses the proposal to introduce individual accounts, which would make a fundamental change to the Social Security program, and other ideas have been proposed. For example, there could be more income taxation of the benefits received by people at higher income levels, or some or all of the proceeds from the federal estate tax could be devoted to Social Security. However, given the magnitude of the continuing funding gap, these two revenue sources could contribute only relatively small portions of the needed funds. From another perspective, several proposals have been made in recent years to enhance Social Security benefits for vulnerable populations, such as very old beneficiaries, workers with very low wage histories, and widows. It was beyond the scope of the committee's charge to assess these or other enhanced benefit proposals. We note, however, that if benefits were enhanced for such vulnerable populations, corresponding reductions in benefits or tax increases would be needed to finance these changes.

17. However, for high earners, Option 1 would reduce the inflation-adjusted level (not just the growth) of currently scheduled benefits for future retirees.

18. Because a later retirement age provides more time for workers to become disabled and to apply for disability insurance and because it delays the age of "conversion" from disability to retirement benefits, raising the Social Security retirement age will increase spending in the disability insurance program. However, the only net effect of delayed conversions on the program's financial position comes from differences in indexing between retirement and disability benefits for this option and two others (see Appendix C).

19. This "progressive indexing" option is not to be confused with a somewhat similar proposal called "progressive price-indexing" that has been proposed and analyzed elsewhere. For a critical analysis of that proposal, see Appendix C and Furman (2005a).

20. The chained Consumer Price Index would replace the older fixed-Weight Consumer Price Index. The newer index reduces the latter's general overstatement of price inflation by roughly 0.3 percentage points per year; see a study by statisticians at the U.S. Bureau of Economic Analysis and Bureau of Labor Statistics (McCully et al., 2007:26-33) and see National Research Council (2002).

21. However, in comparison with currently scheduled benefits, this provision would reduce monthly benefits the most for long-lived beneficiaries, who are disproportionately widows. But note that low- and middle-level workers (and their spouses) generally fare best under progressive indexing—another benefit change under Option 1.

22. Lifetime—not just monthly—benefits are important, too, of course. For instance given the longer longevity projected for 2050, Option 1's delayed retirement ages, relative to the unsustainable current law, produces a greater downward tendency for its lifetime than for its monthly benefits. This helps allow it to sustain program finances without a payroll-tax increase.

23. Throughout this chapter, the illustrations of benefits, earnings replacement rates, and payroll tax paid use the Social Security Administration's definitions of representative workers at different earnings levels. The "low," "medium," "high," and "very high" illustrations are of lifetime earnings levels, scaled to reflect changes in the overall wage distribution over time. "Maximum earners" are defined differently, however, because they reflect steady earnings at each year's taxable maximum, as does "worker at taxable maximum," when the formula for the taxable maximum changes under some of the study's reform options. We note, however, that the Social Security "medium" earning level has been shown to be higher than the actual average level (Mitchell and Phillips, 2006, 2009). However, because our analysis uses the various Social Security definitions of earning levels only for comparison with each other, this finding does not affect the comparisons.

24. We present Social Security earnings replacement rates to gauge the degree to which beneficiaries—especially those without pensions or savings—can rely on Social Security benefits.

25. This is the only instance under Option 2 for which constant-dollar benefits decrease from the 2010 to the 2050 cohorts of new retirees; for details, see Appendix C. For high earners, the real benefits in 2035 under this option would be less in 2035 than 2010; see details in Appendix C.

26. Imposing a second-tier tax without a benefit credit thus tends to move the Social Security program away from its contributory character.

27. Estimates of the revenue from Option 4's tax changes (as for Option 3) rely on projected income distributions. These are included in the actuarial estimates in the current program Trustees' Report (Social Security Administration, 2009d). The Social Security Administration's actuaries have long had to project income distribution for the program's revenue estimates under current law because of the tax paid on some Social Security benefits by relatively upper-income payers of the current personal income tax.

28. By reducing or delaying benefits for future retirees relative to those scheduled under current law, Options 1, 2, and 3 would reduce the program's contribution to income security in old age for all earnings groups; however, the reductions are proportionately larger for those with higher earnings. Option 4 would preserve the program's currently scheduled benefit-growth rates by taxing wages more heavily in the future. Options 2, 3, and 4 would raise taxes for all earnings groups; however, the larger increases in Options 3 and 4 would be borne more by the highest earnings groups. Because payroll taxes do not apply to nonwage income, such as business profits, interest, and capital gains, options that increase payroll tax rates disproportionately affect the people who are most reliant on wage income.

29. As of June 30, 2009, about 90 percent of the population aged 65 and over was receiving Social Security benefits, and about 94 percent of employed people and those who are self-employed were covered under the program (Social Security Administration, 2009a).

7

Options for Defense and
Other Domestic Spending

Although much of the debate about the federal budget focuses on the projected growth in costs for Medicare, Medicaid, and Social Security, they are only three of a vast number of federal programs and activities. Hundreds of other programs—large and small—touch the lives of almost all Americans and implicitly reflect views about federal roles and responsibilities that are often highly contested. The total of spending on these programs is higher than that for Medicare, Medicaid, and Social Security combined and under current policies is projected to remain so until 2014.

Although we group all of these spending programs under the single heading of "defense and other domestic spending," that heading hardly captures the range and diversity of the important public missions they represent. They include enormous expenditures for the military services and weapons, intelligence gathering, and homeland security. They include disability payments and health care for veterans and members of the military; emergency aid in the wake of disasters; a panoply of programs supporting education, training, and income support for the unemployed; and other services to expand opportunity or provide care. They include a host of efforts to improve transportation, the natural environment, manage national parks and forests, protect consumers and foster orderly markets, and aid particular industries and sectors. The range of tools used in this array of programs is similarly diverse, including grants to state and local government, payments to individuals, and extension or guarantees of credit and insurance. The recent downturn has both added to the list of programs and augmented their scale, temporarily increasing their combined spending from less than 10 percent of gross domestic product (GDP) in 2007 to more than 16 percent in 2009—largely because of economic stabilization and recovery initiatives.

SPENDING CATEGORIES AND TRENDS

The vast majority of spending for defense programs, which includes such related functions as intelligence, has to be appropriated on an annual basis—that is, it is "discretionary." In 2008, approximately 57 percent of spending on "other domestic" programs (i.e., nondefense programs other than Medicare, Medicaid, and Social Security) was discretionary. The remaining 43 percent was set by permanent law—that is, it was "mandatory."

Most mandatory programs are so-called "entitlements" that provide payments or other benefits to people eligible by law to receive them. Examples include food stamps, benefits for disabled veterans, federal spending on unemployment compensation, cash refunds from the Earned Income Tax Credit, and federal civilian and military employee retirement payments. Examples of non-entitlement mandatory spending include Temporary Assistance to Needy Families and some payments to farmers and for deposit insurance.

The domestic discretionary category is very broad and diverse. It includes the federal judicial system; homeland security; commerce-related activities; education, training, and employment, low-income housing aid, and other social service programs; science research and development, space exploration, and other technology programs; energy assistance; natural resource protection and other environmental programs; and transportation.[1]

Debates About Spending

In addition to being diverse, the domestic components of this category are often controversial. The value of domestic spending is very much in the eye of the beholder. Arguments about excess federal spending often center on items in this category that are regarded as wasteful, either because the program's purposes are not valued (or are regarded as obsolete) or because the programs are not believed to be effective in achieving their stated ends. Critics may argue, for example, that programs providing support for low-income people are excessively generous or encourage dependency, and that domestic spending includes unnecessary and sometimes unproductive subsidies to interested business or industry groups. They would say that politics seldom lead to efficient allocation.

On the other side of the debate, proponents of domestic spending stress that it includes useful public investments (even as skeptics may take issue with the word "investment") as well as essential services. Advocates contend that many domestic appropriations build economic capacity through infrastructure investment, new technology, education, and strengthened rule of law. Advocates argue that low-income support programs are not only appropriately compassionate but maintain health and help develop productive skills. When much of the federal government was shut down by a funding crisis in the mid-1990s, many Americans felt inconvenienced or even seriously hurt by the absence of routine services they previously took for granted—such as the processing of passports, and open and staffed national parks.

On the defense side, differences of opinion as to the budgetary implications of true security are often intense. We do not know when hostilities may emerge or what future threats will materialize. At the most aggregate level, defense spending is much like purchasing insurance; there is always uncertainty as to how much is enough (perhaps more so than in other parts of the budget), especially given the costs. This uncertainty is exacerbated because some defense spending—such as that for major new weapons systems—is often supported (at times against the best advice of military and civilian experts) because it serves a domestic constituency whose jobs depend on it.[2]

But the issues also run to a deeper level of detail. Programs that would provide defense against a national adversary in a conventional kind of conflict may or may not prove useful in an asymmetric war against terrorism. Specific policies, such as the war in Iraq, fuel intense arguments over spending priorities. Questions regarding the allocation of a given level of spending among new hardware, maintenance and supplies, troop levels, and human resources can be controversial. In this chapter, we present a wide range of alternative levels of defense spending, reflecting not only conflicting views about the best use of defense resources, but also fundamental differences regarding the role of the United States in preserving world peace.

Defense and other domestic spending is not projected to grow as a share of GDP under the study baseline. Indeed, it is projected to fall significantly as a percentage of GDP over the next decade before stabilizing at a level more than 2 percentage points lower than in 2008. Nevertheless, it can be argued that further spending reductions (relative to the baseline) are appropriate. To the extent that fiscal sustainability is addressed through spending reductions, finding all of the needed savings in health care and Social Security will be difficult and, in any event, may take some considerable time to achieve. Savings in defense and other domestic programs may therefore be necessary. Putting all spending programs on the table is also consistent with the notion of "shared sacrifice," which may be an important political element in fashioning a responsible fiscal program for the future. Some may also assert that the growth in the large entitlement programs reflects such urgent needs that cutting other areas of the budget, along with raising taxes, is necessary to accommodate it.

The counterargument is that cutbacks in defense and other domestic programs, which are already slated in the baseline to grow slower than the economy and much slower than other parts of the budget, could threaten important national objectives. Even if ineffective or low-priority programs are targeted for the greatest cuts, if spending slows too rapidly it will be difficult for the government to accommodate needs related to population growth, to make new investments needed for future growth, and to deal with potential new international and environmental challenges. Given that defense and other domestic spending is not the driving factor behind the projected fiscal crisis, difficult choices for the actual cost drivers—Medicare, Medicaid, Social Security—are necessary and inevitable. Distracting attention from the large entitlement programs (as well as revenue needs) could be counterproductive. Tough decisions in those areas, on the other hand, could allow additional resources to be allocated to important defense and other domestic needs.

Consistent with the notion that there can be multiple paths to fiscal sustainability, this chapter discusses options for defense and other domestic spending that run the gamut from deep cuts to significant expansions (all relative to the study baseline). As with other policy discussions in this report, these options are meant to be illustrative and not exhaustive.

Spending Trends

Both the defense and other domestic components of this category of spending grew in real terms from 1962 to 2008. However, as Figure 7-1 shows, defense spending is now a much smaller share of the economy than in 1962, when it was over 9 percent of GDP. Over the same period, other domestic spending rose just slightly as a percentage of GDP.

Under the study's baseline projections (see Chapter 1), overall defense and other domestic spending falls to 8.6 percent of GDP by 2019 and re-

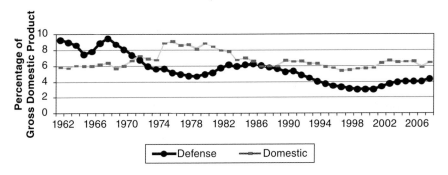

FIGURE 7-1 Defense and other domestic spending as a percentage of GDP, 1962-2008.

mains at approximately that level from 2020 on. This is approximately the same share of the economy it held in 1998, when it was at its lowest share of GDP in the post-1962 period.

Other domestic spending represented 5.9 percent of GDP in 1962 and 6.4 percent in 2008. With the exception of a brief period in the 1970s, it has stayed between 5.4 and 7 percent of GDP. In 2009 it spiked to around 12 percent of GDP because of the economic downturn of 2008-2009 and the policy response to it. The American Recovery and Reinvestment Act of 2009 includes spending for (among other things) infrastructure, credit support for defaulting homeowners, and extended unemployment and health benefits. Spending also was swelled temporarily by extraordinary interventions to stabilize financial markets, the government's assumption of responsibility for Fannie Mae and Freddie Mac, and aid to floundering banks and auto companies.[3] If the economy recovers as projected, other domestic spending will fall back to about 6 percent of GDP in 2010 and then drift down to just over 5 percent of GDP by 2019, remaining around that level from 2020 on. That percentage would be lower than the lowest figure for domestic spending in the post-1962 period, a 5.4 percent share in 1997.

Defense spending represented 4.3 percent of GDP in 2008. In the study baseline, declining troop levels and growth with inflation put it at 3.4 percent of GDP by 2019 (which was about its share in 2002), a level at which it remains from 2020 on.

FOUR OPTIONS

As noted above and throughout this report, the costs that are driving the budget toward unsustainability are (primarily) those for health care and (secondarily) Social Security. The savings that can be achieved in those programs will determine whether there will be more or less room for spending in the rest of the budget at a given level of revenues. Similarly, a willingness to tax more (or less) will leave more (or less) room for all categories of spending. Therefore, a variety of approaches to defense and other domestic spending could be consistent with the goal of putting the federal budget on a sustainable path. The four spending paths discussed below are illustrative of the plausible range of possibilities, at least in terms of level and categorical composition; see Figure 7-2. The rationale for allocating spending, for each option, across subcategories (defense, domestic discretionary, other mandatory) is discussed in Appendix D.

The lowest illustrative option would put spending 20 percent below the baseline by 2019 and hold it at approximately that level thereafter. This would require reductions of a depth unprecedented in modern U.S. history, straining the bounds of political feasibility. Such reductions would mean that many familiar domestic programs would be scaled back or eliminated,

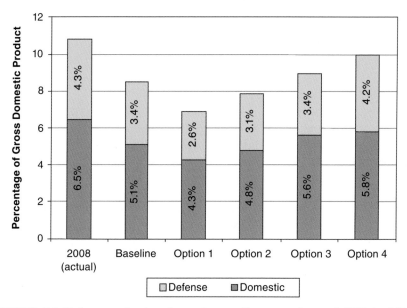

FIGURE 7-2 Defense and other domestic spending as a share of GDP in 2019 under four options.

NOTE: Tables D-1, D-2, and D-3 in Appendix D present further spending details for the defense, domestic discretionary, and other mandatory subcategories.

certain federal responsibilities would be turned over to state and local governments, and the nation's capacity for military intervention would be curtailed.

At the other end, the highest spending option would put spending 16 percent above the baseline by 2019 and hold it at approximately that level thereafter, making room for major new public investments and other program expansions (not all which of may be productive, of course), creating a robust capacity to deal with future military challenges, and potentially make it easier to respond to now-unforeseen emergencies or opportunities. Although spending would be well above the baseline in that year, it would still be lower as a percentage of GDP than in 2008. This option may nevertheless be politically challenging, given all of the other pressures and constraints affecting the budget.

The two options intermediate to the lowest and highest spending ones illustrate additional ways of apportioning resources within the defense and other domestic spending category. The first intermediate option (Option 2) cuts spending by 8 percent relative to the baseline by 2019 and holds it at around that level (as a share of GDP) thereafter, whereas the second intermediate option (Option 3) expands it by 5 percent and holds it at approximately that share of GDP after 2019.

Option 1: Cut Spending by 20 Percent

Option 1 makes deep cuts to defense and other domestic spending, putting overall spending 20 percent below the study baseline by 2019 and, at 6.9 percent of GDP, considerably below the 8.6 percent share of 2008. This represents a reduction (relative to the baseline) of approximately $361 billion in 2019—one that has no precedent in modern U.S. history. Domestic spending falls to 4.3 percent of GDP, well below its 5.4 percent share of 1997 and the 5.1 percent share projected in the baseline. Defense spending falls to 2.6 percent of GDP, an unprecedentedly low level of spending that is well below the baseline projection of 3.4 percent for that year. It is also below the 3 percent share of 1999-2001, which was the lowest share in the post-1962 period.

Cutting spending on any program is always politically contentious. This option would impose substantial pain on virtually all defense and other domestic programs. Based in part on published analyses, it illustrates ways of reducing or eliminating spending for programs that may be regarded by some as ineffective, unproductive, or not essential to the purposes of the federal government. The option also calls for further unspecified cuts in order to achieve additional necessary savings. Reductions of this magnitude have not been feasible to date and are likely to be achieved only if deficit reduction—accompanied by strong skepticism about federal spending—becomes a national priority.

The committee's illustrative choices to achieve such deep cuts come in three parts: (1) to eliminate or substantially reduce program spending in specified domestic areas, (2) to require additional unspecified cuts in other domestic areas, and (3) to redefine defense needs.

Elimination of or Substantial Reductions in Specified Domestic Programs

Option 1 makes substantial cuts to domestic programs through three broad illustrative policy changes.

The first policy change is devolution, which would combine cuts in federal grant programs with delegations of authority to state and local governments (see Appendix D for details). A number of social service, elementary and secondary education, and employment and training programs would be folded into block grants providing greater responsibility and control to states and localities, who (some would argue) might better manage those functions.[4] However, their combined funding would also be reduced by

50 percent, which would require states and localities to come up with additional funds and use resources more effectively in order to maintain the same level of activity; they may or may not be able to do this. Examples of affected programs include those for special education, training and employments services, and aging services.

The second policy change would be to remove commercial subsidies and reduce "low-value" activities. This option selectively draws on a list of potential budget savings identified by the Congressional Budget Office (2009b) to illustrate the sorts of cuts that might be made.[5] This option would reduce the federal government's role in subsidizing particular activities or sectors of the economy for which the private sector arguably could do a better job. For example, many trade promotion and foreign market development programs would be eliminated, along with subsidized financing vehicles such as the Overseas Private Investment Corporation and the Export-Import Bank. User fees for subsidized benefits and services would also be increased. Some have argued that these programs were created at the behest of private interest groups and use public resources largely for those groups' private gain. Similarly, this option would curtail federal spending on activities that may be judged to have relatively low social returns. Payments to producers of certain agricultural commodities, funds for money-losing timber sales, and funding for beach replenishment come under this heading. The caveat, of course, is that what constitutes a low-value activity is often in the eye of the beholder.[6]

The third policy change is to use a smaller inflation adjustment in indexed programs. The standard consumer price index (CPI) may overstate the effect of inflation on households because it does not account for the adjustments that people make in their spending patterns to compensate for changes in the relative prices of different goods and services.[7] The Bureau of Labor Statistics has calculated an alternative measure of inflation, called the chained CPI, which does reflect such consumer behavior.[8] A chain-linked CPI for cost-of-living adjustments for indexed programs would reduce the growth of benefits for a number of the other mandatory programs, chiefly federal civil service and military retirement, veterans cash disability benefits, railroad retirement, and Supplemental Security Income. The Congressional Budget Office furnished the committee with an estimate of the savings that would result by 2019 from using a chain-linked CPI for cost-of-living adjustments for indexed programs.[9]

Additional Unspecified Cuts in Domestic Programs

The specified cuts discussed above would put domestic spending approximately 7 percent below the baseline by 2019. However, reaching the target for this option would require still further cuts. Accordingly, addi-

tional unspecified cuts (which could be similar in kind to the sorts of specified cuts discussed above and described in Appendix D) would also have to
be imposed; these would reduce domestic discretionary spending by another
9 percent, leaving it 16 percent below the baseline by 2019.

A Redefinition of Defense Needs

In this option, defense spending would be sharply reduced from 4.3
percent of GDP in 2008 to 2.6 percent of GDP by 2019, remaining at approximately that level from 2020 on. This would be below the lowest share
of GDP consumed by the military between World War II and now (which
was about 3 percent), but higher in real terms than the combined amount
spent by U.S. allies in the North Atlantic Treaty Organization (NATO).

The military would have to reallocate funds to match real wage growth
in the economy (keeping in mind the cyclical nature of labor markets) and
pay for rising health care costs (8 percent of the current defense budget
goes for health care, a proportion that is projected to rise in line with the
growth of other health spending). Personnel compensation and support for
those who serve (and their families) is and has been the highest priority of
defense policy over the last five Administrations, with costs rising significantly faster than the overall defense budget. If this priority—which now
accounts for nearly half the cost of defense—is to be maintained under this
low-spending option, the capacity to modernize or replace weapon systems
will be virtually eliminated, and only minimal new investments in research
and development and facility construction will be possible. Reductions of
this magnitude, while preserving essential funds to adequately support the
military forces, will eventually result in demands to recapitalize weapon systems and equipment and increase the operating costs necessary to maintain
existing assets at any acceptable state of readiness.

With such reductions, U.S. defense forces would retain the ability to
mount rapid deployments, although those deployments would be very small
and of short-term duration. The funding levels implied in this option would
not provide the capacity to engage in a mission of the size, scope, and duration of the current Afghanistan campaign, and would not support more
than one emergency response at any given time.

Option 2: Cut Spending by 8 Percent

Option 2 is less stringent than Option 1. It would cut overall defense
and other domestic spending by 8 percent relative to the study baseline, putting it at 7.9 percent of GDP in 2019 and keeping it at approximately that
level from 2020 on. This represents a reduction (relative to the baseline) of
approximately $144 billion in 2019.

This option would leave defense spending at 3.1 percent of GDP a decade from now (at around the 2008 level, excluding war-related spending) and domestic spending at 4.8 percent of GDP. As with Option 1, this option assumes that it is possible to target most cuts to less effective or lower priority programs, while perhaps increasing the productivity of what remains. Although these reductions are politically ambitious by any historical standard, they are sufficiently less onerous than those under Option 1 that there is no need to rely on unspecified cuts; see Appendix D for details.

Domestic Programs

The treatment of domestic programs in this option would be the same as in Option 1, with two exceptions:

1. Federal funding for programs block-granted under the devolution option (see Appendix D for details) would be cut by approximately one-third, rather than one-half.
2. There would be no unspecified cuts in domestic programs.

Defense Programs

In this option, defense spending would be reduced to 3.1 percent of GDP by 2019—lower than the baseline level of 3.4 percent, but markedly higher than the 2.6 percent in Option 1. Spending for defense would be slightly above the 3 percent share of the post-Cold War, pre-9/11 period of 1999-2001. Sustaining the present personnel and support policy emphasis would likely maintain the national capacity for rapid military deployment but have implications for defense-related investment, research and development, and construction projects that are similar to Option 1, albeit less pronounced.

Option 3: Increase Spending by 5 Percent

This "pro public investment" option expands overall category spending relative to the baseline. Spending would reach 9 percent of GDP by 2019 and remain at approximately that level from 2020 on. This spending level, by way of comparison, falls in between the 9.2 percent share in 1996 and the 8.8 percent share in 2001.

In sharp contrast to Options 1 and 2, this option assumes that effective public-sector investments that produce long-term economic growth and social benefits can be identified and are worth pursuing. Domestic spending is expanded to 5.6 percent of GDP (at around the 1999 share), an increase of approximately 10 percent relative to the study baseline; this translates to an increase of approximately $99 billion in 2019. Defense spending follows the study baseline, falling from 4.3 percent of GDP in 2008 to 3.4 percent by 2019.

Domestic Programs

In a number of program areas, expanded spending might be considered an investment in assets that yield economic growth and produce social benefits. This option considers three such areas: human capital development, research and development funding, and infrastructure (see details in Appendix D). These expansions are only indicative of what might be done. For instance, there are a variety of ways to expand early childhood education. Although this option refers to proposals to expand Head Start, the same result might be accomplished by encouraging or permitting public schools to offer pre-kindergarten programs or other forms of preschool programs. The committee's examples merely highlight some of the possibilities.

The American Recovery and Reinvestment Act of 2009 (ARRA) also included numerous activities designated as public-sector investments, temporarily boosting spending for this category starting in 2009. Some of the new spending suggested by Option 3 (and Option 4) may echo the content of ARRA. In contrast to ARRA, however, the expansions in this option are intended to be permanent and focused on long-term returns rather than short-term stimulus.

Defense Programs

Defense spending would follow the study baseline, declining from 4.3 percent of GDP in 2008 to 3.4 percent in 2019 (at its 2002 level) but growing with the economy thereafter. In comparison with Options 1 and 2, force reductions would be smaller and weapons modernization would be more extensive. This would make it possible to sustain present levels of personnel and personnel support and permit more gradual declines in defense-related investment, research and development, and construction.

Option 4: Increase Spending by 16 Percent

This option takes the most expansive view of the appropriate roles and responsibilities of the federal government. Spending would reach 10 percent of GDP by 2019 (close to the 9.9 percent share of 2007 and well above the baseline level of 8.6 percent in 2019) and remain at approximately that level from 2020 on.

Option 4 expands defense spending by approximately 24 percent relative to the baseline, putting it at 4.2 percent of GDP (close to its 4.3 percent share in 2008), and it increases domestic spending by approximately 14 percent relative to the baseline, putting it at 5.8 percent of GDP (slightly below its 5.9 percent share in 2007). This option leaves defense and other domestic spending close to the 9.9 percent share of GDP it held in 2007.

Domestic Programs

Domestic spending is expanded to 5.8 percent of GDP (at around the 1996 share), an increase of approximately 14 percent relative to the study baseline; this translates into an increase of $141 billion in 2019. This option would incorporate the new spending programs of Option 3 (see Appendix D for details) and also allow for other expansions, potentially positioning the federal government to better meet unforeseeable contingencies and emergencies.

Defense Programs

This option expands defense spending by approximately 24 percent relative to the baseline, putting it at 4.2 percent of GDP in 2019 and keeping it approximately at that level from 2020 on. This is slightly below the 2008 level of 4.3 percent (which includes temporary war spending) but well above the baseline level of 3.4 percent. The Defense Department would be able to maintain current force sizes while paying for higher health care costs and keeping up with real wage growth. This option would help sustain the priority for a strong all-volunteer force adequately supported. The military also would have substantial funds for modernization, permitting U.S. forces to replace old weapons and incorporate new technology. These actions would, with near certainty, maintain the current technological superiority enjoyed by the United States. This option would permit the military to prepare for future peacekeeping or protection activities and maintain the ability to engage in large and protracted deployments or prevent another country from becoming a near-peer competitor.

CONCLUSION

Although all four defense and other domestic spending options reduce defense and other domestic spending as a share of GDP compared with its level in 2008, only two of the options would require reductions in spending relative to the baseline rate of growth.

The ability of the budget to support the more generous options will depend on the choices that are made with regard to the three major entitlement programs (see Chapters 5 and 6) and the level of revenues (see Chapter 8). Chapter 9 presents illustrative combinations—consistent with fiscal sustainability—of the policy options discussed in these chapters. As will be seen, the higher defense and other domestic spending options discussed in this chapter are plausible only if they are combined with options to significantly reduce the growth of Medicare, Medicaid, and Social Security spending. Even then, such combinations will require federal revenues to be at levels much higher than the norm of recent decades.

NOTES

1. Although labeled "domestic" here for convenience, this category also includes spending for international programs, such as those for diplomacy and foreign assistance. However, in 2008, international programs accounted for just 4 percent of the spending under this label.
2. While Congress has put a stronger spot light on "earmarks" in an effort to curb such parochial, constituency-based practices, the aggregate effect on the budget in the most aggressive instances of earmarks has been typically less than 1 percent of total appropriations.
3. The timing of these outlays will depend on recording decisions by the Congressional Budget Office and the Office of Management and Budget. It appears that the bulk of costs for the Troubled Asset Relief Program (TARP) and capital assistance to Fannie Mae and Freddie Mac, among other interventions, will be recorded in the 2009 deficit.
4. Devolution might also increase disparities among state and local governments, since certain federal grants would play less of an equalizing role.
5. The committee adjusted for the minor overlap between the programs targeted for devolution and the programs selected from the Congressional Budget Office (2009b) report.
6. The report (Congressional Budget Office, 2009b) from which the committee identified illustrative budget savings contains arguments for and against each of the options.
7. For example, when the price of apples rises, the standard CPI registers that fact as an unalloyed loss of well-being. However, consumers can recoup some of that loss by switching their consumption to oranges or something else; the standard CPI does not capture that effect. See Johnson et al. (2006) and Gordon (2006) for a technical discussion of biases in the CPI.
8. A chained CPI uses spending data from more than one time period to account for substitution behavior on the part of consumers (see Cage et al., 2003).
9. Total savings would amount to $31.3 billion dollars by 2019. The chained CPI is also used in one of the committee's illustrative Social Security options (see Chapter 6 of this report) and in one part of the simplified tax alternative to the current-tax structure (see Chapter 8).

8

Revenue Options

Having considered spending options in the three preceding chapters, in this chapter we consider the options for revenues. Of the committee's four illustrative scenarios for long-term budget sustainability, three would require substantial revenues in addition to the amounts projected under our current-policy baseline. Just *how* additional revenue is raised is an important policy question. At higher tax rates, substantial flaws in the current tax system would be magnified. Therefore, in addition to considering options for higher levels of revenue, the committee has analyzed alternative tax regimes that promise to raise revenues more efficiently and with fewer adverse effects on economic growth. This analysis includes illustrative application of a much-simplified personal income tax structure and of a possible additional revenue source, the value-added tax (VAT), to reach higher revenue levels.[1]

Taxes can be raised in different ways, which distribute the burden differently across people with different levels and sources of income: these differences implicitly embody different concepts of fairness. And different tax regimes can have different overall effects on the economy: for example, most tax experts believe that the current tax code could be reformed in ways that would boost economic growth. The tax system also directly affects how the nation can respond to the increasingly competitive global economy.

The first part of this chapter provides an overview of federal revenues, currently and over time. The second part looks at flaws of the current tax system—its complexities, inequities, and generally negative effect on economic performance—and ideas for reform. The chapter also considers the

U.S. tax system in an international context, which is important to assessing how the U.S. tax regime affects the economy's global competitiveness. It briefly discusses the important but elusive goal of achieving fairness in taxation. In the final part of the chapter, the committee analyzes two alternatives to the current tax system, considering them both as ways to fix flaws in the current system and to raise the additional revenue that would be needed under three of the committee's four scenarios.

THE CURRENT TAX STRUCTURE

Revenue Levels and Sources

For the last half century, federal revenues have fluctuated mostly between 17 and 21 percent of the gross domestic product (GDP), even as tax legislation reduced or increased income tax rates, increased payroll tax rates, and made other changes. The business cycle has substantial effects on the federal budget; and the deep 2008-2009 recession, following major tax cuts early in this decade, has reduced revenues as a share of GDP below historical levels. However, as the economy recovers, revenues are expected to rise gradually back to 17 percent and then higher as the economy grows further. Figure 8-1 shows the recent history of federal revenues as well as the trend projected in the study's baseline.

The largest amounts of federal revenue come from the individual income tax, the corporate income tax, and the payroll taxes that fund Social

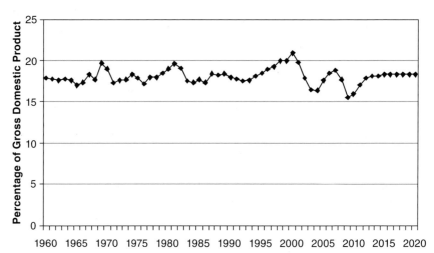

FIGURE 8-1 Federal government revenues as a share of GDP.
NOTE: Data for 2010, 2015, and 2020 are estimates.

Security and Medicare (often referred to as social insurance taxes). These three taxes account for 93 percent of federal revenues. Federal payroll taxes rose rapidly from the 1960s to the 1980s with the expansion of Social Security and the introduction of Medicare, but as a share of GDP they have leveled off since then. While receipts from the payroll taxes were increasing, those from the corporate income tax were declining as a percentage of GDP, leaving total revenues roughly flat. The payroll taxes are earmarked to finance rising current and future health and retirement benefits; corporate income taxes are not earmarked. Therefore, the ostensibly equal exchange of corporate income tax for payroll tax receipts—the latter linked to higher health and retirement spending—arguably left the federal budget worse off for the long term.[2]

Complexity of the Tax Code

The individual income tax is imposed on wages and salaries, returns from savings, small business profits, and other sources of income under a graduated rate structure.[3] In 2009, statutory or explicit tax rates ranged from 10 to 35 percent. A substantial share of low-income workers and families pay no income tax because, with exemptions and the usual deductions, their modest earnings are not subject to even the lowest rate. The corporate income tax imposes a rate of 35 percent on corporate profits, with small corporations paying lower rates.

Average tax rates—which are simply taxes paid divided by total income —are almost always lower than the statutory rates because they include the effects of deductions and exemptions. Yet another important type of tax rate is the "marginal" rate, which is the rate a taxpayer pays on an additional dollar of income. For example, for a person earning $60,000 who pays $6,000 in federal income tax, the average tax rate is 10 percent. But if this person is in the 25 percent federal tax bracket (and no other features of the tax code affect tax liability) then the rate on any additional income earned, the marginal rate, is 25 percent. Because marginal rates determine the after-tax returns from work, savings, and investment, they affect the willingness to undertake such activities.[4]

For the typical individual income taxpayer, with moderate amounts of wage income and modest deductions from an owner-occupied home, the income tax can be relatively simple. But for some taxpayers, particularly small business owners, the income tax is often quite complex. Federal tax rules spanned 70,320 pages in 2009—one measure of their complexity— three times more than in the 1970s (CCH Canadian Limited, 2009).

In part the income tax is so intricate because "income" is difficult to define and measure; partly for the same reason, the current income tax base does not reflect a consistent definition of income. Indeed, the current income tax is probably better thought of as a hybrid of a broad-based income tax and a consumption-based tax. Some types of savings and investment (such as for education) are treated more generously than they would be under a pure income tax, while other types (such as interest on ordinary savings) are fully taxed, as they would be under a pure income tax. Some (such as savings and investment for retirement) are treated as they would be under a pure consumption tax, much more generously than under an income tax. And the rest are treated somewhere in between. These inconsistencies in taxation allow taxpayers to reduce their tax burden by shuffling assets from fully taxed to tax-favored accounts (such as for education or retirement), an activity that reduces taxes collected without significantly increasing total saving or investment.

The complexity of the tax code has steadily worsened over time in part because policy makers have increasingly used it to try to achieve social goals and to aid particular sectors of the economy through narrow reductions in tax liability. For example, the deduction for the interest on home mortgages and other housing-related deductions seek to increase home ownership, and deductions for tuition and other education-related deductions seek to make college more affordable. Such tax provisions intended to benefit specific groups of taxpayers are known as "tax expenditures." The number of these tax expenditures (see Chapter 1) doubled from 67 in 1974 to 146 by 2004 (Government Accountability Office, 2005:4). A new study increases that count to 158, for 2008 (Minarik, 2010).

The number and range of tax expenditures lose large amounts of revenue. Tax expenditures for activities other than business account for roughly 6 percent of GDP (Burman et al., 2008a). For comparison, the individual income tax raises about 8 percent of GDP. These figures suggest that eliminating tax expenditures and broadening the tax base would allow tax rates to be cut nearly in half (Burman et al., 2008a:13). However, the elimination of tax expenditures for specific purposes might lead to demands for greater direct spending for those purposes.[5]

Most experts contend that if the tax code had fewer special provisions, especially those for tax expenditures and lower rates, it would be more conducive to growth and would consume less time and energy of taxpayers to comply with (or avoid).

ISSUES IN TAX REFORM

The current federal income tax is a long way from the simple and neutral system that almost all tax experts—and many taxpayers—favor. They support moving to a tax system that raises needed revenue simply, minimizes both paperwork and economic distortions, and provides a socially desired degree of progressivity. Yet policy makers have been reluctant to do the sometimes politically risky and always unglamorous work of "cleaning up" the code by ridding it of outdated or ineffective provisions and inconsistent definitions. Experience suggests that the people who would lose financially from elimination of the targeted provisions oppose such reform and are more effectively mobilized in their opposition than the larger numbers of people who would benefit from what would be small tax reductions. Often, many taxpayers see their own tax benefits as fair treatment for special circumstances but believe other taxpayers should lose their targeted benefits.

Simplification

Achieving tax simplification would yield five main benefits for individuals, businesses, and the economy.

First, it would reduce the high administrative and compliance costs of the tax code. Americans spend about 7.6 billion hours annually filling out tax forms, keeping records, and learning tax rules (Internal Revenue Service, 2008:3). The Internal Revenue Service (Internal Revenue Service, 2008:4) estimates that the cost of complying with federal income taxes is roughly $200 billion annually.[6]

Second, tax simplification would improve the ability of individuals and businesses to make sound economic decisions: that is, to make decisions that work best for their own finances and for the performance of the economy, rather than to try to benefit from special provisions in the tax code. For example, the large and growing number of tax rules on pensions, savings vehicles, and investment earnings complicate, if not confuse, family financial planning.

Third, simplification would reduce the frequent and often costly errors made by both taxpayers and businesses.

Fourth, it is widely believed that simplification would address the problem that tax complexity leads to noncompliance because taxpayers are confused about what income is taxable and what tax "breaks" exist. Complexity—and its twin, ambiguity—also foster "aggressive" tax planning as both taxpayers and tax advisers try to take advantage of the code. Because complex tax rules are subject to multiple interpretations, they spur taxpayers and businesses to take risks in the hope that their tax-cutting strategies are either legal or are not uncovered by the Internal Revenue Service (IRS) (for a detailed discussion, see Edwards, 2003).

Fifth, complexity can dilute the incentives—thus, the effectiveness—of provisions that seek to advance particular societal goals. For example, it is difficult or impossible for people who invest in housing that qualifies for a tax credit to know for certain ahead of time the exact tax benefit it will yield because it depends partly on their future incomes and tax liabilities.[7]

Because it is difficult to estimate the tax consequences of the particular actions that such tax provisions are intended to reward, they act less as a spur to socially desirable behavior than one might expect while still resulting in loss of revenue.

There are many ideas for tax simplification. One that is frequently mentioned is to replace the income tax with a flat-rate or progressive consumption-based tax system. Revenue estimates have varied quite widely, but it appears that under revenue-neutral reform, switching to a flat consumption-based system might increase U.S. incomes over the long term by about 10 percent (Altig et al., 2001; Auerbach, 1996; Joint Committee on Taxation, 1997; Jorgenson and Yun, 2002; Kotlikoff, 1993). However, a consumption tax at a single flat rate would shift the tax burden among households significantly, which would create winners and losers among different groups of taxpayers.[8]

Economic Efficiency and Growth

Whatever the level of taxes in the future, GDP and incomes would be higher if the tax system were more efficient than it currently is. An efficient tax system is one that minimizes distortions that adversely affect working, saving, investing, spending, and other important economic decisions. A pure income tax would treat different forms of income in the same way, thus broadening the tax base. This would allow lower marginal tax rates without losing revenues, so that economic decisions would be less driven by their effect on taxes owed and be more likely to raise income throughout the economy.[9]

Neutral Treatment of Different Sources of Income

Variations in the way different categories or sources of income are taxed tend to distort wage, price, and profit signals in the economy, thereby diverting resources into lower productivity uses. This is particularly so for variations in taxing different sources of income of one type, such as business profits and capital income. For example, if one industry benefits from a special tax provision, higher after-tax returns in that industry will draw resources to it from other activities that have higher economic value. Except in the case of demonstrated market failure, only equal tax treatment of different economic activities will lead to the most efficient use of scarce resources; see Box 8-1. All of the special provisions in the current income tax code—including the favorable treatment of home ownership (even for vacation properties)—create economic costs or "deadweight losses." These are the losses in "welfare" (economic well-being) that occur when tax rules distort economic behavior: individuals and businesses act in ways that take

---

BOX 8-1
Distortions in the Current Tax Code

Provisions in the tax code that favor one source of income or another can distort private financial decisions.

One example of such a distortion is that there generally is a single layer of income taxation for noncorporate business profits but two layers for corporate profits: returns to corporations' investments are taxed at both the business level and at the individual level, in the form of dividend and capital gains taxes (see Gravelle, 2004).

The tax code also creates numerous distortions for capital investment. For example, for businesses, the system of asset depreciation is distorted by the ad hoc rules that govern the time period over which investment costs are deducted and by price inflation, which lowers the depreciation deduction below replacement costs (Congressional Budget Office, 1997:39; Jorgenson and Yun, 2002:317).

The tax code can distort decisions for personal savings as well. The income tax favors consumption over saving because consumption is not taxed but the returns to saving are, encouraging people to spend their earnings rather than save them. Because policy makers have long recognized the favored treatment of consumption over savings, they have enacted many special provisions for savings. The tax code has different rules for dividends, interest, tax-exempt bonds, capital gains, simplified employee pension plans, individual retirement accounts (IRAs), 401(k) retirement plans, Keogh Plans (which also allow individuals to tax-defer savings from earnings), and other retirement arrangements, life insurance, estates and inheritance, and annuities. Although in some cases these disparate rules may only subsidize the transfer of existing wealth into tax-favored accounts rather than spur new saving, they do reduce the anti-savings bias of the income tax. Yet they are so complex as to defeat most taxpayers' (and some specialists') understanding of them.

---

advantage of the tax code rather than in ways that bring true benefits for the individual or business. That is, tax-induced distortions risk reducing the long-term benefits that arise when individuals use their incomes as they choose. They thus interfere with the wise choices of both individuals and businesses for income, consumption, savings, investment, and production.

Marginal Tax Rates

Marginal tax rates are the rates that individuals and businesses pay on an additional dollar of income, or save for any item (such as an itemized deduction) for which there is a tax preference. The economic distortions in the tax code are magnified when marginal tax rates are high or differ among otherwise similar economic options. The economic waste ("deadweight loss") to economic performance from the current tax code is directly related to marginal tax rates. As marginal rates rise, these efficiency losses rise more than proportionally, roughly as the square of marginal tax rates. Because of this distortion, tax reform efforts in the past, such as the bipartisan Tax Reform Act of 1986, focused on reducing marginal tax rates.

If marginal tax rates are cut, the tax base will expand as people reduce their tax avoidance and increase their productive activities (Feldstein, 1995). One series of studies has estimated that a permanent 5 percentage point reduction in marginal tax rates accounts for a 10 percent increase in capital expenditures.[10]

Given the adverse effects of high marginal tax rates from a growth or efficiency perspective, policy makers should want the lowest possible tax rates that raise the amount of government revenue desired. This consideration becomes particularly important for this study because the adverse effects of high rates would be magnified at the higher levels of revenue needed to achieve long-term fiscal sustainability under three of the committee's four scenarios.[11]

International Context

Globalization is transforming separate but intensely competing national economies into a single world economy through rising cross-border trade and investment, migration of workers, and transfers of technology, with important implications for the tax system.

Most people are aware of globalization because of growing international trade. But the growth in trade has been dwarfed recently by the growth in international investment. Although the value of global trade has tripled since 1990, the value of global investment flows has increased 10-fold (as measured in nominal dollars between 1990 and 2006).[12] These investment flows have put pressure on governments to restrain tax levels and reform tax systems with an eye to international competitiveness. The United States has a lower overall tax burden than many other advanced industrial countries. The total of federal, state, and local taxation in the United States equaled 28 percent of the economy in 2006, in comparison with an average for the countries in the Organisation of Economic Co-operation and Development (OECD) of 36 percent; see Figure 8-2. Although Japan and Korea have levels of taxation similar to the United States, most nations in Western Europe have higher tax burdens.

As OECD government budgets generally increased in size during the 1970s and 1980s, largely to finance increased services and social benefits, income and payroll taxes were the major sources of additional revenues. But in recent decades, many countries have greatly expanded their taxes on general consumption, such as VATs. In Europe, the average VAT rate rose

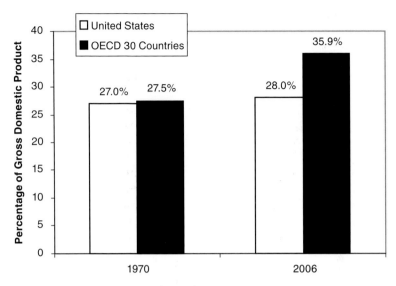

FIGURE 8-2 Tax revenues as a share of GDP.

over time to its current level of about 20 percent (European Commission, 2009).

Perhaps the most striking changes in tax policies in the OECD countries have been the dramatic reductions in income tax rates since the 1980s. Following the lead of Britain and then the United States, all major industrial nations cut their statutory individual and corporate tax rates (Organisation for Economic Co-operation and Development, 2008a).[13]

For corporate taxes, the situation between the United States and the OECD countries is quite different. The United States now has the second highest marginal (roughly, "statutory") corporate tax rate in the world (only Japan has higher rates); see Figure 8-3. The World Bank ranks the United States as 76th best in the world in terms of the burden of business taxes and business tax compliance costs (World Bank and Pricewater-houseCoopers, 2007:47).[14]

Some fiscal experts argue that international tax competition is productive because it encourages governments to reform their tax systems and reduce low-priority spending (see, e.g., Edwards and Mitchell, 2008).[15] However, not all tax competition is so high-minded. Some very small countries with minimal public-sector needs have explicitly striven to attract corporate "headquarters"—which can be nothing more than mailboxes—by establishing very low corporate tax rates. In effect, the corporations and the country split the tax savings between them.

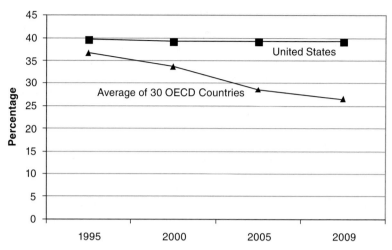

FIGURE 8-3 Top corporate tax rates in the United States and 30 OECD countries.

Whatever the underlying motivation, there is concern that unless U.S. taxation is competitive with the nation's trading partners, businesses will shift their investment and reported profits abroad. In particular, multinational corporations, which account for a majority of U.S. merchandise exports, can shift investments to minimize tax payments and distortions (Mataloni, 2007:44; data for 2005). If U.S., foreign, and multinational corporations reduce their activity in the United States because of relatively high corporate taxes (not building new factories here, for example), one of the likely effects would be lower wages for average American workers, implicitly compensating for the higher taxes paid here.[16] At the same time, tax competition to attract capital reduces tax rates on corporate income, capital gains, dividends, and high incomes in general, and thereby perhaps unintentionally constrains tax systems to be less progressive. The conflicting concerns of legitimate international tax competition and a race to the bottom on taxes on capital raise complex issues that will be important for all tax policy decisions in the coming decades.

Fairness

Every citizen and taxpayer supports tax fairness although it is quite possible that no two people agree on precisely what that is. And the literature on the subject is huge.[17] Taken in the abstract, interpretations can be quite philosophical, with questions ranging from the proper ratio of the tax burden of the richest citizen to the poorest, to whether it is more morally proper to tax income or consumption.

In a practical context, the distinctions that have to be made are between making "fair" choices to collect the same amount of revenue as is collected now and making "fair" choices to distribute additional taxes (e.g., to close the budget gap described in this report). In raising an unchanged level of revenue, some people want a tax system that is more progressive, that is, that places greater burdens on those at higher incomes. Other people want less progressivity. One argument for changing the tax system but not changing its current level of progressivity is that this approach would minimize the number of "winners" and "losers" from the tax change. Also, taxpayers have made long-term commitments—borrowing money to buy homes or invest in their own businesses, for example—and increasing their taxes in the short run is unfair or, at least, painful.

When the goal is to increase the overall amount of revenue, however, fairness issues are more contentious. Furthermore, there is no clear and simple benchmark—such as maintaining the current distribution of burdens—that can be used as a starting point for public debate.

In this chapter generally, the committee models either the current tax law or a simplified alternative with tax rates chosen to replicate the level and distribution of revenues of the current law and then increases revenues by simply increasing all tax rates proportionately. Such an approach holds no particular claim to superiority and in an actual legislative process surely would be challenged from all sides. However, we find it a straightforward starting place for the kind of discussion that this report seeks to begin and support.

There are practical choices that may conflict with some conceptions of fairness. One issue, noted above, is the international competition for investment on the basis of after-tax income from investments. If international competition—whether arguably efficient or a shortsighted "race to the bottom"—forces lower taxes on incomes from capital, that would tend strongly toward the perhaps-unintended consequence of reducing the progressivity of the tax system.

Another issue is the current negative income tax burden on comparatively low-wage workers. (That is, because of "refundable" credits—discussed below—many low earners receive checks rather than paying taxes through withholding or otherwise.) In the 1960s and early 1970s, some argued for increasing the personal exemption and standard deductions to cut the tax burden for families with poverty level incomes, and, at the same time, to reduce the administrative and compliance burden on those families and the IRS by eliminating the obligation to file a return. In the mid-1970s, however, this approach was expanded with the introduction of "negative income taxes," in the form of the Earned Income Tax Credit (EITC). The EITC eliminated the burden of the Social Security payroll tax for poor families, and provided a kind of wage supplement that did not add to employers' costs and so would not fuel inflation. However, it totally reversed the simplification advantage of removing low earners from the rolls; it actually made their tax returns much more complex than those for the average middle-class taxpayers. The administrative complexity grew as necessary safeguards were added against fraud. (And, there were concerns about possible under-withholding of tax for families whose wage incomes increase modestly during a year.) These issues have been compounded over the years as other tax credits have been made refundable.

If budget deficits prove to be as large as feared and significant revenue increases are enacted, it may be hard to raise enough revenue without some tax increases on the current large share of the household population that now does not pay income taxes—about 45 million—either because they receive a refund or owe no taxes, but instead actually receives negative income taxes.[18] This would be a significant reversal of the recent policy trend of increasing the progressivity of the tax code.

Many other issues involving the economic efficiency, complexity, and ease of administration of the tax system may make it difficult to pursue any conception of fairness in taxation. The many objectives of tax policy, including fairness and revenue sufficiency, are necessarily to some degree in conflict, and the difficulty of resolving such conflicts is one of many reasons that tax reform is both technically complex and politically challenging.

ILLUSTRATIVE TAX OPTIONS

Three of the committee's four scenarios for sustainability would require raising considerable additional revenue. In two of the scenarios the levels would approach or exceed the share of GDP in some other wealthy nations (see Chapter 1 for current international comparisons). If income and payroll tax rates were simply raised while retaining the current tax structure, the adverse effect on growth would likely be more severe than if a simplified tax structure were adopted; see, e.g., Congressional Budget Office (1997), Feldstein (2006), and Hubbard (1998). Table 8-1 provides an overview of the committee's illustrative tax options, in line with the illustrative scenarios for a sustainable fiscal future outlined in Chapter 4 and detailed in Chapter 9. Possible increases in payroll taxation for Social Security and for the hospital insurance portion of Medicare, discussed in previous chapters, are also shown. The discussion below considers possible changes to federal income taxes under the current federal structure of personal and corporate income taxation or a simplified income tax structure and with the possible addition of a VAT. The two alternative tax structures are applied to reach each of the four future revenue levels and paths required by these scenarios.

TABLE 8-1 Federal Tax Structure and Revenue Levels Under the Committee's Four Paths

Path	Current Tax Structure	Simplified Tax Structure
Low Spending and Revenue: Revenues remain at 18-20% of GDP through 2050, to about 22% by 2080.	Income taxes remain at roughly 10% of GDP. Payroll taxes: Medicare remains at 2.9% for both employers and employees with no limit; Social Security tax remains at 12.4% for employers and employees, up to an indexed earnings cap.	Income taxes remain at roughly 10% of GDP; personal income tax reformed with a broader base, lower rates, and two brackets; corporate rate cut to 25%. Payroll taxes same as at left.
Intermediate-1: Revenues rise to about 23% of GDP by 2050; edge up to about 24% by 2080.	Current income tax cuts expire and all tax rates rise above current law. For example, for 2050, the top personal rate of 35% rises to 37.2%, and the capital gains rate of 15% rises to 15.9%. Medicare payroll tax is doubled. Social Security payroll tax raised in steps to 13.3% in 2060; same cap.	Similar individual income tax rates as above, but tax-bracket thresholds and standard deduction adjusted to increase revenue. For example, by 2080 the two rates are 7.4% and 18.4%, and the capital gains rate is 11%. Payroll taxes same as at left.
Intermediate-2: Revenues rise to about 25% of GDP by 2050 and to about 26% by 2080.	Current tax cuts expire and income tax rates rise (more than above). For example, for 2050, the top personal rate rises to 40.9% and to 42.5% by 2080; the capital gains rate rises to 17.5% percent and to 18.2% by 2080. Medicare tax doubled. Current Social Security tax raised in steps to 14.5% in 2075; same cap. Second-tier Social Security payroll tax added for any earnings above cap in current law; rises to 3% in 2060.	Somewhat higher individual income tax rates than immediately above; tax brackets and the standard deduction are also adjusted. For example, by 2080 the two rates are 8.7% and 21.8%, and the capital gains rate is 13.1%. Payroll taxes same as at left.
High Spending and Revenue: Revenues rise to about 28% percent of GDP by 2050 and after that date to about 32%.	Current tax cuts expire and income tax rates rise higher than above. For example, for 2050, the top personal rate is 50% and the capital gains rate is 21.4%. VAT added around 2020; rate rises to 14.6% by 2080. Medicare tax doubled. Current Social Security tax raised in steps to 14.7% in 2080; cap raised. Second-tier Social Security tax added for any earnings above raised cap and rises to 5.5% in 2075.	Higher individual tax rates than above; tax brackets and deductions adjusted. For example, by 2080 the two rates are 11.5% and 28.7%, and the capital gains rate is 17.2%. No VAT. Payroll taxes same as at left.

Current Tax Structure

One way to raise more revenue is simply to increase the statutory tax rates under the current tax structure, which now range from 10 to 35 percent. In the "high spending and revenues" scenario that approach pushes income tax rates so high that the committee has concluded that current levels of tax avoidance and negative economic effects would reach unacceptable levels. "Unacceptable" is defined differently by different experts, but the committee concluded that to avoid damaging effects on growth, the top income tax rate should not exceed 50 percent for people with the highest incomes.[19] With the revenue required for the "high" scenario, that level would be reached by about 2020 under the current tax structure. At that time, we assume that policy makers would add to the current income tax a VAT similar to that in Europe. Thereafter, because we assume that personal and corporate income taxes cannot rise further, we assume for purposes of illustration that the VAT's rate would rise to supply whatever additional revenues are needed.[20]

The economic burden imposed by a VAT could be minimized if it were imposed on a very broad base of all consumption. Nevertheless, in most countries, the VAT has a narrower base that excludes significant categories of consumption (such as food), for both technical and political reasons. In the 15 core countries of the European Union (EU), the average VAT tax base is about 40 percent of GDP.[21] We assume that a VAT in the United States would have the same breadth as this European average.

Overall, the tax levels and structures in the United States and the EU countries are noticeably different. In 2006, the tax-to-GDP ratio in the United States was 28 percent, compared with 39.8 percent in the 15 core nations of the EU (Organisation for Economic Co-operation and Development, 2008b:96). Taxes on "general consumption" were 7.9 percent in the United States and 19.2 percent in the 15 EU countries. Thus, in a rough sense, Europe's higher social spending and larger governments are funded by higher general consumption taxes, the VAT.

One way to view the typical European approach is as using relatively regressive VATs, with burdens falling disproportionately on lower-income people, to pay for more redistributive social spending than in the United States, such as larger child allowances and higher unemployment benefits. Following this reasoning, if the United States adopted a VAT, it might be seen as taking only half of the European social bargain.

For simplicity, we do not assume an explicit period of transition to a VAT—that is, a slow phase-in of increasing tax rates—but rather propose a VAT rate to provide the revenue needed at any given time. The committee recognizes that adding a VAT would impose disparate combined tax burdens on different age groups. For instance, middle-aged and elderly people who have saved without the benefit of current tax subsidies, having already paid income tax on earnings when earned, would pay a VAT on those same earnings when they are spent as consumption, perhaps in retirement.[22] Although the result could be unexpected double taxation of a portion of the earnings of that group, some analysts believe this would be appropriate because these groups benefit from Medicare and Social Security. (And some analysts believe that this or similar problems would inevitably accompany any major change in the tax system and can be mitigated or avoided with fine adjustments in the exemptions, rates, and other parameters of the tax law.)

Under the low scenario we rely on both the current tax structure and all the details of current tax law. The greater demands of the three other scenarios are met by proportionately increasing tax rates for: (1) the six regular tax brackets; (2) capital gains and qualified dividends; and (3) the two brackets of the alternative minimum tax (AMT).[23] In other words, for the three scenarios that include spending above the revenue baseline, the current tax *structure* is retained, but not its detailed tax *rates*. Proportionately increasing tax rates is one rule-of-thumb method for an even-handed distribution of any additional tax burden, but it is by no means the only possible approach, and, like any other, it would be controversial.

Figure 8-4 displays the top statutory rates over time for the current tax structure under the committee's four scenarios. (Table E-1 in Appen-

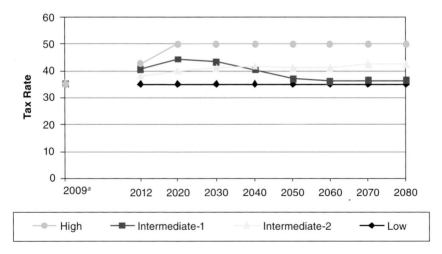

FIGURE 8-4 Current tax structure: top personal income tax rates for the committee's four scenarios.

[a]Under current law.

dix E shows all the personal income tax rates, as well as the VAT rate.)
Specifically:

- Under the low scenario, because all personal income tax rates stay
  at the 2009 level, the top rate remains 35 percent.
- The intermediate-1 scenario requires more revenue initially than
  the intermediate-2 scenario because it is oriented to the more immediate spending of human capital investment programs, rather
  than to Medicare or Social Security.
- Because the intermediate-2 scenario is oriented more to the programs that serve the elderly, especially Medicare, its spending initially rises more slowly than spending under intermediate-1, but it
  rises faster than in intermediate-1 after about 2030. After about
  2040, all personal income tax rates under the intermediate-2 are
  higher than under intermediate-1.
- Under the high scenario, the top personal income tax rate rises to
  50 percent by 2020, which the committee assumes is a practical
  maximum. (The other rates also rise proportionately.) In 2020 and
  thereafter, a VAT is added to the tax structure. With the increasing
  revenue needs over time in this scenario, the single rate of the VAT
  rises from 0.9 in 2020 to 14.6 percent in 2080.[24]

Simplified Tax Structure

Rather than continuing to base tax law on the current structure of
the income tax, policy makers could act to reform and simplify it (see
Table 8-1, above). This section considers the effects of a simplified tax
structure under each of the committee's four illustrative scenarios. The current tax structure discussed in the preceding section and the broader-based
or simplified tax structure discussed here represent two "bookends," with
many possibilities in between.[25]

Assumptions

The committee's illustrative version of a simplified tax would replace
the current six tax brackets for individuals with two. With few deductions
or credits, individual income tax rates could be lowered and still yield the
same revenue because the tax base would be broader. The only deductions
or credits would be the current EITC and child tax credit, both for low-
income, working filers, and both refundable for those with no net income
tax liability. As currently, those "taxpayers" would receive a check for the
net amount of the credit. To help meet international tax competition, the
corporate tax rate would be reduced from the current generally applicable
35 percent rate to 25 percent.

The two-bracket simple income tax loosely echoes the Tax Reform Act of 1986, which broadened the income tax base and reduced statutory rates. The committee's simplified tax is a somewhat more "pure" tax reform than the 1986 act because it eliminates many more deductions, exemptions, and credits. Such a plan was recently analyzed by the Tax Policy Center of the Urban Institute and the Brookings Institution (Burman et al., 2008b).[26]

The committee's simplified tax plan would be revenue neutral and approximately distributionally neutral in 2012. In other words, it would raise the same amount of money as under the current tax system, and it would generally retain the same relative burdens on various broad income groups as would occur under current tax law projected to 2012. Some analysts prefer more precisely mirroring the current-law distribution of the tax burden: for the same total revenue yield, this approach would require more tax brackets. In the committee's scenarios that require additional revenue, the distribution of that additional revenue burden will inevitably be controversial.

For the low scenario, the committee's illustrative simplified tax structure in 2012 would have these basic features:

- individual tax brackets of 10 and 25 percent ("lower" and "upper" or "first" and "second" brackets, respectively);
- application of the upper tax bracket to incomes above $73,100; and
- a standard deduction that is almost doubled from the current level, to $17,000 for joint filers or $8,500 for others.

For all scenarios, the simplified tax structure would have these features:[27]

- no itemized deductions;
- retention of the current 15 percent rates on capital gains and qualified dividends;
- elimination of almost all deductions and credits, except pro-savings tax features such as IRAs, 401(k) retirement plans, and Health Savings Accounts;
- elimination of the mortgage interest deduction for own-occupied homes (see below); and
- retention of a simplified EITC and child tax credit for low-income workers and their families.[28]

One tax expenditure that would be dropped is the deduction for mortgage interest on owner-occupied homes, for those who itemize deductions. Although it would be appropriate to have a mortgage interest deduction in a system in which the economic benefit of living in an owner-occupied home, that is to say, implicit rent, is taxed, it is not appropriate in our system.

The mortgage interest tax expenditure roughly equals in cost those for pensions. Unlike those for pensions, which are generally considered pro-savings, however, the home mortgage interest deduction is generally considered pro-consumption. Critics also note that it is generally regressive because people at higher incomes tend to itemize deductions, have more mortgage interest to deduct, and are in higher tax brackets, which increases the benefit of each dollar in interest that is deducted. These critics also note that mortgage interest deductibility tends to lead to overinvestment in houses and diverts savings away from business investment that would help promote an internationally competitive economy.

As an element of a possible broader reform of health care and for fairness, for all scenarios, the simplified tax structure establishes a dollar cap on the level of insurance that employers provide as health benefits that is not subject to the income tax. As noted in previous chapters, the cost of this insurance is currently not taxable to either employers or employees, and it is not subject to either income or payroll taxation. As an open-ended subsidy, it provides an incentive for employees (especially, well-paid employees) to receive compensation in the form of "gold-plated" insurance coverage, which tends to drive up health costs. Because the value of this provision to the taxpayer increases with taxable income, it is highly regressive. It is currently the most costly tax expenditure in the system.

Capping the level of employer-paid health insurance that is excludable from personal income taxation would raise revenue and help limit this source of medical inflation. Under the committee's simplified tax structure, the cap would be the average cost of such plans for 2009: an estimated $5,370 for single coverage and $13,226 for family coverage. The cap would rise with general price inflation, which has generally risen much less rapidly than inflation in medical prices or medical spending.[29] If medical inflation continued at a high rate, the cap would raise increasing amounts of revenue over time.

The committee's simplified tax would make no changes to the business tax base except repeal of the special manufacturing deduction added in 2004.

A major tax reform of this sort could bring difficulties and uncertainties, especially during the transition to it. However, if major tax reform is done thoughtfully, potential problems can be minimized. More importantly, potential problems would have to be weighed against the demonstrated inadequacies of the current tax system, which derive both from its structure and its high rates.

The committee offers this simplified tax structure—a major tax reform —in keeping with a basic premise of this study: that the serious and funda-

mental long-term fiscal problem facing the United States demands fundamental (and bold) long-term solutions. More specifically, if revenue levels
must rise, then the current tax code's distortions and inefficiencies will be
magnified by higher rates, so that consideration of tax simplification becomes both more urgent and more necessary.

Implementation

Under the simplified tax structure, statutory rates for the personal income tax would be markedly lower, for a given revenue level, than under
the current tax approach; see Figure 8-5 (see also Tables E-1 and E-2 in
Appendix E). Moreover, with simplified taxation, the rates of its upper and
lower brackets (i.e., the second and first brackets, respectively) generally
decrease over time except under the high scenario after many years. By
contrast, under the current tax structure, the top and other rates increase
over time for the intermediate-2 and high scenarios.[30] For the high scenario
under the current tax structure, rates rise to their deemed maximum in
2020, at which time a VAT is imposed and its rate rises thereafter as needed
to generate required additional revenue.

Under the simplified tax structure, personal income tax rates generally
decrease over time because of the broader tax base of simplified taxation and the elimination or reduction of costly tax expenditures, including interest paid on home mortgages and, especially, employer-sponsored
health insurance. With growth in real income, these tax expenditures would

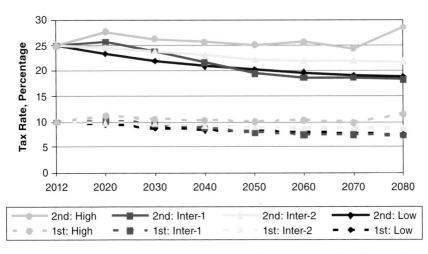

FIGURE 8-5 Personal income tax rates for the first and second brackets under a
simplified tax structure for the committee's four scenarios.

otherwise be increasingly costly. The general decline in rates for personal income taxes adds to the strength of this approach in minimizing both the distortion of economic decisions and the tax system's negative effects on work and saving incentives.

Effects of the Options on Distribution of the Tax Burden

Figure 8-6 and Table 8-2 show the degree to which the combined federal tax burden is shouldered by each of five income quintiles (i.e., fifths), under the current and simplified tax structures. (The combined federal tax burden comprises the major federal taxes [see Appendix E], including the payroll taxation and VAT summarized in Table 8-1.)[31] To get a clearer picture of how people with the highest incomes would fare under an alternative tax structure, data for the top quintile are supplemented by data for the top 10 percent and 5 percent of the income distribution. Also, reflecting current tax *rates*—not just the current *structure*—current law is used as a benchmark (see Appendix E for more detailed information). As described above, the combined tax burden on each group includes income taxes and payroll taxes for all scenarios and, in the high scenario under the current tax structure, the addition of a VAT.

Two indicators are used to gauge the relative burden of taxation on different income groups because they convey different insights. One indicator is the percentage shares of combined federal taxes, which are shown in Figure 8-6 for 2050 for each income group. This is a relative measure of tax burden. As a tax system becomes more progressive, higher quintiles shoulder an increasingly greater share of the total tax bill. The second indicator is the percentage change (increase or decrease) in net, after-tax income, compared with the tax baseline, for 2012, 2050, and 2080, for each group, which is shown in Table 8-2. This is a measure of how deeply the taxes will "bite." Change in after-tax income gives another view of how a new tax policy affects each income group, one that makes particular sense when, as here, the revenue requirement is being varied.

In looking at Figure 8-6 and Table 8-2, it is important to remember that much changes over the long time span of the projections. Although the committee's revenue illustrations are designed for approximately unchanged tax distributions at the start (2012), the relative burdens can diverge over time, for at least three reasons. First, the economy is growing. Growth in real incomes puts taxpayers into higher personal income tax brackets— particularly with the six brackets in the current tax structure—and also affects the amount of payroll tax paid.[32] With only two brackets for regular income and no AMT, this "real bracket creep" generally raises proceeds of the simplified income tax far less than under the current structure.

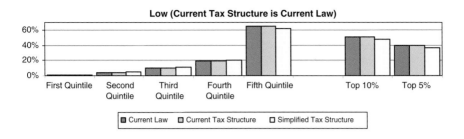

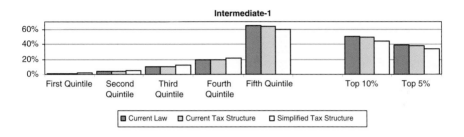

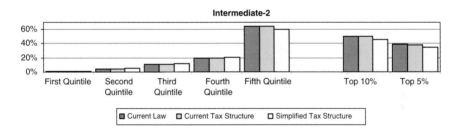

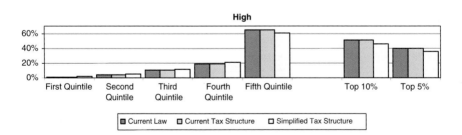

FIGURE 8-6 Distribution of the percentage share of combined federal taxes by relative income in 2050 for the committee's four scenarios.

TABLE 8-2 Percentage Change in After-Tax Income Under the Committee's Four Scenarios in Comparison with Current Law for Selected Income Groups, in percent

Group	2012		2050		2080	
	Current Tax	Simplified Tax	Current Tax	Simplified Tax	Current Tax	Simplified Tax
Low Scenario						
First Quintile	NA	0.1	NA	–2.0	NA	–2.6
Third Quintile	NA	0.7	NA	–1.0	NA	–1.7
Fifth Quintile	NA	–0.1	NA	2.1	NA	2.7
Top 5%	NA	0.2	NA	3.1	NA	3.6
Intermediate-1 Scenario						
First Quintile	–0.5	–0.6	–2.2	–4.8	–1.8	–5.4
Third Quintile	–1.8	–1.8	–3.5	–6.2	–3.9	–6.7
Fifth Quintile	–3.7	–2.1	–3.5	–0.1	–3.1	0.5
Top 5%	–4.2	–0.6	–3.0	2.0	–2.5	2.5
Intermediate-2 Scenario						
First Quintile	–0.5	–0.3	–2.3	–4.9	–2.3	–5.9
Third Quintile	–1.3	–0.6	–4.6	–6.7	–6.7	–9.3
Fifth Quintile	–2.3	–1.3	–6.2	–2.9	–7.8	–3.8
Top 5%	–2.5	–0.3	–6.0	–1.2	–7.3	–2.0
High Scenario						
First Quintile	–0.6	–0.8	–4.8	–6.2	–7.0	–9.2
Third Quintile	–2.2	–2.8	–9.8	–11.0	–14.4	–18.1
Fifth Quintile	–4.9	–2.6	–15.0	–7.5	–18.0	–13.5
Top 5%	–5.7	–0.8	–16.2	–6.0	–17.6	–11.7

NOTE: NA = not applicable.

Second, the needed revenue paths of the four scenarios also affect the distribution of taxation. The level and path of payroll taxation vary with the scenario, as do other details that also affect the distribution of payroll tax payments.[33] And the VAT added in the high scenario under the current tax structure also has distributional effects—it is less progressive than either form of personal income taxation. In practice, there is no doubt that tax rates and other parameters of the tax system that affect tax distributions would be adjusted multiple times over the decades covered in these simulations and projections.

The third source of change in the tax distribution over time has to do with how the various personal income tax rates are adjusted in the implementations of the two tax structures. For simplicity, we have assumed that the various rates within each personal income tax bracket are adjusted proportionately to each other. Notably, capital gains rates and those on ordinary income are not only raised and lowered together, but are raised or lowered by the same proportion. All of these assumed changes potentially contribute to changes in the distribution of tax burdens. (Appendix E provides additional data for all the years projected.)[34]

The committee's modeling—like most such analysis—specifies that higher tax rates would modestly reduce taxable incomes. However, it does not model the likely reductions to GDP if tax rates rise. Again, this follows the practice in most such analyses.

Although the distributions of our scenarios' *initial* tax burdens—that is, in 2012—are modeled to be approximately the same as current law would be in that year, the distribution of tax burdens can change over time if additional revenue is raised. Given the complexity of the tax system changes we analyze, it is perhaps surprising that even for many years in the future, the overall distribution of tax burdens changes only modestly across the scenarios and across tax regimes.

Looking first at the percentage share of the combined federal tax burden (Figure 8-6), for the current tax structure in 2050, in all scenarios the relative burdens stay about the same as under current law. This is in large part because the current tax structure is modeled closely on current law. The first (i.e., bottom) quintile shoulders about the same burden as current law (1.2 percent of total taxes paid), at all revenue levels. The same is true for that middle (or third) quintile, for which shares of the combined burden vary between 10.4 and 10.8 percent. The top quintile generally continues to pay 64 to 65 percent of the total burden. However, especially under the intermediate-1 scenario, those in the top 5 percent pay somewhat less: 38.1 percent, compared with 39.3 percent under current law.

With only two tax rate brackets to fine-tune the distribution in the simplified tax structure, combined federal taxation tends to move somewhat away from the current degree of tax progressivity and—partly since the implementation of simplified taxation changes only restrictedly—that divergence tends to increase over time. Table 8-2 shows that in 2050 for each scenario, the simplified tax "bites" the first and third quintiles somewhat more, and the fifth somewhat less. That is, under the current tax structure, the first and third quintiles have a bigger drop in after-tax income than under the simplified tax structure, while the reverse is true for the fifth quintile. (The same relationships appear in Figure 8-6.) These distributional effects of the tax structures tend to increase in time, as shown by the columns for 2080.[35]

Some details and implications of how the simplified income tax structure is modeled here may help explain the distributional differences shown. Under the current tax structure, many single-earner families in the lower quintiles get a tax break by the "head of household" filing status, which is not included in the simplified tax structure. In the simplified tax approach, real income growth makes more and more filers at the low end of the distribution subject to income taxation. The simplified tax structure also eliminates itemized deductions, which currently benefit some middle-level tax filers who would, under simplified taxation, claim the standard deduction. Although the amount of the standard deduction in the simplified structure rises through time with the price level, incomes tend to increase faster, so its projected tax benefit diminishes over time, which is another cause of the distributional difference between the current and simplified tax structures.

Among high-income taxpayers, the effects of the tax treatment of income from capital gains remain significant.[36] The distribution of this income source is extremely skewed: in recent years the top 0.1 percent of taxpayers has received roughly half of all capital gains. Table 8-2 shows that under both the current and simplified tax structures—but especially for the latter—the top 5 percent generally fares much better than the top 20 percent. For the implementation of both tax structures, the capital gains rate is adjusted proportionately to the rates on ordinary income, but the resulting reduction in progressivity is greater with the simplified tax structure.[37]

Although the simplified tax structure moves the federal tax system somewhat away from its current progressivity, it would remain highly progressive. In 2050, for instance, the first quintile would pay 1.2-1.3 and 1.5-1.7 percent of combined taxes under the current and simplified structures, respectively, for the different scenarios; for the middle quintile, taxes would be 10.4-10.8 and 11.2-12.2 percent, respectively; and for the top 5 percent the share of all taxes would vary between 38.1 and 39.4 percent for the current tax structure and between 33.7 and 36.5 percent under the simplified tax structure.[38] If these distributional results were judged to differ more than is desired from the current progressivity of the tax burden, the tax liabilities could be adjusted by using somewhat more elaborate procedures than the committee used to fine-tune the tax parameters, such as the exemptions, standard deductions, numbers of tax rate brackets and their tax rates.

The committee chose a simple tax structure that started by approximately replicating the current distribution of the tax burden. This choice does not reflect the committee's position on any particular distribution of the burden. Rather, our goal was to show ways to raise the revenues required by the spending scenarios. If policy makers and others prefer a somewhat more or less progressive system, it can be achieved with relatively minor changes in the parameters of the committee's version of a simplified system.

Whatever the tax structure or the population group, all the committee's scenarios except the low one reduce the after-tax incomes of taxpayers. To one degree or another, all taxpayer groups would shoulder the increased tax burden in the three scenarios that include substantial increases in federal spending.

CONCLUSIONS

This chapter's illustrative options demonstrate some of the broad choices for modifying the federal tax system in order to collect the revenues needed in the committee's four paths to fiscal sustainability. For the scenarios requiring higher revenues, increases in payroll taxation can be combined with increases in personal and corporate income taxation, which is feasible both to raise the needed revenue and approximately retain the current tax burdens. Our illustrations show that there is enough flexibility in the current personal income tax structure so that a VAT (a new, major tax) would need to be added only in the high spending and revenue scenario under this current tax structure. Tax policy that simplifies the current corporate and personal income taxes can achieve the highest required revenues without adding a VAT.

The illustrations show that well into the future, a simplified income tax structure (combined with higher payroll taxes) yields extra revenue by eliminating or modifying current tax expenditures. Enough extra revenue comes from such base broadening that a new tax like a VAT need not be added, even at the highest illustrated revenue level. In fact, by and large, under a simplified income tax structure, the marginal rates of personal income taxation would start low and decline over time and still provide the necessary revenue. In contrast, if the current tax structure (including tax expenditures) is retained, these rates would start higher and generally increase over time to meet the revenue requirements.

The debate over whether and how to raise revenues to pay for a given level of future spending offers an opportunity to consider alternatives to the current tax system that could be more efficient, simpler, and more conducive to economic growth. In any tax regime, high marginal tax rates tend to distort economic decisions, tend to lower growth, and—especially for personal and corporate income taxation—tend to reduce incentives for work and investment. But unavoidably difficult tradeoffs in values are implicit in the choice between the current tax structure and a simplified tax structure for personal income taxation.

After a transition, the committee's illustrative policies, which use straightforward approaches to setting the rates, exemptions, and other parameters of the tax law, show somewhat less progressivity in combined federal tax burdens under the simplified tax structure than the current tax structure for each of the illustrative paths of revenue needs. And this difference in the distribution of tax burdens tends to increase over time, despite the similar starting points used.[39]

The simplified tax structure's reduction in progressivity might be mitigated or avoided by adjustments or additions to its details—such as raising the capital gains tax rate relative to that on ordinary income, adjusting the indexation of the standard deduction, and other changes that would have beneficial tax effects on low- and moderate-income single-earner families. Rather small changes to combined marginal tax rates—single percentage points—could change the conclusions of this distributional analysis. The simple illustrations here stop short of such fine tuning, which would surely be a part of an actual legislative process.

The current tax structure—characterized by complexity and many narrow tax expenditures—and current tax rates have resulted from past policy debates and reflect the current balance of political interests. Higher revenue levels, accompanied perhaps by bold changes to establish a simplified tax structure for the personal income tax or introduce a VAT, would require different tradeoffs and a new consensus. The options presented here suggest, in broad outlines, the kinds of changes in tax structure that may be required if a decision is made to achieve fiscal sustainability by raising revenue levels to match higher future spending, taking into account the effects of such changes on efficiency, growth, and the distribution of tax burdens

NOTES

1. Other new federal taxes that have been proposed by some people include a carbon tax and increasing federal taxation on gasoline and diesel fuel. For simplicity, we considered only a VAT, which many countries have implemented successfully. A national sales tax might be possible in the United States, but we have not estimated this possibility in our scenarios. We also note that taxes are one kind of government revenue: customs duties and a miscellany of other receipts account for the remainder.

2. Controlling health care spending—including employer-provided care—is likely to have an indirect effect that would raise *taxable* compensation, boosting both payroll and personal income tax revenues in the future (compared with the baseline). This effect is likely because employers (often facing international competition) would probably have to defray increased health insurance costs out of taxable pay. Controlling health care costs would mitigate this reduction in taxable compensation, which would then be higher than otherwise. We have not attempted 75-year modeling of this indirect link between controlling health care spending and tax revenue, just as we do not model the macroeconomic consequences of alternative structures of the personal income tax. On the general relationship between health cost inflation and taxable compensation, see Nyce and Schieber (2009).

3. Personal income taxes also are paid by Subchapter S corporations, a few of them quite large.

4. Average tax rates can affect other aspects of behavior, too. Average rates for the committee's illustrative options are discussed below.

5. The arithmetic of tax expenditure dollars is complex—the figures shown are just simple examples. An estimate of the revenue loss of a particular tax expenditure makes sense only in reference to a particular tax base and rate schedule.

6. Income tax compliance costs have been variously estimated at between 10 and 20 percent of revenues collected. Such estimates typically apply a per hour wage rate to the estimated number of hours that Americans spend on tax compliance activities.

7. We note, however, that because there is no cap on the mortgages that receive favorable tax treatment, there is an incentive to overinvest in housing relative to other assets.

8. Any kind of tax reform or tax simplification would be complicated. Moreover, the transition to a simplified structure is itself risky, difficult, and costly; see Congressional Budget Office (1997).

9. In addition to the more general (i.e., theoretical) studies cited throughout, the Joint Committee on Taxation routinely applies its two macroeconomic models to estimate how major tax changes would effect the overall economy (see, e.g., Committee on Ways and Means, 2009b:531,538; Joint Committee on Taxation, 2005).

10. Martin Feldstein (2006) briefly summarizes most of this literature. For more detail, see also Carroll et al. (1998, 2000a, 2000b) and Gentry and Hubbard (2004). On the effect on the equilibrium (i.e., steady-state) level of the capital stock see Joint Committee on Taxation (2005). Robert H. Frank presents evidence that somewhat higher marginal tax rates do not alter behavior or undermine productive activities (2005). Roughly similar, but a very different form of analysis, an international statistical comparison of economic growth rates found no association with the level of taxation, controlling for other potential and actual influences (Lindert, 2003).

11. The efficiency effects of tax changes are only one consideration. Below, we analyze the distributional consequences of illustrative tax structures.

12. Data on trade data are the average of imports and exports from the International Monetary Fund (2007a); data on investment are the average of inflows and outflows of portfolio and direct investment from the International Monetary Fund (2007a).

13. The total combines national and subnational governments. From 1995 to 2006, the average top individual income tax rate in the 30 OECD countries fell from 48 percent to 41.9 percent, and the comparable rate in the United States fell from 46.7 percent to 41.9 percent.

14. Another study compared 80 countries. It found that the United States had the 18th highest marginal effective tax rates on business investment for 2008, behind such countries as India, Canada, Italy, and Germany (Chen and Mintz, 2008:2-3).

15. This is a controversial matter. Other fiscal experts are concerned that a "race to the bottom" in tax rates would go too far and result in cutting back important government services. Some jurisdictions, including Ireland, Hong Kong, and the Cayman Islands, have become tax havens and offer very low or zero income tax. Policy makers have expressed concern that such jurisdictions attract tax avoidance activities. However, some economists argue that tax havens have generally positive effects on the world economy. Hines (2006), for example, argues that by helping firms reduce their taxes on reported profits in high-tax countries, havens may help increase real investment in high-tax countries. He also argues that tax havens nearly always have good governance structures.

16. However, the contrary view (see the preceding note) deemphasizes this focus on the effects of high tax rates and views corporate tax competition as really an international "race to the bottom"—a zero-sum attempt to attract mobile capital. The result, according to this view, is a restriction on every nation's tax tools that makes all tax systems less progressive, with a lighter burden on capital and a heavier tax burden on labor, which is less mobile.

17. For a reasonable start, see Blum and Kalven (1953).

18. In 2006, at least 20 million returns, or about 15 percent of the total number filed, entailed negative tax liability. The number of tax returns with precisely zero liability was about 25 percent larger, 25 million than the number with negative liability (Internal Revenue Service, 2009:Table 2)

19. Only 4 of 30 OECD countries now have top income tax rates that exceed 50 percent.

20. For simplicity and because its revenue yield is dwarfed by that of the personal income tax, we have not explored increasing the proceeds from the corporate income tax by broadening its base—without raising the statutory rate. Although we have mentioned the corporate tax's statutory and marginal tax rates, its *average* rate—influenced by exclusions from taxable income—is important too, especially in comparison with other countries. Just as the simplified tax's broadening of the personal income-tax base can increase proceeds while lowering statutory and average rates, so can broadening the base of the corporate income tax.

21. In 2006 the typical VAT rate for the 15 countries was 19.8 percent. For details of VAT rates, see European Commission (2009); for VAT revenues, see Organisation for Economic Co-operation and Development (2008c).

22. However, Social Security benefits are indexed to price inflation, so these benefits would be protected from this aspect of the transition to a VAT. Similarly, the actual services paid for by Medicare and Medicaid would not diminish after a VAT, although out-of-pocket medical spending would rise. (A dollar spending cap for Medicare, Medicaid, or both [see Chapter 5] would need to take the price effect from a VAT into account.)

23. The AMT is indexed to price inflation but, in time, real growth in incomes makes more taxpayers subject to it. The price-indexed thresholds of the tax brackets are retained in our approach, as are the current tax expenditures.

24. In fact, it is not worthwhile to set up a VAT structure to collect at the low rate of 0.9 percent. For simplicity, these data reflect the financial pressures on the tax system structure, not short-term administrative responses. At least in the later years of the scenarios, it appears that no practical VAT with the base we have specified could *replace* the personal income tax: it would be in addition to it. A national sales tax might be possible, but we have not estimated this possibility in our scenarios.

25. The simplified tax would retain the current tax's "worldwide" treatment of cross-border income flows by continuing to tax American companies on foreign profits.

26. The Tax Policy Center modeled both the illustrative current tax and simplified tax policies for the committee. For more information on the center's microsimulation model and how it is applied to model the federal tax system, see, especially, Rohaly et al. (2005) and Burman et al. (2008c).

Because of the need to revise and extend the model to project two very different tax approaches almost 75 years into the future, this aspect of the committee's study used certain aspects of slightly earlier data, assumptions, and scenarios than presented in Chapter 9. (The only exception is that Figure 8-1 uses the baseline data in Chapter 9.) Three differences are noteworthy.

First, although both chapters rely heavily on Congressional Budget Office (CBO) projections, the revenue projections here use certain long-term assumptions, such as inflation rates, that CBO made before it made those that we use in Chapter 9. (For example, for the years after 2018, this chapter's long-term inflation rate assumptions were those made August 2008, while those in Chapter 9 use CBO's subsequent June 2009 assumptions.) However, the somewhat different projections used have little or no effect on the comparison here of the study's illustrative revenue policies because these are modeled as *changes* from the study baseline, not as absolute levels.

Second, (except for Figure 8-1) this chapter's revenue baseline differs somewhat from the comprehensive baseline applied to Chapter 9 and described in Appendix B. However, both baselines do assume that most of the 2001 and 2003 tax cuts are permanent and extend the 2009 treatment of the AMT and the estate tax, and both baselines project future revenue collections at 18 to 22 percent of GDP during the 75-year projection period.

The third difference of note relates to the assumed timing. Both chapters assume revenue changes start in 2012, and Chapter 9 assumes spending changes start then, too. However, the revenue needs that drive this chapter's data were based on preliminary modeling that delayed spending reforms. Especially for the earlier years, delaying the spending reforms tended to result in higher debt service generally and, in some instances, higher noninterest spending before spending reductions took place. Consequently, this chapter's resulting tax policies generate slightly higher revenues than needed for the scenarios of Chapter 9. This "error" is on the side of prudence. But this small difference has little or no effect on this chapter's *comparison* of the eight illustrative revenue policies—since they are all affected the same way by the projected revenue needs.

27. For each instance of a simplified tax structure, the second (or "upper") tax bracket applies to incomes exceeding those for the first ("lower") bracket Our illustrations vary both the personal tax rates and the thresholds for these brackets (see Appendix E).

28. The simplified tax structure is designed to start with approximately the same relative burdens as current law projected to 2012. That is done by adjusting its parameters then, specifically, the tax bracket thresholds, the standard deduction, and the child tax credit. Over time, other parameters are also adjusted to meet revenue needs, such as the tax rates for the two brackets and the rate on capital gains and qualified dividends. Although the simplified tax is designed for approximate distributional neutrality in 2012, its tax burdens might shift over time to meet revenue needs. Because of this possibility, the study compares the later projected burdens of the current and simplified taxes against each other.

29. The cap would be indexed using the chained consumer price index (CPI)—generally considered more accurate than older versions of the CPI (see Chapter 6). The chained CPI would also be used to index future payments in Option 1 for Social Security (discussed in Chapter 6).

30. In the low scenario, current tax structure rates stay fixed, by the design of this scenario.

31. Other measures of the distribution of the federal tax burden are useful as well. One is tax paid as a percentage of income, which is also the average tax rate; see Tables E-13 through E-18 in Appendix E. Also, the estimates of the future distribution of tax burdens rely heavily on projection of the income distribution, which in turn relies on CBO long-term projections. For estimation, the income breaks between the quintiles are as follows (in 2009 dollars): 20 percent, $19,429; 40 percent, $37,634; 60 percent, $65,903; and 80 percent, $112,079. That is, the top quintile comprises people with annual incomes above $112,079, and the bottom quintile comprises those with incomes below $19,429. The top 10 percent group starts at $162,348, and the top 5 percent at $227,254.

32. The payroll tax would be affected in a variety of ways under the illustrative Social Security options of Chapter 6 (summarized in Table 8-1, above). The intermediate-2 and high scenarios not only increase the Social Security payroll tax, but they also move its relative burdens in the progressive direction. Currently, the excess of annual earnings above $106,800 is exempt from Social Security payroll taxation, but both options would impose an additional tax (at a lower rate) above the current tax cap. Moreover, the high scenario would raise the current tax cap so that additional upper-level earnings would be subject to taxation at a higher rate. Although payroll tax increases first become effective in 2012, they would be phased in very gradually, so that, for a given revenue level above "low," the distributional differences between the current and simplified tax structure almost exclusively reflect the change in income tax structure.

33. For details on effects of the payroll tax over time, see note 32.

34. These results show changes in tax distributions for future projections on the basis of commonly used assumptions about the level and distribution of income, both total

income and by source. As in the recent past, economic developments—financial booms and busts, technological innovations—will result in differences from these projections in unforeseeable ways. Still, both the distributional findings for tax structures and the various scenarios are based on the same set of economic projections.

35. For a given scenario—such as high—the differences in the distribution of combined taxes between the current and simplified taxes very likely would reflect the different structures of the personal income tax. The differences in the distribution *do not* reflect the payroll tax, because the current and simplified taxes for a given scenario include the same payroll taxes (see Table 8-1). Another point refers only to the high scenario. With the current tax structure only, this scenario includes a VAT that would rise from 8.1 percent in 2050 to 14.6 percent in 2080. The rising VAT likely explains why—for the top 5 percent—the difference in after-tax income between the current and simplified tax structures is 7.5 percentage points in 2050, but narrows somewhat to 5.9 percentage points in 2080.

36. Whatever the tax structure, increasing the gap between the marginal tax rates for capital gains and ordinary income expands the incentive to shelter income as capital gains. Such sheltering (i.e., tax avoidance) is both inequitable and inefficient. The current gap between the top statutory rate on ordinary income (35 percent) and the 15 percent rate on capital gains is 20 percentage points. Under the current tax structure for the intermediate-2 scenario in 2050, these percentage rates are 40.9 and 17.5 respectively, which increases the gap, to 23.4 percentage points. For the same scenario under a simplified tax structure, rates of 22.2 and 13.3 mean a smaller gap than at present, of 8.9 percentage points. The gap in the tax rates for ordinary income and capital gains can be reduced by taxing capital gains more heavily, but that risks curtailing investment and international competitiveness.

37. This appears in the disaggregated findings for the top quintile—not shown here—into the 80-90, 90-95, and 95-99 percentile groups, as well as the top 1 percent and 0.1 percent groups. Although, in absolute terms, those findings are very sensitive to the projected income distribution, they do show the high-end effects of tax structure, given the income projection.

38. Historically, lower maximum tax rates have led upper-income taxpayers to exert less effort converting their taxable incomes into nontaxable forms because there is less financial incentive for them to do so.

39. However, this comparison of relative tax burdens under the three of the scenarios (not the low one) shows that taxes increase for all taxpayer groups in all years.

9

Multiple Paths to Sustainability

The nation's long-term fiscal situation requires action soon. The choices required are difficult. Given competing pressures for higher spending and lower taxes, consensus on forceful action will be difficult to achieve. A major objective of this report is to indicate spending and revenue policy choices that, in the right combinations, could put the federal government on a fiscally sustainable course.

This chapter shows how the policy options described in the previous chapters can be combined to create four illustrative spending-and-revenue paths, each meeting the tests of fiscal sustainability presented in Chapter 3 (see Figure 9-1). One would sharply reduce spending growth (relative to the baseline) to keep revenue requirements close to the recent historical level. Another path—with substantially higher revenue requirements—would expand spending for defense and other domestic programs, allow Social Security spending to grow as it would under current policies, and require a more modest slowing in the growth of Medicare and Medicaid. Two intermediate paths illustrate a possible tradeoff between new spending on public investments and spending for elderly oriented entitlement programs.

These four paths do not by any means exhaust the panoply of potential policy solutions to the fiscal challenge, but they do provide some sense of the lower and upper bounds of the available choices and embody a range of philosophical values and views on government. The paths also illustrate the difficulty of the decisions facing the nation: each requires decisive changes in federal spending, and three of the four require higher revenues. To allow time for a national discussion on these difficult decisions, and recognizing the risk of introducing major changes too early in the expected economic

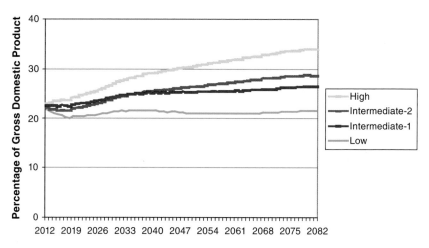

FIGURE 9-1 Projected federal spending under the committee's four scenarios.

recovery, the committee's four scenarios are designed to begin in fiscal 2012. The process of making painful choices, however, must begin now.

In the study baseline, the ratio of the debt to the gross domestic product (GDP) is projected to reach about 65 percent in 2011 and continue rising (see Chapter 1 for a description of the study baseline; see details in Table F-2 in Appendix F). In contrast, in all four of the committee's paths, revenues are adjusted so the debt-to-GDP ratio declines to 60 percent by 2022 and stays at that level thereafter; see Figures 9-2 and 9-3 (also see Tables F-3 and F-4 in Appendix F). The next four sections provide the substantive details of each of the four paths; technical details on their construction are in Appendix F.

LOW SPENDING AND REVENUES PATH

The low path illustrates how revenue needs could be held close to their historic levels by adopting the low spending options for each of the three policy areas: see Figure 9-4 and (for the difference in spending and revenue levels between the low scenario and the study baseline) Figure 9-5. (For details; see Tables F-5 and F-6 in Appendix F.) Medicare and Medicaid spending growth would be allowed to exceed the economy's growth rate only to accommodate the increasing number of people eligible for these programs due to changes in the age and gender composition of the population. Achieving this zero percent excess cost growth rate would require "strong medicine." In the near term, it likely would entail direct reductions in the

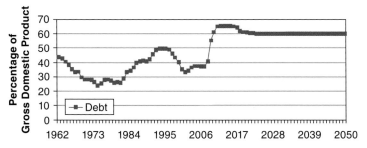

FIGURE 9-2 Projected federal debt under the committee's four scenarios.

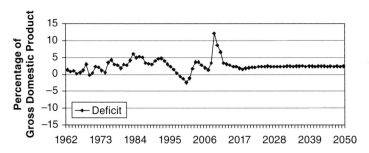

FIGURE 9-3 Projected federal deficits under the committee's four scenarios.

growth of federal health spending, although systemic reforms that improve incentives, information, and efficiency might allow these painful and distortionary restrictions to be loosened eventually. Social Security growth would be reduced to a level that would allow payroll taxes to be maintained at current rates while putting the program on a course to solvency; benefit changes would be designed to have least effect on people with lowest earnings. Merely to allow these health and retirement programs to grow with the size of eligible populations and the economy while keeping revenues near the current level, the proportion of the economy's resources devoted to all other federal responsibilities would have to be sharply reduced.

Federal revenues could remain at approximately 18.5 percent of GDP through 2025, but would have to increase to 19.2 percent by 2035 and fluctuate around that level through 2083. (For comparison, in the study baseline federal revenues are projected to reach 18.3 percent of GDP in 2019, 18.9 percent in 2035, and 21.8 percent in 2083.) On this path, the combined revenues of all U.S. governments—including those of the state and local levels at about the same proportion of federal revenues as now—

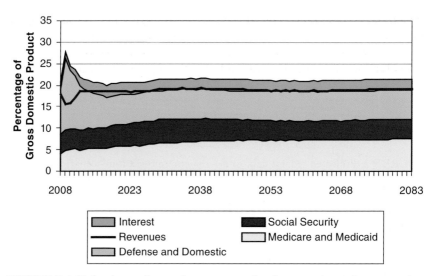

FIGURE 9-4 Federal spending and revenues under the committee's low scenario.

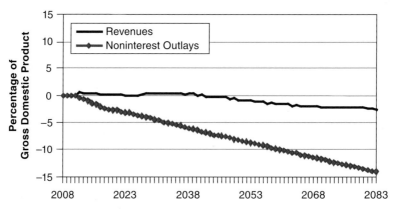

FIGURE 9-5 Deviation from the study baseline for revenues and noninterest outlays under the low committee's scenario.

would stay below the current average of advanced economies belonging to the Organisation for Economic Co-operation and Development.

HIGH SPENDING AND REVENUES PATH

At the other end of the spectrum, the substantial revenue increases assumed in the high path allow a smaller (though, in the longer term, still substantial) reduction in the growth of health spending, Social Security spending sufficient to provide currently scheduled benefits, and higher spending on other domestic and defense programs; see Figures 9-6 and 9-7 (for details see Tables F-11 and Table F-12 in Appendix F). Medicare and Medicaid spending would increase at a decreasing rate, eventually achieving zero percent excess cost growth. Current benefit levels would be maintained for future Social Security recipients. The share of resources allocated to all

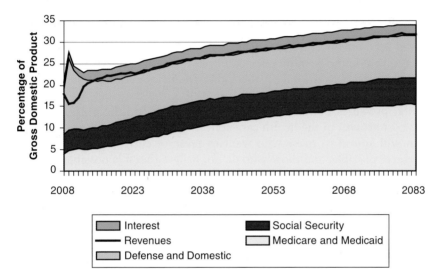

FIGURE 9-6 Federal spending and revenues under the committee's high scenario.

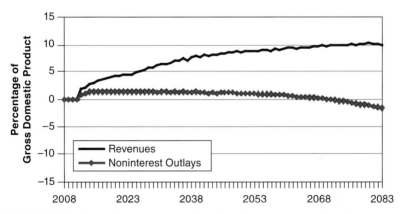

FIGURE 9-7 Deviation from the study baseline for revenues and noninterest outlays under the committee's high scenario.

other federal responsibilities would be slightly below the level as a percentage of GDP in 2008, but still a significant expansion relative to the study baseline.

To support the spending policies under this scenario, revenues would have to reach 22.4 percent of GDP in 2019, 25.9 percent in 2035, and 31.7 percent in 2083—the last being an approximately 45 percent increase over the study baseline revenue share of 21.8 percent for that year. There is little doubt that the current tax structure could not be used to collect revenues at these levels, making extensive structural reforms and new revenue sources (such as a value-added tax) necessary. If state and local revenues grow proportionately, by the end of the projection period the U.S. public sector would account for about one-half of the U.S. economy—a share about as large as that in the Scandinavian countries or France today.[1] Such comparisons are subject to the caveat that other countries may find themselves on a higher future spending trajectory as well, given that they are subject to similar pressures both from an aging population and the pressures of excess cost growth in the health care sector. The high revenues and spending path will appeal to those who want to preserve current program benefits wherever possible, and those who do not believe that it is possible to curtail health spending growth substantially without harm to health outcomes. This scenario also may appeal to those who anticipate that the nation will need major new public investments to maintain robust growth or to address international or environmental crises.

TWO INTERMEDIATE SPENDING AND REVENUES PATHS

Two intermediate scenarios illustrate ways of making tradeoffs among different spending priorities. The intermediate-1 path can be characterized as focused more on public-sector investments, while the intermediate-2 path dedicates more resources to elderly oriented entitlement programs; see Figures 9-8, 9-9, 9-10, and 9-11 (for details, see Tables F-7, F-8, F-9, and F-10 in Appendix F). Relative to the high spending path, both scenarios would curtail the growth of Medicare and Medicaid through a combination of direct spending reductions and systemwide reforms. Similarly, the intermediate-2 path would curtail the inflation-adjusted growth of Social Security benefits. The intermediate-1 path would place tighter limits on the growth of these elderly oriented programs than the intermediate-2 path—although not to the same extent as the low spending path. (Although the intermediate-1 path would reduce Social Security benefit growth for most, those with higher earnings would experience slight real cuts relative to the benefits scheduled under current law.) Compared to the baseline, the intermediate-1 path also expands the resources dedicated to other federal functions (though not to the same extent as the high path), while the

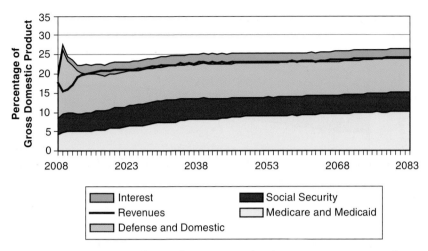

FIGURE 9-8 Federal spending and revenues under the committee's intermediate-1 scenario.

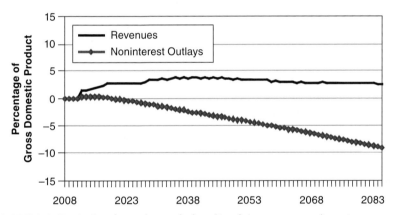

FIGURE 9-9 Deviation from the study baseline for revenues and noninterest outlays under the committee's intermediate-1 scenario.

intermediate-2 path cuts back on commitments in these areas (though not to the same extent as the low path). The intermediate-1 scenario, in other words, does more to constrain spending on the elderly to allow the federal government to take on some new responsibilities, make selective public investments for the future, and maintain defense spending at the baseline level. The intermediate-2 scenario, in contrast, gives priority to protecting the health and benefits of the elderly at the expense of reductions in defense and other domestic spending.

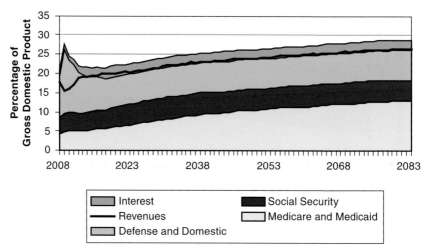

FIGURE 9-10 Federal spending and revenues under the committee's intermediate-2 scenario.

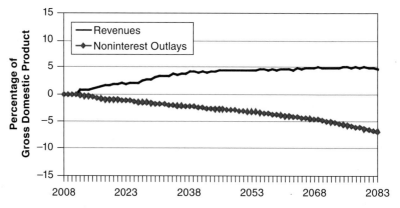

FIGURE 9-11 Deviation from the study baseline for revenues and noninterest outlays under the committee's intermediate-2 scenario.

Revenue requirements would initially be slightly higher for the intermediate-1 than the intermediate-2 scenario. However, as the costs of Social Security and (especially) Medicare and Medicaid begin to escalate, this gap becomes progressively smaller and disappears by 2035. Thereafter, the revenue requirements for the intermediate-2 path are higher than those for intermediate-1. Revenue levels for the intermediate-1 and intermediate-2 scenarios are at 21 and 20.1 percent of GDP in 2019, 22.6 percent (for both) in 2035, and 24.2 and 26.4 percent in 2083. If state and local revenues grew at the same rate as federal revenues over the 75-year projection period, the share of the economy accounted for by the entire public sector in both scenarios would eventually equal or surpass the current average of the countries in the Organisation for Economic Co-operation and Development.[2]

SUMMARY OF THE PATHS

All four paths presented in this chapter would put the federal budget on a sustainable course. Medicare and Medicaid spending as a share of GDP is reduced relative to the baseline in all four; the range of variation, however, is quite large. Social Security spending as a share of GDP is lower than the baseline in three scenarios and unchanged in a fourth. Spending on other federal programs as a share of GDP is higher than the baseline in two scenarios and lower than the baseline in two others. Revenues as a share of GDP are higher than the baseline in three scenarios and remain near or slightly above their recent historical average in a fourth.

The committee recognizes that it is not wise to introduce major deficit reduction during a downturn or early in a recovery. Therefore, our illustrative scenarios introduce the first policy changes in 2012. As one benchmark for assessing the realism and potential economic impacts of such changes, we have compared the magnitude of the changes, as percentages of GDP, with those that were enacted in 1993 as part of the Clinton Administration's economic plan. For the paths presented in this study, savings from policy changes would be about twice as large in the first year as those that were estimated when the 1993 plan was enacted (1.1 percent and 0.5 percent, respectively), but much closer in magnitude by the fifth year (1.9 percent and 1.5 percent, respectively).[3] The past is at best an imperfect guide to the future. Still, it is noteworthy that passage of the 1993 fiscal plan was followed by sustained economic growth, which most people believe was aided by an accommodative monetary policy. The lesson may be that a responsible fiscal policy can reassure financial markets and create room for the Federal Reserve to lower interest rates, helping to offset the contractionary effect of tighter fiscal policy.

It is important to note, as mentioned in Chapter 2, that in estimating these scenarios we have made no effort to estimate how different mixes of spending and tax policies could alter future economic growth. The absence of clear evidence about the relationships between policy choices (even those that substantially change levels of spending and revenues) and economic growth makes it impractical to model those effects (Kobes and Rohaly, 2002), even though some understanding of these relationships would be part of the ideal development of budget policy. Therefore, readers will need to form their own judgments about whether certain policy mixes (e.g., those that include prudent public investments) will be more likely to yield higher future growth than others (e.g., those that promote the formation of private capital).

The committee's scenarios illustrate that it is possible to construct any number of plausible spending and revenue paths over a wide range of ideological orientations and policy preferences, each consistent with long-term fiscal sustainability. The scenarios demonstrate that a person who is seeking to protect specific values and interests can find a preferred approach, although not one that is pain-free. The scenarios demonstrate that any path to sustainability will require difficult choices in most policy areas. For example, even the least constrained spending scenario (with high revenue requirements unprecedented in U.S. history) will ultimately require a nontrivial change in the growth trajectory for federal health spending. The illustrative scenarios also suggest that it may not always be easy to label paths to sustainability as "conservative" or "liberal." For example, the intermediate-1 and intermediate-2 paths have the same revenue requirements in 2035, but they allocate federal resources quite differently.

Putting the federal budget on a fiscally sustainable path is not just an accounting exercise; distributional implications are also important. Although it would be useful to estimate how the four illustrative scenarios vary in their impact on people at different income levels, options for health, defense, and other domestic programs do not lend themselves to distributive analysis: the Medicare and Medicaid spending trajectories are not tied to fixed combinations of specific reforms; defense is a public good whose distributive implications are all but impossible to estimate; and the components of the aggregate-level options for other domestic programs are explicitly illustrative and, by definition, incomplete. Therefore, although the committee estimated in Chapter 8 the effects of different revenue levels and tax structures by income level, it was unable to perform such an analysis on the spending side (with the exception of Social Security in Chapter 6)—let alone quantify the joint impact of revenue and spending choices. The one thing that can be said with certainty, however, is that by moving away from the unrestrained practice of borrowing to pay for current spending, all four scenarios leave future generations better off than they would be otherwise.

Consequences of Delayed Action

The committee's analysis and projections are based on an assumed "starting date"—that is, the year when policy changes will begin to affect spending and revenues—of 2012. Policy makers will have to judge, based on the condition of the economy and other factors, whether to make changes of the proposed magnitude beginning in 2012. They might choose, for example, to postpone some of the first-year changes by a year or more. Delay would mean, however, that the risks of carrying a larger debt would be extended and the eventual cost to the budget of a policy adjustment would be larger. To estimate the consequences of delayed action, we have modeled 5- and 10-year delays (see Appendix F for additional details).

Delayed action would result in higher near-term deficits, which would result in a higher debt. This higher debt, in turn, would require more interest to service, adding further to deficits and debt.

If action is delayed until 2017, the debt-to-GDP ratio will have risen to 72.1 percent by 2016, rather than 64.9 percent had remedial action begun in 2012. Using the intermediate-2 scenario as the basis for estimating the cost of a 5-year delay (other scenarios yield very similar results), revenues would peak at 22.3 percent of GDP rather than 21.2 percent (see Table F-13 in Appendix F; for comparison with revenues, see Table F-9 in Appendix F). In other words, revenues would have to be about 5 percent higher at their peak if budget reforms are delayed just 5 years.

The estimated consequences of a 10-year delay in addressing the fiscal challenge—to 2022—are more than twice as severe as those for a 5-year delay. Again using the intermediate-2 scenario as a basis, a 10-year delay in remedial action would allow debt to rise to nearly 83 percent of GDP before remediation begins (see Table F-14 in Appendix F; for comparison with revenues, see Table F-9 in Appendix F). Because of the additional revenue needed to reach the target debt-to-GDP ratio thereafter, revenues would have to be about 12 percent higher at their peak than in the intermediate-2 scenario.

The consequences of a delay of 10 years are more than twice as severe as those for a delay of 5 years for two reasons. First, because of compound interest on the additional debt, doubling the years of delay more than doubles the addition of debt. A doubled delay to attain a sustainable debt-to-GDP ratio would thus require more than twice as large an increase in revenue, even with everything else unchanged. Second, during those 10 years the number of Social Security, Medicare, and elderly Medicaid beneficiaries would have been increased by retirement of additional baby boomers. Thus, such a delay would put program spending on a permanently higher trajectory even when the same specific policy reforms are eventually introduced. Although even a 5-year delay would add greatly to the difficulty of reaching sustainability, a 10-year delay would more than double the difficulty of putting the nation's budget on a sustainable path.[4]

How delay makes it more difficult to achieve sustainability can also be assessed in a second way, as requiring a bigger reduction from projected spending (compared with the baseline), rather than as a further increase in revenue. To stay within the revenue bounds of the intermediate-2 scenario (i.e., which assumes policy changes are introduced in 2012), a 5-

year delay would require steeper spending reductions. For instance, Social Security, Medicaid, and Medicare would have to be cut to the level of the intermediate-1 scenario, and domestic and discretionary spending would have to be cut even further—to that of the low scenario (see Table F-15 in Appendix F; for comparison with revenues, see Table F-9 in Appendix F). The combination of delayed—but more deeply cut—spending paths requires a revenue path that is close to that of the intermediate-2 scenario without a delay, but a delay means lower levels of public services.

However, if spending reductions were delayed by 10 years, *no* combination of the reduced spending paths we have modeled could be sustained and hold needed revenue within the bounds of the intermediate-2 scenario (see Table F-16 in Appendix F; for comparison with revenues, see Table F-9 in Appendix F). Despite the lowest spending paths the committee has estimated (as part of the low revenue and spending scenario), with a 10-year delay the revenues required are markedly higher than with the intermediate-2 scenario. In contrast, the intermediate-2 scenario without delay leads to lower taxes *and* more public services. This projected outcome is another indication that a 10-year delay is far worse than one of 5 years.

As noted in Chapter 6, the illustrative Social Security reforms were designed both to achieve a financially stable program and to contribute to the sustainability of the federal budget as a whole, and to do so without raising payroll taxes or reducing benefit growth more than required to ensure the program's long-term solvency. Having already considered consequences for the whole federal budget if these specific, detailed changes to Social Security are delayed 5 or 10 years, what is the consequence for that program's solvency? As shown in Tables F-17 and F-18 (in Appendix F), none of the illustrative reforms if delayed comes close to achieving solvency (see Tables C-1 and C-2 and the accompanying text in Appendix C). Relative to reform undertaken starting in 2012 (i.e., not delayed), delayed Social Security reform helps the program's finances much less for two reasons. First, on-time reforms affect more baby boomers than delayed reforms, which is important because the illustrative benefit-growth reductions are restricted to *new* retirees. Second, delaying increases in payroll taxation raises less revenue than needed for program solvency, particularly because of the slower growth of the labor force that is projected. Overall, our analysis shows that to achieve budget sustainability with delay, reforms would have to be tougher—deeper spending reductions or higher tax increases or both—which would make delayed reform more politically difficult than more immediate reform.

Another consequence of delay cannot be modeled. That is the heightened risk that the nation's creditors—especially, those abroad—will recognize that the United States has no credible plan to restore fiscal stability and so demand higher interest rates on their loans or even broader economic changes. With higher interest rates, and thus more of the budget devoted to debt service, the available revenues for programs would shrink, and the options for corrective action on the spending side would become still more difficult.

The Political Challenge

Given the magnitude of the fiscal challenge facing the nation and the costs of delay in meeting it, action would seem to be urgent. Yet the difficulty of the choices required, the nature of the U.S. political system, the record of most recent efforts to address the nation's fiscal health, and continuing pressures for higher spending and lower taxes all suggest that early and decisive action will be difficult.

One way to increase the likelihood of appropriate and timely action would be to adopt budget process reforms such as those described in the next chapter. Budget reforms, while not sufficient in themselves to cause leaders to address the long-term fiscal challenge, can encourage and support those willing to make tough choices. The final chapter of the report addresses the kinds of actions needed by the nation's people and leaders to avoid a fiscal catastrophe.

NOTES

1. If state and local revenues remained at about their current percentage of GDP rather than growing in line with federal revenues over the projection period, total U.S. government revenues would be about 45 percent of GDP after 75 years. For projections of U.S. state and local government revenues and spending through 2050, see the Government Accountability Office (2007a).

2. International comparative statistics on public revenues and expenditures are available from the Organisation for Economic Co-operation and Development (2009). These estimates are based on National Income and Product Accounts concepts, which generally result in higher figures for both revenues and spending compared to U.S. federal budget concepts and the corresponding estimates used in this report. However, for purposes of the general comparisons made here, we are assuming that estimates using the National Income and Product Accounts and U.S. federal budget concepts remain roughly proportional to one another across time and with changes in levels.

3. The 1994-1998 percentages use GDP as estimated by the Congressional Budget Office (1994).

4. Part of the added budget cost arises from additional health and Social Security benefits. However, another part arises from a delay in controlling price inflation in health care costs.

10

Fiscal Stewardship:
A Budget Process for the Long Term

Herbert Stein, chair of the Council of Economic Advisers under Presidents Richard Nixon and Gerald Ford, famously said: "If something cannot go on forever, it will stop." But there is a corollary—how it stops matters.

As detailed throughout this report, significant dividends would be realized by addressing the fiscal challenge that faces the nation before it forces precipitous and hasty actions in the face of intense economic, social, and political pressures. If started early enough, changes in social, economic, and fiscal policy commitments can be phased in gradually, giving the American public time to make adjustments in their own retirement and savings plans and their expectations about the role of government in their lives. Whether change arrives through a gradual process of timely course corrections or as a rude shock from economic forces over which the United States will have little control may depend on whether the nation can reform the way it makes budget decisions.

The best-designed budgeting process cannot make the hard choices easier. But once those choices have been made, a well-designed process can support leaders who are prepared to meet the long-term fiscal challenge. The committee has concluded that the federal government's current budget process does little to facilitate the actions needed to address the nation's fiscal challenge and would do little to preserve any hard-won gains achieved by those actions.

Any budget is a plan for the fiscal future, but the way the federal government currently formulates its budget is weighted toward the past. Established programs and tax expenditures favor the interests and needs of current generations in the competition for resources, at the possible expense of future generations. The budget process needs to represent not only the interests and needs of the moment, but also those of the future. If the needs of today's taxpayers are not properly balanced with those of tomorrow's, future generations may suffer a loss in living standards and may have to contend with a severe economic crisis.

In this chapter the committee discusses a set of budget process reforms that would promote and sustain a new regime of more responsible budget stewardship. Specific reforms are proposed that would provide both policy makers and the public with a clear picture of the long-term implications of budget proposals, provide incentives for the President and Congress to act responsibly, and promote accountability for their actions or for their failure to act. Better process cannot provide political will, but it can reinforce the resolve of leaders who are prepared to face the long-term fiscal challenge and act as responsible stewards.

We offer what we believe are the essential elements of a reformed budget regime that focuses attention on the long-term challenge. In the next section we first provide the context with a brief discussion of the political challenge of instituting such reforms. The rest of the chapter presents the elements of a proposed new budget regime, one that would add information, set medium- and long-term fiscal goals, and enhance accountability by policy makers for meeting those goals.

THE POLITICAL CHALLENGE

Budgeting is always an exercise in hard choices. In any democracy, it is especially difficult to allocate fiscal sacrifice. The groups that benefit from specific tax and spending programs are almost always more organized than the general public that would benefit from responsible budget changes.

Tackling long-term fiscal challenges is even more daunting and politically challenging. Taking on programs that drive long-term deficits raises vexing challenges for the current generation of decision makers. Today's voters must be convinced to make sacrifices in current consumption and promised government benefits in order to reduce the probability of a future crisis and to improve the living standards of the next and future generations.

Rather than facing the proverbial wolf at the door, taking on the nation's long-term fiscal challenge is, as once suggested by Charles Schultze (former chair of the Council of Economic Advisers), more akin to dealing with the termites in the woodwork—a problem that is not immediately apparent but can bring the entire house down if not dealt with proactively. For example, if policy makers wait until the Social Security trust fund is insufficient to pay benefits, the federal deficit will already have grown to a level that will damage economic growth and saddle the budget with ever-growing interest payments. The information needed to address Social Security's unsustainability is available now, but nothing in the process requires that it be recognized and addressed now, when it could be dealt with much more easily than later.

The nature of budgeting also has changed in recent decades in ways that complicate the exercise of budgetary discipline and resolve. Before the 1960s, the lion's share of spending was provided through discretionary appropriations. The appropriations committees, largely controlled by members with relatively safe seats, took a fiscally conservative and incremental approach to the budget, keeping spending growth from outpacing revenues. Since then, however, as the scope of government benefits grew to meet human needs, most spending came through open-ended entitlements, which are not subject to annual review or to budgetary caps. There has also been an increase in open-ended tax expenditures on the revenue side, which are also subject to neither annual review nor caps.

Leadership

Some observers believe that the political risks of tough choices are so high that only an economic crisis will compel leaders to change the nation's fiscal course. And history suggests that political leaders rarely step forward to lead such an effort as long as there are no obvious and compelling economic or political consequences today of current policies. If the historical pattern holds, it presents a bleak prospect for meeting the current challenge, because, as the committee's analysis shows, waiting for a crisis will cause unprecedented economic and political harm to the nation.

Other evidence is more encouraging, however. The recent history of developed nations indicates that deficit reduction and major policy reform are not politically impossible tasks for the leaders of advanced democracies. Some nations have made substantial reforms in their own pension and tax systems in the past 20 years (see Penner, 2007). One recent study of the past 40 years of fiscal history in nations of the Organisation of Economic Co-operation and Development (OECD) found that incumbent governments that institute policies to reduce deficits are rewarded with reelection (Government Accountability Office, 1994; see also Brender and Drazen, 2008). Although deficit reduction is never easy, leaders who take decisive action can then position themselves as taking measures necessary to protect the nation's economy and finances and protect the interests of the next generation.

The United States, too, has taken some significant steps in recent years to change the course of fiscal policy. In 1983, the National Commission on Social Security Reform (known as the Greenspan Commission, after its chair) formulated convincing analyses and arguments that led to political consensus for reforms to Social Security. The reform, which included both tax increases and reductions in benefits for retirees, did not fully solve the program's sustainability problems but it greatly ameliorated them.

Similarly, in 1990, the nation adopted a budget agreement that constituted significant deficit reduction, to be followed by similar action in 1993; see Box 10-1. That agreement, engineered by leaders of both major parties, helped turn the federal government from then-chronic deficits to a 4-year period of budget surpluses.

These examples illustrate how leaders can confront politically charged fiscal challenges (see Light, 1995). The 1990 example provides both a positive and a cautionary message. It created budget process rules that for almost 10 years brought discipline to budget decisions. But the rules were eroded when budget surpluses seemed to make budget discipline less important. Partly as the result of the abandonment of those rules, the budget surpluses soon disappeared.

These infrequent examples of far-sighted leadership can provide guidance for how to break through long-standing gridlock to produce major

---

BOX 10-1
The 1990 Budget Agreement

In 1990, the nation faced a budget crisis brought on in part by a projected deficit far in excess of the targets established by the Gramm-Rudman-Hollings Balanced Budget and Emergency Deficit Control Act of 1985 (Pub.L. 99-177). That act had established annual deficit targets and required an automatic cancellation of budget resources for many programs if the target for a given year was exceeded. The projected deficit for fiscal 1991 was so far in excess of the legislated target, and the resulting automatic cuts would have been so severe, that leaders began bipartisan negotiations to find new targets and a new approach to budget discipline as an alternative to one they considered unworkable.

Under this pressure, President George H.W. Bush and Democratic congressional leaders negotiated a set of tax increases, cuts in entitlements, and limits on discretionary appropriations. These policy actions were supported by enactment of procedural reforms incorporated in the Budget Enforcement Act of 1990. The act legislated dollar caps on discretionary appropriations spending for fiscal 1991-1995 (later extended through 2002) and instituted a new pay-as-you-go (PAYGO) regime that required any new tax cuts or entitlement expansions to be offset by other benefit cuts or tax increases over the following 5 (later 10) years. The 1990 actions were updated in 1993 with another set of major cuts and tax increases, along with extensions of the budget process rules. The budget rules, constraints on discretionary programs, and PAYGO offsets were observed through much of the decade, until the emergence of budget surpluses. Ironically, of course, those surpluses were partially brought about by these earlier actions.

fiscal reforms (see Fabrizio and Mody, 2006). One interesting lesson from this history is how leaders can take advantage of how the public views most major fiscal issues. On fiscal issues, the public is not of one mind, but at least two. A July 2009 *New York Times*/*CBS News* poll confirmed what other polls and research has consistently shown: a majority of people want the deficit to be reduced but about the same majority do not want spending cut or taxes increased. This ambivalence provides an opportunity for leaders to reframe issues to appeal to the latent public support for fiscal restraint, and a sustainable longer-term fiscal path.

The Role of Process

Political leadership is essential to fiscal reform, but the rules and institutions of the budget process can make important contributions. They determine the kinds of information available and how it is used, shape incentives for action, and establish accountability for the results of those actions (Meyers, 2009). Budget processes frame the most important decisions made by a political system in a given year: how much of the economy to devote to government through taxes and how to allocate spending of limited resources.

No one should expect any budget process to persuade legislators to endure severe political pain. But well-designed rules can nudge them in the right direction and can provide political "cover." They can say that, contrary to their personal preferences, "The rules made me do it."

But budget processes are produced by the same system that produced the problems they seek to address (see Anderson and Sheppard, 2010). When major budget enforcement measures were adopted in 1990, they were designed to lock in deficit reduction achieved through negotiated revenue and spending policy agreements. In other words, policy makers first made the difficult decision that deficit reduction was imperative. Then, with considerable difficulty, they negotiated an agreement to achieve it. The new rules were negotiated last, and they were designed primarily to prevent the Congress from allowing the hard-won package of deficit reductions to erode over time. A properly designed budget process can highlight the important consequences of different courses of action and can force leaders to acknowledge explicitly and take responsibility for the long-term consequences of their decisions. Far-sighted and strong budget rules can also help leaders take on both near- and long-term deficits by providing fiscal targets and restraints.

BUDGET REFORM FOR RESPONSIBLE STEWARDSHIP

The long-term fiscal outlook depicted in this report argues for a new way to use the budget to institutionalize a long-term perspective and provide leaders with the tools needed to forestall looming fiscal crisis. Consistent with the history of budget process reform, there is reason to believe that a more forward-looking process can help to support the initiatives of those leaders who are willing to make the case for fiscal responsibility.

The committee favors reforming the budget process to make it more focused on the long term and to establish a new system of responsible budget stewardship. The current budget process is focused primarily on the short term. It uses a 5- or 10-year time frame as the primary period for the baseline, and the costs of most proposals are factored into the decision process only for that period. While existing congressional rules enforcing discretionary spending ceilings and PAYGO offsets may prevent new actions that make deficits worse, the current regime does not prompt Congress or the President to go beyond current baselines to achieve deficit reduction. It contains nothing that requires changes in major drivers of the long-term fiscal outlook—Medicare, Medicaid, Social Security, and tax policy. Moreover, the current process sets no explicit fiscal goals or targets for long-term deficits or debt. Budgetary costs are largely presented on a current cash basis, which is misleading for programs whose present commitments imply future costs that are much larger than their current cash effects on the deficit. As with most OECD nations, existing long-term sustainability analyses are not integrated into the budget process in the near term (Anderson and Sheppard, 2010). Given this orientation, it is not surprising that the process has not encouraged leaders to deal with the looming problem.

Recent actions have expanded the time horizon for budget decisions in certain areas, providing a possible model for broader reforms. The 2003 Medicare prescription drug legislation instituted a funding warning that requires the President to propose changes when the portion of general revenue financing exceeds 45 percent, although Congress has undermined the provision by eliminating the requirement for expedited congressional review. The Senate has included a "four decade" rule for new mandatory spending that requires the Congressional Budget Office (CBO) to estimate costs for the subsequent four decades, bolstered by a point of order that can be raised on the floor. Although this provision has entered into debates on occasion, it is still too soon to know whether it will provide significant institutional self-restraint.

The rest of this section discusses three major areas in which reform is needed to highlight the long-term implications of current programs and to encourage decision makers to act now to place the budget on a sustainable long-term path: information, goals and targets, and accountability.

Information on Long-Term Implications of Current Decisions

A first step for reform of the budget process would be better information about the fiscal future. Such information would provide a strong foundation for other reforms. With better information, the long-term outlook and related analyses would be highlighted as part of the budget process. The President could use long-term analyses to provide an annual fall report on the fiscal state of the nation and to develop a budget for the following fiscal year. Congress could use long-term projections to develop its annual budget resolution, set enforceable medium- and long-term budget targets, and use these to guide its annual choices in appropriations and reviews of mandatory spending and tax policy.

More broadly, new and more prominent information about the long-term implications of current and proposed policies—with appropriate caveats about the uncertainties that surround any such projections—could be used by the public to assess whether a proposed budget meets the tests of fiscal prudence presented in this report, to assess the long-term implications of pending budget proposals, and to hold leaders accountable for the long-term consequences of their budget choices.

Information alone cannot be expected to change ingrained practices. However, like the slow effect of water dripping on stone, the gradual introduction of new fiscal measures and better information can, in fact, highlight and elevate the long-term dimension of major policy debates.

Better information on the long-term outlook and consequences of today's budget choices can also help leaders reach the right choices. The seriousness of the projected long-term fiscal challenge has been no secret to policy makers. CBO, the Government Accountability Office (GAO), and the U.S. Office of Management and Budget (OMB) all prepare annual assessments of the budget outlook decades ahead.

In the past decade, a growing number of countries have independently adopted some version of long-term fiscal projections as part of their budget planning. Long-term fiscal projections provide a way to assess and discuss the sustainability of current public policies by quantifying the long-term fiscal consequences of those policies, as well as the effects of demographic and other changes on selected summary fiscal indicators. Their use is still limited to a relatively small number of industrialized countries, and it is too early to assess whether they have affected budget choices. (See Appendix G for a summary of information from 12 OECD countries on long-term fiscal projections.)

In the United States, the presentation and consideration of such information is divorced from the decision-making process: it is presented separately from and at different times than CBO's reports on the 10-year budget outlook. Adding or enhancing information, developing new metrics, and changing how information is presented and used in developing the federal budget could increase the visibility of and accountability for the long-term consequences of budget choices.

The committee offers three proposals for more long-term information in the budget process: integrating treatment of long-term budget projections into annual budget documents and making them prominent; expanding use of information on fiscal exposures in CBO and OMB budget reports; and increasing the use of accrual accounting.

Integration of Long-Term Budget Projections

Although OMB, CBO, and GAO all prepare long-term budget projections, these are not highly visible. OMB's analysis appears in the *Analytic Perspectives* volume of the President's budget. CBO's long-term analysis is prepared on a different cycle than its regular budget baseline reports and update. GAO updates its reports throughout the year, but must wait for updated data from CBO and the annual Social Security and Medicare Trustees reports. All of the reports provide important information on the budget's long-term trends, but nothing in the current annual budget process requires that this information be used in that process, so these reports are easily ignored.

As a first step, OMB and CBO could readily integrate presentation of their long-term fiscal outlooks with their near-term budgetary baselines by updating and publishing long-term projections in their initial and midyear budget reports. It would also be very valuable if the long-term impact of the President's budget policies became a regular section of the main budget volume, with long-term projections included in that volume's *Summary Tables*. In the same vein, it would be very valuable if CBO's long-term outlook were updated every time the agency updates its budget baseline. Other countries do a better job of highlighting their long-term outlook in ways that are hard for policy makers and the public to ignore: Australia is one example; see Box 10-2.

Information on Fiscal Exposures

Some of the largest federal programs have costs that grow exponentially over the long term. Their longer-term cost projections are not disclosed in either budget authority or outlay columns in the budget. GAO has coined the term "fiscal exposures" to refer to such activities, which include federal insurance and operations and maintenance for newly acquired capital, as well as long-term spending estimates for the pension and health benefits of current employees. Some of these exposures are defined as liabilities in federal financial statements; but others, such as Social Security, Medicare, and Medicaid, are not. Yet all of them will require future expenditures that are not fully reflected in near-term or even 10-year projections that are prepared routinely by CBO and others (see Government Accountability Office, 2003). OMB's *Analytical Perspectives* volume includes reporting on assets and liabilities, but it does not include the same range of commit-

BOX 10-2
Australia's Experience with Long-Term Budgeting

Australia is one of the leaders in long-term budgeting. The figure immediately below shows how the long-term budget outlook improved in Australia between the first intergenerational report made in 2002 (IGR1) and the second 5 years later (IGR2).

Australian Intergenerational Report, 2007: Comparison of IGR1 and IGR2 Projections of Primary Balance

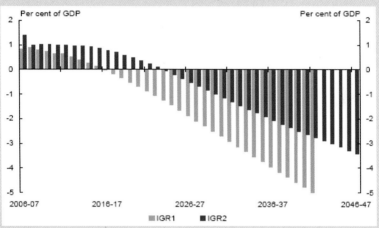

NOTE: Since IGR1, there have been some changes in projection methodologies incorporating new data and modeling approaches.

Australia's Operation Sunlight

On April 16, 2006, the then Shadow Minister for Finance released a discussion paper entitled "Operation Sunlight—Enhancing Budget Transparency" setting out recommendations to enhance budget transparency and accountability. The report, revised in 2008, proposes that the Australian government, among other things:

- Produce an Intergenerational Report every 3 years with greater disaggregation of expenditure information at the program level;
- Investigate the utility of a whole-of-government triple-bottom line (economic, environment, and social) chapter in the Intergenerational Report;
- Make it mandatory for all new programs subject to significant demographic risk be assessed and reported over a 40-year horizon consistent with the Intergenerational Report; and
- Extend the length of forward estimates presented together with the budget from 3 to 6 years (including the budgeted fiscal year) for programs likely to be subject to demographic pressures.

SOURCE: Commonwealth of Australia (2007). Reproduced by permission.

ments as GAO's analyses. CBO's budget reports do not include estimates for such exposures.

As an initial small step toward greater awareness of the longer-term dimensions of fiscal exposures, the magnitude of such commitments could be noted in the schedules of the President's budget. Ideally, OMB would work with agencies to implement an exposure concept, by recording the net present value of future costs for specific program activities in the budget for which such information is relevant, appropriate, and feasible. Government Accountability Office (2003) recommended that such information be recorded in a column alongside the more familiar outlays and budget authority recorded for all programs.

More broadly, both policy makers and the public would be well served if OMB and CBO were required to produce annual reports on fiscal exposures, which would serve as counterparts to GAO's analyses. These three agencies could work together to assess methodological issues in estimating these exposures.

Accrual Accounting

The federal budget mostly relies on cash accounting to estimate the amount and timing of program costs. That accounting is generally the most appropriate measure to capture the current-year effects of federal fiscal policy on the economy and on the borrowing needs of the Treasury. However, for selected programs, cash accounting provides misleading signals to federal policy makers about the financial costs of commitments that extend far beyond the current year.

Cash understates the longer-term costs of some programs that represent long-term contracts. For these programs, costs may arise far in advance of when cash is needed to satisfy obligations: for example, federal deposit and pension benefit guarantee insurance programs often show up as earning surpluses on a cash basis in the budget, even though their underlying risks and longer-term deficits are known to actuaries and auditors. In these cases, an accrual approach should be considered using the best methods available to estimate accruing costs.

An accrual approach would record the net present value of long-term contractual commitments in the year they are made, regardless of the actual flow of cash payments. In 1990, the federal government adopted such an accrual approach to replace the cash approach for loan and loan guarantee programs—recognizing that near-term cash flows understate the magnitude and risks associated with loan guarantees and overstate the commitment implied by direct loans. Accrued net present value better captures the underlying costs to the federal Treasury over the longer term and records these costs as outlays (and therefore as part of the deficit calculation) at the time the commitment is made. Using present value accounting to move forward the time when the cost of long-term commitments is recognized in the budget improves incentives for policy makers to take timely action if it is needed to address their costs.

The federal government similarly could adopt accrual budgeting for such commitments as federal employee pension and retiree health care costs, which are currently recognized as liabilities on the federal financial balance sheet. It would also be valuable to consider adopting accrual approaches to estimating the budgetary costs of such contingent liabilities as insurance programs. Moving to accrual for insurance would require additional research and complex modeling to capture the longer-term risks assumed by government for uncertainties, such as natural disasters and other unpredictable events.

Fiscal Goals and Targets

The committee believes that establishing a set of fiscal goals and targets is essential to gaining control of the fiscal future. Setting fiscal goals is a critical first step in institutionalizing consideration of the long-term outlook. Above all, it would force acknowledgement of the unsustainability of current policies.

In recent years, many nations have adopted fiscal targets and frameworks that helped them become fiscally responsible. In New Zealand, for example, the adoption of overall fiscal targets, in concert with market pressures, reframed policy debates; see Box 10-3. Sweden followed a similar approach. Fiscal targets had an impact not through formulaic cuts, but by providing a compelling way to frame budget debates on the basis of the long-run implications of current budget choices. In both countries, earlier fiscal and economic crises made fiscal goals important, and leaders risked criticism if their fiscal outcomes fell short.

In the United States, Congress last set overarching fiscal goals under the 1985 Gramm-Rudman-Hollings Act, which prescribed declining deficit targets for the federal budget. However, the goals were applied in a mechanical fashion that proved to be politically unsustainable, as unprecedented economic fluctuations moved the goals further away regardless of the actions taken by the policy makers. Chastened by this experience, policy makers turned to spending targets under the Budget Enforcement Act (BEA) of 1990, with a focus on holding themselves accountable for decisions they controlled, namely, the overall size of discretionary spending and new entitlements and tax cuts. Although this approach was more realistic and feasible for the United States, the BEA regime did not address the growth of spending or revenue losses for existing programs. That is, it prevented legislative acts from making things worse when in force, but contained no

BOX 10-3
New Zealand's Budget Principles

New Zealand, since 1994, has followed a legally enshrined set of budget principles, and the Government is legally required to assess its fiscal policies against these. The principles include: reducing public debt to prudent levels; once these have been achieved, maintaining them by ensuring that, over a reasonable period of time, operating expenses do not exceed operating revenues; sustaining a net worth that provides a buffer against adverse events; managing fiscal risks prudently; and pursuing policies that contribute to stable, predictable future tax rates. It is left to the government to interpret terms in the law such as "prudent" and "reasonable." A government may depart from the principles if it specifies its reasons and a plan to return to the principles in a specified period of time. Every 4 years the government presents a statement of New Zealand's "long-term fiscal position," including a 40-year budget projection and accompanied by a "statement of responsibility, signed by the Secretary of the Treasury, attesting that his Department used its best professional judgments about the risks and outlook (Anderson and Sheppard, 2010).

mechanism for significantly improving the long-term outlook. Subsequently, the abandonment of overarching fiscal policy goals and targets has left Congress and the President without a framework to assess the long-term consequences of current policy or new proposals. Nor does it reward them for doing so.

The setting of long-term fiscal targets could be adapted to the current budget process. As explained in Chapter 3, the committee judges that a 60 percent upper limit on the ratio of debt to the size of the economy (as measured by the gross domestic product, GDP) would be an appropriate fiscal goal for leaders to put in place over the next two decades. Formal adoption of such a goal now can help leaders develop fiscal policies to constrain the exponentially growing levels of debt implied by the nation's current fiscal path.

A practical question is how to integrate such long-term fiscal goals into a budget process that is predominately focused on the near term. The long-term outlook is the starting point for formulating alternative fiscal policy targets that would create a more sustainable fiscal future. However, no one would suggest that the federal government should prepare a detailed budget for the next 50 or 75 years. Rather, since the federal budget is prepared annually, long-term goals should serve as a guide for the formulation of policies that would lead to a sustainable debt level over the next 10 or 20 years. In the United States, any such fiscal target would have to be renewed with each administration and each Congress.

A frequent review of the fiscal targets would allow the problem to be addressed iteratively, in politically manageable bites. The target may need to be adjusted and phased in over the near term, for instance, to avoid precipitous fiscal actions that might jeopardize the economic recovery. In such major policy areas as health care, progress will in all likelihood proceed in iterative stages. Thus, although the next budget offered by the President or approved by Congress will likely not contain sufficient specific proposals to eliminate the excess growth of health costs, it could include actions to make progress to that end and make a commitment to continue to address the problem in the long run.

In the United States, assuming that inflation remains under control, annual deficits that average around 2 percent of GDP would be consistent with maintaining a debt-to-GDP ratio of 60 percent. As discussed in preceding chapters, simply meeting a 2 percent deficit target will become more fiscally ambitious over time unless actions are taken to modify the growth paths of the major entitlement programs or to adjust tax revenues—the key drivers of the long-term outlook.

Medium- and long-term fiscal targets could be established in the annual congressional budget resolution and then used to assess both the President's budget and the congressional policy actions. The budget resolution and accompanying committee reports would have to explicitly address the nature of the policy actions that Congress will take to achieve the debt target over the next 10 and 20 years. CBO could be required to review this section and provide its own estimate of the impact of these proposed policies on the debt target. A new congressional procedure (point of order) could be considered to reinforce the establishment of debt targets in the budget resolution.

CBO's report also could assess the implications of these policy changes on the long-term outlook over the next 50 years. Although budget resolutions may not provide sufficient detail to generate detailed estimates over the long term, a report that provided even some assessment of the budget resolution's impact on the long-term target would provide useful insights. Such a report could, at a minimum, assess whether the budget resolution would make the long-term outlook better or worse.

Accountability

Fiscal targets and goals are not self-enforcing. Rather, a framework is necessary to hold leaders accountable for meeting targets. As difficult as reaching agreement on targets might be, sustaining commitment over time is even more difficult.

The accountability framework the committee proposes has four elements. First, it would require the President to provide an accounting of the long-term fiscal outlook and the administration's plans to address it. Second, it suggests that longer-term fiscal goals should be reinforced through a budget enforcement regime that would help ensure that the goals cannot be ignored without consequences. Third, it would ensure a periodic review of the major drivers of long-term deficits on both the spending and revenue sides of the budget. Fourth, it would require that beyond the 10-year budget projection period, the long-term fiscal effects of new proposals for spending or tax cuts be fully offset. Taken together, these reforms would establish a budget regime in which the President and Congress share political accountability for presenting and enacting budgets that take greater account of the implications of today's policies for the federal government's long-term fiscal outlook.

Although reforms such as providing better information and setting fiscal goals can increase attention to these issues, the commitment of elected officials will be critical to bringing about definitive actions to deal with the nation's fiscal challenge. While the panel is not endorsing specific steps, all panel members agree that stronger public accountability for the consequences of deficits both near and long term is needed.

The committee is aware that there are many other proposals for enforcing accountability for fiscal goals. For instance a balanced budget amendment to the Constitution has been prescribed by some as an inescapable restraint on political officials. Although almost all the states have such a requirement, a provision like this would not give the national government sufficient flexibility to take necessary actions to stabilize the economy, which calls for deficits at some times and surpluses at others. In addition, although balanced budget requirements seem to promise certain discipline, they have, in fact, been undermined by creative fiscal accounting in many states—a pattern that is very likely to be repeated in many ways at the national level. Moreover, for all the reasons discussed in Chapter 3, we believe that a budget's projections for the debt provide a more appropriate indicator of its potential economic impact than whether the budget is balanced or not.

Presidential Accountability

In the U.S. system, presidents are uniquely held publicly accountable for the performance of the economy. Political scientists observe that the state of the economy is a critical factor in a president's approval ratings and the results of subsequent elections (Lewis-Beck and Stegmaier, 2008). Consequently, presidents often initiate policies and programs to try to ensure good economic outcomes in time for their own reelection campaigns, for their party's midterm elections, and for their legacies. Enhancing presidential ownership of the long-term fiscal challenge ultimately depends on whether the public holds the president accountable for long-term fiscal outcomes. One way to shape those expectations is to require presidents to account for the nation's future fiscal outcomes annually in a highly visible forum. The president could report on the long-term fiscal outlook, based on outcomes through the most recently completed fiscal year and the proposed or enacted budget for the current year. Until fiscal sustainability is assured, this report might take the form of an address in the fall to a joint session of Congress. The president's annual statement of the nation's fiscal outlook would be a reference point for everyone concerned with the sustainability of the federal budget. Such a fiscal accounting might come to be widely anticipated as a basis for assessing how well the president and Congress have done in delivering on the fiscal goals and targets set earlier in the year. It would also be a well-publicized starting point for development of the coming year's budget proposals for the long run.

Reinforcing Accountability for Meeting Goals and Targets

There is considerable controversy over whether fiscal goals and targets would constitute an effective spur or constraint on policy makers. Both in the United States and other countries, experience with fiscal rules—which use a summary indicator of fiscal condition to bind political decisions by the executive or legislature—has sometimes been discouraging. In order to have a meaningful impact on fiscal decision making, policy makers should face consequences if they ignore such goals. However, designing a budget enforcement regime is always challenging since it requires constraining the subsequent choices of political officials who are free to ignore or modify their own constraints in a democratic system.

Nonetheless, the committee believes that any fiscal policy regime has to specify consequences if fiscal results fall short of targets. Although political leaders may choose to ignore fiscal goals in the future, they should none-theless at least be held accountable in some public way for doing so. The existence of a budget enforcement regime that specifies specific sanctions for shortfalls may have an independent effect on the fiscal policy decisions of policy makers.

Reaching fiscal goals and debt targets calls for a budget process that will enable Congress to enact laws to reduce spending and increase revenues. Fortunately, the existing budget process has features that would enable Congress to do so. Specifically, the current budget reconciliation process provides the budget committees and leadership with a vehicle to require the committees to develop the broad legislation that can achieve major budgetary savings for the near and longer term. Reconciliation bills have the advantage of overcoming the fragmentation of the committee process by imposing overarching fiscal savings targets assigned to committees, and with deadlines and consequences. Moreover, reconciliation bills have the additional advantage of being governed by special rules in the Senate that limit debate and are not subject to filibusters.

In addition, the fiscal goals articulated by the President and Congress can be reinforced as they have in the past by discretionary spending caps and PAYGO rules that constrain the Congress from adopting new spending and revenue provisions that would jeopardize its targets. PAYGO would require offsetting legislated changes to increase entitlement spending or reduce taxes that would increase the deficit or reduce the surplus with changes that would reduce spending or increase revenues. After 1990, annual caps on appropriated spending and PAYGO were successful at restraining spending increases and tax cuts for several years, making a contribution to the balanced budgets achieved for 4 years starting in 1998. These rules are currently enforced through congressional points of order. However, the underlying statutory framework that provided for fallback budget sequesters when the rules are breached was allowed to expire in 2002. A good first step would be to reinstitute these caps and PAYGO requirements in statute, along with the potential sanction of budget cuts should the rules be violated.

However, PAYGO and caps will generally not by themselves be sufficient to enforce debt targets. They do not control for the growth of spending or declines in revenue under existing programs, such as Medicare and Medicaid. Accordingly, an accountability framework must include some kind of look-back process where the fiscal targets can be compared with actual levels of deficits and debt achieved at the end of the fiscal year.

Two of many possible options for imposing accountability if results do not meet a target or goal are automatic fall-back actions and a soft constraint. Automatic cuts or revenue increases could be triggered if the president and Congress fail to achieve the fiscal target. Both the trigger and the automatic mechanism used to determine the required spending cuts or tax increases would have to be carefully designed, and Congress and the president should be able to waive the trigger during economic or national security crises. (As noted above, the 1985 Gramm-Rudman experiment of enforcing balanced budget goals with automatic cuts failed to gain support, partly because the fiscal goals were unworkable and unrealistic, covering a relatively narrow range of programs.) Automatic fall-back cuts would need to be applied to a broad range of both spending and revenues to have a strong base for savings and to promote the principle of equal sacrifice. In contrast to an automatic approach, a soft constraint would call on Congress to either take subsequent action to meet the target or to go on record that the target is unreachable. Such a mechanism relies on the power of shame to trigger action through the budget process. Although this approach does not involve the complexity of fall-back cuts, it is also a weaker constraint that can be more easily ignored.

Periodic Review of the Drivers of the Fiscal Challenge

Given the importance of Social Security, Medicare, Medicaid, and tax policy for the long-term outlook, they will require special attention to ensure accountability. Those three programs represent open-ended commitments not only to present beneficiaries and taxpayers, but also to future ones. Although some entitlement programs employ trust funds that do have limitations, in most cases those limits only become a real constraint years after the programs are known to impose a net burden on the budget.[1]

There are many approaches to promote periodic review of the major drivers of the fiscal challenge, three of which are frequently mentioned: sunsets, benchmarks, and triggers.

- With sunsets, Congress would set legislated dates for specified major entitlements and tax expenditures, but excluding such programs as Social Security and federal pensions, which represent very long-term commitments. An approaching sunset would periodically provide an incentive for reexamination of a program's costs and benefits. Although periodic reviews might increase prospects for reining in features with fast-growing costs, they do not guarantee that reforms will actually occur. Some people object to this approach because setting sunset dates increases uncertainty on the part of individuals and businesses that rely on the programs in planning the use of their own resources.
- Another approach to ensure that policy makers periodically address the three major entitlement programs and tax expenditures would be to establish benchmarks or targets for them. If spending exceeded these targets or revenues fell short, the budget process could require the President or Congress to propose and Congress to vote on measures that would close the gaps as soon as they are identified.
- Congress could also enact provisions that automatically trigger actions if specified benchmarks or targets for the three major entitlement programs and major tax expenditures are not met. The use of triggers is controversial among experts. Soft triggers would require Congress or the President to either explicitly ignore the limit or take some action to address it.[2] Alternatively, a hard trigger would automatically implement specific spending cuts or revenue increases (Penner and Steuerle, 2007). Other nations have used various triggers or "automatic balancing mechanisms" tied to long-run projections for some or all parts of their budgets with good results (Penner and Steuerle, 2007); see Box 10-4.

The committee notes that it is difficult to design fall-back mechanisms if targets are not both appropriate and realistic. A hard trigger, for example,

---

BOX 10-4
Automatic Balancing Mechanisms in
Canada, Germany, and Sweden

In Canada, an automatic balancing mechanism was introduced in 1998 and mandates action if:

- An actuarial projection concludes that the Canada Pension Plan is not financially sustainable; and
- An agreement between the central government and the provinces on necessary courses of action cannot be achieved.

Financial sustainability is defined relative to the ability to maintain a specific level of contribution over a period of 75 years. Should the level of contributions exceed a figure established by law, the automatic balancing mechanism would affect changes in both contributions and pensions. In this situation, the contribution rate would be increased by half of the excess of the steady state subject to maximum annual increase. The remainder would be covered by a freeze of pensions payable over a 3-year period.

In Sweden, an actuarial income statement and balance sheet of the non-financial, defined, pay-as-you-go, contribution scheme has been made every year since 2001. In addition, an automatic balancing mechanism can temporarily abandon the indexation of pension rights and current benefits to average wage growth if the stability of the scheme is threatened. Stability of the system is defined by a balance ratio that relates to the scheme's assets and liabilities. A balance ratio of less than 1 means that the scheme is out of balance (i.e., liabilities exceed assets), and earned pension rights and current benefits are reduced according to the balance ratio rather than the average wage. This will continue as long as the balance ratio is less than 1.

In Germany, a sustainability factor linked to the national dependency ratio that is applied to the rate of indexation of benefits was introduced in 2005. In contrast to the triggers in Canada and Sweden, it is permanently activated—and may only be deactivated by an act of parliament—until the social security pension is sustainable under a determined contribution rate. Since 2008, the German government must report every 4 years how to meet targets for replacement and contribution rates.

---

must accomplish two seemingly conflicting goals: to be sufficiently punitive and unpalatable to force Congress and the President to achieve fiscal actions through the regular process; and to be sufficiently realistic and feasible to be regarded as credible if the target is not met through the regular process.

In 2008 a bipartisan coalition of budget experts embraced hard triggers for Social Security and Medicare (Brookings-Heritage Fiscal Seminar, 2008). The coalition's proposal sets limits on growth for these programs, enforced by automatic cuts in benefits and premiums when those limits are exceeded. A coalition of opposing experts argued that this proposal was unbalanced in its selection of what programs should be subject to fiscal discipline, exaggerated the power of numerical targets to force decisions on how to balance spending and revenues, and would fail to address the growth of tax expenditures that also jeopardize the fiscal outlook (Aaron et al., 2008). Complex design choices would have to be faced in establishing any triggers, including how the triggers are activated, the resulting actions, how triggers can be adjusted for economic downturns, and the frequency of reviewing the trigger mechanism to reflect changes in the programs and in the overall budget outlook.[2] Substantial work would be needed to determine if triggers would be equally effective on the spending and revenue sides of the federal ledger. Revenue triggers, which could take the form of surtaxes or delays in indexing and other scheduled revenue-reducing provisions, would present novel design challenges, as none have yet been developed, enacted, or applied.

In the U.S. political system, it should be noted that even a hard trigger is not automatic—Congress cannot bind its own future actions, let alone those of future Congresses. The Medicare program illustrates the differential fortunes of soft and hard triggers. Premiums for Medicare Part B (doctors' insurance) are automatically established each year to equal a fixed percentage of projected costs for the coming year, and those levels have not to date been overturned by Congress. In contrast, the triggers that require reductions of doctors' fees under the Part B program have been routinely overturned.[3]

The concept of triggers itself has triggered significant debate, among committee members as well as in the broader policy community. Proponents argue that such provisions would not allow these fast-growing determinants to grow automatically: the current system places the political burden on those trying to slow growth in costs or benefits. In contrast, a hard trigger would force program advocates to act to override the triggered changes. But opponents argue that triggers could negatively affect beneficiaries. Moreover, some analysts object to the lack of accountability by elected officials that are inherent in triggers. For instance, many would argue that cuts to doctors' fees for Medicare have substantive effects on the availability of care for the elderly that should be debated on their merits as they occur rather than being subject to triggers.

Consideration of the Long-Term Costs of New Policies

Meeting debt targets will require the President and Congress to more carefully consider the long-term cost implications of new spending and revenue proposals. To bring consideration of long-term costs into the decision-making process, policy makers need to have access to information about the long-term cost (or savings) effects of a proposal when it is under consideration. They also have to be able to object to long-term costs they view as unwarranted through a point of order or other procedural measure. Current rules for consideration of proposed mandatory spending and tax policy changes generally limit estimates to a 10-year period, even if the proposed change has substantial implications for the budget's long-term outlook. Yet a different rule is well within recent policy tradition: the Senate has already incorporated such a point of order in its rules, requiring policies to be deficit neutral in each decade over the next 40 years. Both the Senate and House have weak rules that attempt to restrain actions that would worsen the Social Security deficit. CBO does not currently provide quantitative estimates of costs beyond 10 years, but it does provide a qualitative judgment about whether proposals would increase or decrease the deficit over the longer term (Elmendorf, 2009).

The 1990 PAYGO requirement that mandatory spending and revenue proposals not increase future deficits was enforced not only by the rules of the House and Senate, but also by a back-up requirement that, if congressional action increased net spending over a 5- or 10-year period, covered entitlement programs would be cut to the extent needed to eliminate the increase. It may be useful to consider a comparable procedure for longer-term costs as well. Although establishing the precise order of magnitude for long-term costs may be difficult, it may be possible to create formulaic reductions in spending or increases in revenues if proposed new legislation would increase the deficit beyond the 10-year period on the basis of CBO's qualitative assessment. Like the 1990 act, a specified formula could provide greater incentives to observe long-term fiscal neutrality in considering new legislation.

CONCLUSION

Given the serious threat posed by long-term imbalances in the nation's projected spending and revenues, simply waiting for a crisis to force leaders to deal with the fiscal challenge would be irresponsible. Rather, the committee concludes that reforms to the budget process are needed now to help hold leaders accountable and to support responsible action. Just as in the battle to curb cigarette smoking, information, public framing, expert studies, and political entrepreneurs will all be important in elevating the priority devoted to meeting the nation's fiscal challenge. The breadth and scope of the changes required will call for both budget process reforms to galvanize the attention of political leaders and public engagement strategies that mobilize the attention of broader publics at the grassroots level.

Nothing can force leaders to take on this challenge absent support from the public. However, once hard decisions have been made, enhanced information, fiscal targets, incentives for prudent action, and procedures to enhance accountability could make a difference. The reforms and options outlined in this chapter could help.

NOTES

1. Trust funds, such as Medicare Part A (hospital insurance), become a net fiscal drain on the budget when they are contributing less cash from dedicated taxes than they are spending, which is often long before their fund runs out of Treasury securities that enable them to pay benefits in full. Even though the fund may be technically solvent, the budget incurs a net financial burden as fund-held Treasury securities are redeemed to cover cash deficits.

2. If the trigger concept is extended to tax expenditures, there would be particular challenges, including the several years' lag before data on revenue losses become available and the large number of exogenous factors that affect tax expenditure revenue losses, including changes in tax rates and other tax expenditures.

3. This softer trigger, which requires expedited consideration of Medicare reforms, has been ignored or bypassed by the House in both years that such a review was triggered. Currently, the Medicare program has a trigger that is activated when the general revenues that support the program exceed 45 percent of the total program. Because the trigger was activated for fiscal 2009, the President included in his budget proposals to bring Medicare below the threshold, but Congress took no action in response.

11

What Should Be Done Now?

The members of the study committee disagree about many questions of policy. We hold widely differing views, in some cases, about the priority to give different categories of spending, about who should pay for government and how much government they should pay for, about the proper division of responsibilities between federal and state and local governments, and even about the fundamental purposes of government.

What we firmly agree on is the need for strong action now to adjust the long-term relationship between federal government spending and revenues—the urgent need to put the budget on a sustainable path. We also agree that this is going to be one of the biggest political challenges the nation has ever faced.

WHY IS THIS SO HARD?

Two defining characteristics of the long-term fiscal challenge distinguish it from other budget or policy problems and make it difficult for people, including leaders, to grapple with:

- The pain of cutting spending, increasing taxes, or both, is immediate, while the gain of avoiding a fiscal train wreck—and its devastating consequences—is in the future.
- Because all fiscal projections are inherently uncertain, the long-term benefit that will result from the short-term pain cannot be precisely specified.

It is tempting, given uncertainty about the future, to discount the problem and hope that it will diminish, if not go away. People can use the lack of precision inherent in all projections to deny troubles ahead.

When faced with immediate pain and uncertain gains, the natural and perhaps rational reaction is to do nothing, to delay. In the case of an unsustainable U.S. fiscal policy, the costs of delay are not immediately obvious. They are insidious, and the time in the future when remedial action becomes unacceptably painful or no longer possible cannot be pinpointed. Moreover, a potential signal of unsustainable policies—higher pricing of U.S. Department of the Treasury borrowing to finance current spending—may have been masked during the recent downturn by the market's perception that alternative investments are even riskier. If so, interest costs could increase before policy makers have had time to act. As described in Chapter 1, increased interest costs could lead to escalating problems: first, crowding out or forcing abandonment of other government functions and priorities as interest payments swallow greater shares of the federal budget; and later, decreasing wealth, slowing growth, and reducing future standards of living.

Even if everyone becomes convinced today of an urgent need to act, differences in values and perceptions of what government should do and how to pay for it would constrain possible agreement on what to do. Policy disagreements are bound to be intensified by the need to limit what government will be able to do in the future. The likely unwillingness of many to consider the interests of future generations—perhaps because of profound disagreements regarding what those interests are or what sort of government should be bequeathed to the future—will complicate choices.

Reaching agreements to minimize and share the inevitable pain may require a change in political culture toward less partisanship, more openness to compromise, and more trust and honest communication between people and their leaders. To the extent that compromises can be found and choices can be made that allow public resources to be used more productively, the needed policy changes can be a positive sum game. But to the extent that some government programs will be eliminated or scaled back, it will not be a net gain for everyone. To forge agreement on a plan that moves the budget to a sustainable path, attitudes and practices will have to change. Realistically, such changes will take time. The committee recognizes that at least some delay in fully responding to the nation's fiscal challenge is likely, although we stress that delay means the challenge will only loom larger.

In sum, tackling the fiscal crisis is perhaps the toughest kind of political problem. Given its characteristics, quick, decisive action to put the nation's budget on a sustainable course may be improbable. Yet if action is not taken in the near future, the nation will face a calamity, and the possible actions will be fewer and far more disruptive than what is now possible. Thus, now is the time to debate alternatives, to choose, and to act. If this is done, the nation's fiscal course can be corrected in ways that avoid the worst pain.

WHY IS DELAY RISKY?

Although waiting is a normal reaction to any difficult problem, in this case it is especially risky. Consider two possibilities and their potential consequences: (1) that the fiscal problem proves to be overblown or self-correcting or (2) that the problem is as serious as the committee (and most analysts) argue. Even if these two outcomes were equally likely, it is probable that the costs of acting too late or ineffectively would be much greater than the costs of acting too soon and too precipitously.[1]

Consider first the costs of acting to address what proves—contrary to all current evidence—to be an exaggerated fiscal challenge. Some people point to the risk of having taken large and difficult choices that raise taxes or reduce the government's ability to address many urgent needs but that later prove to have been unnecessary. A too stringent fiscal policy could slow the growth of the U.S. economy or even tip the economy into another downturn. This would, in turn, require a corrective policy response—either easing fiscal policy or relaxing monetary policy or both. Yet the probability is high that the political system would adjust without difficulty. As at the end of the 1990s, the problem of projected endless surpluses tends to be self-correcting.

Now consider the costs of failing to act in the face of a serious fiscal challenge. The first risk is that of having to take bigger and much more difficult steps later to put the budget on a sustainable course. At the same time, the risks of a disruptive financial crisis would continue to grow. As detailed in earlier chapters, such a crisis could take the form of higher interest rates on U.S. Treasury debt that would complicate corrective action by draining resources for government programs; or it could take a more disruptive form. The risk would be compounded if, for instance, standard population projections underestimate growth of the elderly population.[2] After a tipping point that is inevitable but impossible to pinpoint, there will be no simple fiscal strategy to bring revenues and spending into alignment. If that point were reached, the social and economic costs of delay would explode.

So, there are two possible ways to err. One kind of error—overreacting—is readily reversible; the other—underreacting—may not be. That is, the committee has concluded that the risks of error in dealing with the fiscal challenge are asymmetric. Even in the face of great uncertainty, the safer course is to take decisive action soon to change the nation's fiscal course.

Despite the seriousness and scope of the budget challenges, however, there are a number of reasons for optimism and for believing in the efficacy of action:

- If action is taken soon, the nation can preserve Social Security and Medicare for future generations close to their current form, although not without lowering the rate of growth of benefits and/or raising additional revenues to finance them. Even under the low spending and revenues scenario outlined in Chapter 9, monthly Social Security benefits rise in real terms for most workers. That is, even if benefits are sharply reduced relative to current law, most future Social Security benefits will still be higher, after inflation, than today's benefits.

- For Medicare and Medicaid, it is more difficult to forecast future costs because of the many factors that drive health care spending, but benefits are likely to continue to cover at least the big ticket health care items for senior citizens. Thus, the fiscal challenges facing the United States by no means imply the devastation of these programs that have been so instrumental to the well-being of senior citizens and to reducing the proportion of seniors who live in poverty.

- Although the demographic pressures facing the United States are serious, they do not look overwhelming, based on standard projections of labor force participation, future retirement ages, immigration, and other relevant factors (cf., Social Security Administration, 2009d). The U.S. challenge from this source is less formidable than that facing most other major industrialized nations—many of whom will see much greater imbalances between their working and nonworking populations and sooner than the United States.[3]

- Given its relatively low current tax levels, in comparison with other industrialized countries, the United States has more leeway than most of its peers to raise revenues, should it take that route, provided that the tax system is reformed to make revenue collection more efficient and to promote economic growth.

Just as an ordinary household can meet its budget challenges by taking charge, gathering information, and seeking financial advice, the people of the United States and the nation's leaders should feel empowered and moved to action, not to despair. The nation's problems are not insurmountable, but the sooner action is taken the more likely is success.

HOW CAN THIS REPORT HELP?

One product of the committee's study is a framework for analyzing and addressing the long-term budget challenge, presented in Chapters 2 and 3. We believe this framework can contribute to how people think about the fiscal challenge and, therefore, what solutions they will consider. Psychologists have studied the effects of framing on cognition (see, e.g., Kahneman,

2002). The proper framework can enable one to use structured reasoning in place of immediate perceptions or intuition, leading to better judgments. Groups who use a common framework are more likely to find areas of agreement. In this case, how the budget problem is presented, and in what context it is viewed, will affect the ability of everyone to recognize its essential character and therefore the urgent need for action.

The Committee recognizes, however, that merely describing the problem and putting it in proper perspective is not sufficient. Therefore, this report uses the framework to develop illustrative budget paths to sustainability. These examples—combining major policy options described in Chapters 4 through 8—show how one can apply the framework to construct a very broad range of plausible paths meeting the primary tests of fiscal prudence presented in Chapter 3, leading to budget sustainability. The committee hopes that these scenarios are used as a starting point for vigorous rational debate and early action.

WHAT CAN EVERYONE DO?

When the President proposes a budget and as Congress considers a budget resolution or adopts a budget, everyone should apply the six tests of fiscal prudence detailed in Chapter 3. Because they are central to the committee's analysis, we repeat them here:

1.   **Does the proposed federal budget include policy actions that start to reduce the deficit in the near future in order to reduce short-term borrowing and long-term interest costs?**
2.   **Does the proposed budget put the government on a path to reduce the federal debt within a decade to a sustainable percentage of gross domestic product (GDP)?**
3.   **Does the proposed budget align revenues and spending closely over the long term?**
4.   **Does the proposed budget restrain health care cost growth and introduce changes now in the major entitlement programs and in other spending and tax policies that will have cumulative beneficial fiscal effects over time?**
5.   **Does the budget include spending and revenue policies that are cost-effective and promote more efficient use of resources in both the public and private sectors?**
6.   **Does the federal budget reflect a realistic assessment of the fiscal problems facing state and local governments?**

The first tests are particularly hard for nonexperts to apply by themselves. Therefore, the committee urges the Congressional Budget Office, the U.S. Office of Management and Budget, and other organizations to regularly publish projections of the long-term effects of the President's budget and alternatives that can be used by anyone to assess the extent to which the proposals are sustainable.[4]

People can also use the six tests to analyze not just the entire budget but major policy proposals and legislation that affect the budget—to assess their effects on the long-term outlook. To help such assessments, we also urge the Congressional Budget Office, the Office of Management and Budget, and other organizations to extend their analyses beyond the standard horizon to consider long-term effects of proposed legislation. Interested people and groups also can construct their own preferred budgets, using as a starting point the analysis of options for major spending categories and revenues in Chapters 4 through 8. And in looking at analyses of proposals, everyone should be skeptical of the estimates of budget effects provided by advocates of a particular proposal and search for analyses of such proposals prepared by those who do not have a vested interest in their enactment.

People can communicate their views on all of these matters to political leaders and policy makers. It is important for leaders to know that their constituents, armed with the facts and working with the right framework, can support leaders who advocate policies contributing to a sustainable federal budget.

Finally, constituents can reward leaders who make the difficult choices needed for long-term budget sustainability. The U.S. political system, with its frequent elections, tends to reward lawmakers who support programs and policies that have short-term benefits while ignoring long-term consequences. By their own behavior at the ballot box and in direct communication with leaders and policy makers, people who understand the long-term fiscal challenge and recognize that it requires hard choices can push leaders to pay attention to the need to meet the long-term challenge.

WHAT SHOULD LEADERS DO?

Leaders obviously have a responsibility to lead and to present budgets and policy proposals consistent with a budget that is sustainable over the long term. Committee members are well aware of just how difficult it will be for leaders to gain broad popular support for any combination of policies that would put the nation on a sustainable path. The committee urges leaders to use the study's framework to address the fiscal challenge in a manner that promotes public support for rational and creative action. It may be too difficult—given the nature of the fiscal challenge and the habits of partisanship—for leaders to develop specific policies in a single year's budget sufficient to accomplish the entire, large task of aligning spending and revenues. However, the coming year's budget should show a credible commitment to policy changes that substantially bend the curve toward sustainability and an explicit commitment to the goal of aligning revenues and spending over the long term. The committee's scenarios allow some time for debate and response and for correction of the short-term economic situation by assuming that policy changes take effect beginning in 2012.

Only if the process is supportive of forward-looking and prudent fiscal policy choices can this problem be solved. If the current federal budget process is found to be a hindrance rather than a help—too short-sighted and cumbersome—then the first step for leaders may be to change it. The committee's ideas for how to establish a new budgeting regime of that is forward-looking and provides incentives and means of accountability to encourage responsible, far-sighted actions, are presented in Chapter 10. Reforms can help leaders act as responsible stewards of the interests of the nation's children and grandchildren. The committee favors reforming the federal budget process to use better information about the long-term budget outlook as a basis for setting medium- and long-term fiscal goals and to consider adoption of new procedures to hold leaders accountable for responsible fiscal stewardship.

It is not the job of a group of experts, but rather the job of leaders and the people, acting through the political process, to make the necessary choices. Those leaders who recognize the seriousness of the challenge will realize that all other important policy goals are hostage to first putting the budget on a sustainable course. Their job must be to lead a creative national dialogue, beginning now and pressed vigorously, to help the United States find a way to a sustainable fiscal future.

NOTES

1. Greater uncertainty implies the discounting of future costs and benefits at a higher rate. The higher the discount rate, the smaller future costs and benefits appear when compared to costs and benefits in the near term. Great uncertainty would therefore favor a decision to delay action unless the distribution of expected outcomes between the two alternatives were asymmetrical. For an interesting analysis of this issue applied to global warming policies, see Nordhaus (2008), especially Chapter 9.

2. A new set of population and life expectancy forecasts for the United States, with a focus on transitions that will take place by mid-century, illustrate potential budget effects of hypothesized accelerated advances in biomedical technology that either delay the onset and age progression of major fatal diseases, or slow aging itself. "Results indicate that current forecasts of the U.S. Social Security Administration and U.S. Census Bureau may underestimate the rise in life expectancy at birth for men and women combined, by 2050, by from 3.1 to 7.9 years. As such, there could be 164 to 419 million more person-years-of-life lived among the population aged 65 and older by 2050 than current government estimates predict, and cumulative outlays for Medicare and Social Security could be higher by $3.2 trillion and $8.3 trillion" (Olshansky et al., 2009). If such an alternative forecast proves correct, the policy adjustments needed to attain budget sustainability would have to be much larger than portrayed in this report.

3. The share of the U.S. population over 65 is projected to rise from 12 percent in 2000 to 20 percent in 2050 in the United States, but in the same year it is projected to reach 25 percent in France, 30 percent in Germany, 33 percent in Italy, and 37 percent in Japan (Census Bureau, 2007).

4. One difficulty in setting standards for assessing budgets over the long term concerns the proper horizon for projecting policy effects and assessing sustainability. A good discussion is by Ulla (2006:160-162), who argues that, although "the possibility to forecast beyond the next 50 years may be low . . . going beyond 50 years may provide information to help reformulate present entitlement programmes and build a strategy to deal with future challenges." The Social Security and Medicare actuaries focus on a 75-year horizon, long enough to encompass the lifetimes of most people who are already alive.

References

Aaron, H.J. (2007). Budget crisis, entitlement crisis, health care financing problem—Which is it? *Health Affairs, 26*(6), 1,622-1,633.

Aaron, H.J. (2009). *Interpreting the Trustees' Reports.* National Academy of Social Insurance Briefing, May 15. Available: http://www.nasi.org/usr_doc/Henry_Aaron_NASI_Presentation_05_15_2009.pdf [December 2009].

Aaron, H.J., and Reischauer, R. (1998). *Countdown to Reform: The Great Social Security Debate.* New York: Century Foundation.

Aaron, H.J., Altman, N., Apfel, K., Blum, J., DeLong, J.B., Diamond, P., Greenstein, R., Horney, J., Kogan, R., Lew, J., Moon, M., Ooms, V.D., Reinhardt, U., Schultze, C., Solow, R., and Van de Water, P. (2008). *A Balanced Approach to Restoring Fiscal Responsibility.* Washington, DC: Center on Budget and Policy Priorities.

Abt Associates Inc. (1997). *Medicare Cataract Surgery Alternate Payment Demonstration: Final Evaluation Report.* Cambridge, MA: Abt Associates Inc.

Achenbaum, A. (1986). *Social Security: Visions and Revisions.* New York: Cambridge University Press.

Altig, D., Auerbach, A.J., Kotlikoff, L.J., Smetters K.A., and Walliser, J. (2001). Simulating fundamental tax reform in the United States. *American Economic Review, 91*(3), 574-595.

American Academy of Actuaries. (2007). *Social Security Reform Options.* Public Policy Monograph. Washington, DC: American Academy of Actuaries.

Anderson, B., and Sheppard, J. (2010). Fiscal futures, institutional budget reforms, and their effects: What can be learned? *OECD Journal on Budgeting, 2009*(3).

Antos, J.R., and Rivlin, A.M. (2007a). Rising health care spending—Federal and national. In A. Rivlin and J. Antos, eds., *Restoring Fiscal Sanity 2007: The Health Spending Challenge.* Washington, DC: Brookings Institution Press.

Antos, J.R., and Rivlin, A.M. (2007b). Strategies for slowing the growth of health spending. In A. Rivlin and J. Antos, eds., *Restoring Fiscal Sanity 2007: The Health Spending Challenge.* Washington, DC: Brookings Institution Press.

Apfel, K., and Flowers, B., eds. (2007). *Big Choices: The Future of Social Security.* Austin: University of Texas.

Association of State Dam Safety Officials. (2002). *The Cost of Rehabilitating Our Nation's Dams.* Lexington, KY: Association of State Dam Safety Officials.

Auerbach, A.J. (1994). The U.S. fiscal problem: Where we are, how we got here, and where we're going. In S. Fischer and J. Rotemberg, eds, *NBER Macroeconomics Annual,* pp. 141-175. Cambridge, MA: National Bureau of Economic Research.

Auerbach, A.J. (1996). Tax reform, capital allocation, efficiency, and growth. In H.J. Aaron and W.G. Gale, eds., *Economic Effects of Fundamental Tax Reform.* Washington, DC: Brookings Institution.

Auerbach, A.J., and Gale, W.G. (2009). *The Economic Crisis and the Fiscal Crisis, 2009 and Beyond.* Available: http://www.taxpolicycenter.org/UploadedPDF/411843/_economic_ crisis.pdf [December 2009].

Auerbach, A.J., Gokhale, J., and Kotlikoff, L.J. (1991). *Generational Accounts—A Meaningful Alternative to Deficit Accounting.* NBER Working Paper 3589. Cambridge, MA: National Bureau of Economic Research.

Baltagi, B.H., and Goel, R.K. (1990). Quasi-experimental price elasticity of demand in the United States: 1960-1983. *American Journal of Agricultural Economics, 72*(2), 451-454.

Baltagi, B.H., and Griffin, J.M. (1995). A dynamic demand model for liquor: The case for pooling. *The Review of Economics and Statistics, 77*(3), 545-554.

Barry, C., Cullen, M.R., Galusha, D., Slade, M.D., and Busch, S.H. (2008). Who chooses a consumer-directed health plan? *Health Affairs, 27*(6), 1,671-1,679.

Berenson, R.A. (2005). Which way for competition? None of the above. *Health Affairs, 24*(6), 1,536-1,542.

Bergsten, C.F., ed. (2009a). *The Long-Term International Economic Position of the United States.* Special Report 20. Washington, DC: Peterson Institute for International Economics.

Bergsten, C.F. (2009b). The dollar and the deficits, how Washington can prevent the next crisis. *Foreign Affairs, 88*(6), 20-38.

Biggs, A.G. (2008). Entitlements: Not just a health care problem. *Health Policy Outlook* (7). Washington, DC: American Enterprise Institute. Available: http://www.aei.org/docLib/ 20080923_0723380HPOBiggs_g.pdf [December 2009].

Biggs, A.G., and Springstead, G.R. (2007). Alternate measures of replacement rates for Social Security benefits and retirement income. *Social Security Bulletin, 68*(2), 1-19.

Blank, R. (2007). Improving the safety net for single mothers who face serious barriers to work. *The Future of Children, 17*(2), 183-197.

Bloom, D.E., Canning, D., and Sevilla, J. (2001). *The Effect of Health on Economic Growth: Theory and Evidence.* NBER Working Paper 8587. Cambridge, MA: National Bureau of Economic Research.

Blum, W.J., and Kalven, H. (1953). *The Uneasy Case for Progressive Taxation.* Chicago: University of Chicago Press.

Boards of Trustees. (2009). *2009 Annual Report of the Boards of Trustees of the Federal Hospital Insurance and Federal Supplementary Medical Insurance Trust Funds.* Washington, DC: U.S. Government Printing Office.

Bohn, H. (1995). The sustainability of budget deficits in a stochastic economy. *Journal of Money, Credit, and Banking, 27*(1), 257-271.

Boots, S.W., Macomber, J., and Danziger, A. (2008). *Family Security: Supporting Parents' Employment and Children's Development.* New Safety Net Paper 3. Washington, DC: Urban Institute.

Bott, D.M., Kapp, M.C., Johnson, L.B., and Magno, L.M. (2009). Disease management for chronically ill beneficiaries in traditional Medicare. *Health Affairs, 28*(1), 86-98.

Bowman, K. (2008). *Attitudes Toward the Federal Government*. Washington, DC: American Enterprise Institute.

Bowman, K. (2009). What do Americans think about taxes? *Tax Notes*, April 6. Available: http://www.taxanalysts.com/www/website.nsf/Web/FederalTaxNews?OpenDocument [December 2009].

Brender, A., and Drazen, A. (2008). How do budget deficits and economic growth affect reelection prospects? Evidence from a large panel of countries. *American Economic Review*, 98(5), 2,203-2,220.

Brookings-Heritage Fiscal Seminar. (2008). *Taking Back Our Fiscal Future*. Washington, DC: Brookings Institution and Heritage Foundation.

Brown, J.R., and Apfel, K.S. (2006). Point/counterpoint: Would private accounts improve social security? *Journal of Policy Analysis and Management*, Summer, 679-690.

Brownstein, R. (2009). Financial risk cuts deeper, poll finds. *National Journal*, April 25, 1.

Buiter, W.H. (2006). *The "Sense and Nonsense of Maastricht" Revisited: What Have We Learnt About Stabilization in the EMU?* Paper based on a public lecture given in the Seminal Contributions to the Political Economy of European Integration Seminar Series, School of Economics. January 5. Available: http://www.nber.org/~wbuiter/sense.pdf [December 2009].

Burman, L.E. (2006). *Taking a Checkup on the Nation's Health Care Tax Policy: A Prognosis*. Statement before the U.S. Senate Committee on Finance. Available: http://www.taxpolicycenter.org/UploadedPDF/900934_burman_030806.pdf [December 2009].

Burman, L.E. (2008). *A Blueprint for Tax Reform and Health Reform*. Statement before the U.S. Senate Committee on Finance. Available: http://tpcprod.urban.org/UploadedPDF/901167_Burman_reform.pdf [December 2009].

Burman, L.E., Toder, E., and Geissler, C. (2008a). How big are total individual income tax expenditures, and who benefits from them? *American Economic Review*, 98(2), 79-83.

Burman, L.E., Leiserson, G., and Rohaly, J. (2008b). Revenue and distributional effects of the individual income and estate tax provisions of Senator Thompson's plan for tax relief and economic growth. *Tax Notes*, 196-208.

Burman, L.E., Lim, K., and Rohaly, J. (2008c). *Back from the Grave: Revenue and Distributional Effects of Reforming the Federal Estate Tax*. Washington, DC: Urban Insitute-Brookings Institution Tax Policy Center. Available: http://www.taxpolicycenter.org/publications/url.cfm?ID=411777 [July 2009].

Butler, S.M. (1998). Medicare price controls: The wrong prescription. *Health Affairs*, 17(1), 72-74.

Cage, R., Greenlees, J., amd Jackman, P. (2003). *Introducing the Chained Consumer Price Index*. Paper presented at the Seventh Meeting of the International Working Group on Price Indices, Paris, France, May. Available: http://www.bls.gov/cpi/super_paris.pdf [December 2009].

Cannon, M.F. (2006). Pay-for-performance: Is Medicare a good candidate? *Yale Journal of Health Policy, Law, and Ethics*, 7(1), 1-38.

Cannon, M.F. (2009a). *Fannie Med? Why a "Public Option" Is Hazardous to Your Health*. Washington, DC: Cato Institute.

Cannon, M.F. (2009b). *Yes, Mr. President: A Free Market Can Fix Health Care*. Washington, DC: The Cato Institute.

Carpenter, C. (2007). *How Do Workplace Smoking Laws Work?: Quasi-Experimental Evidence from Local Laws in Ontario, Canada*. NBER Working Paper No. 13133. Cambridge, MA: National Bureau of Economic Research.

Carpenter, C., and Cook, P.J. (2008). Cigarette taxes and youth smoking: New evidence from national, state, and local youth risk behavior surveys. *Journal of Health Economics*, 27(2), 287-299.

Carroll, R., Holtz-Eakin, D., and Rosen, H.S. (1998). *Entrepreneurs, Income Taxes, and*

Investment. NBER Working Paper No. W6374. Cambridge, MA: National Bureau of Economic Research.

Carroll, R., Holtz-Eakin, D., Rider, M., and Rosen, H.S. (2000a). *Income Taxes and Entrepreneurs' Use of Labor.* NBER Working Paper No. 6578. Cambridge, MA: National Bureau of Economic Research.

Carroll, R., Holtz-Eakin, D., Rider, M., and Rosen, H.S. (2000b). *Personal Income Taxes and the Growth of Small Firms.* NBER Working Paper No. 7980. Cambridge, MA: National Bureau of Economic Research.

Cawley, J. (2007). The cost effectiveness of programs to prevent or reduce obesity. *Archives of Pediatric and Adolescent Medicine, 161,* 611-614.

CCH Canadian Limited. (2009). *Standard Federal Tax Reporter.* Alphen aan den Rijn, The Netherlands: Wolters Kluwer.

Cebul, R., Rebitzer, J., Taylor, L., and Vortuba, M. (2008). *Organizational Fragmentation and Care Quality in the U.S. Health Care System.* NBER Working Paper No. 14212. Cambridge, MA: National Bureau of Economic Research.

Census Bureau. (2002). *Demographic Trends in the 20th Century.* Washington, DC: U.S. Census Bureau.

Census Bureau. (2007). *International Data Base.* Available: http://www.census.gov/ipc/www/idb/ [December 2009].

Census Bureau. (2009). *2009 Statistical Abstract.* Washington, DC: U.S. Census Bureau.

Centers for Medicare and Medicaid Services. (2009a). *National Health Expenditures by Type of Service and Source of Funds, CY 1960-2007.* Available: http://www.cms.hhs.gov/NationalHealthExpendData/02_NationalHealthAccountsHistorical.asp#TopOfPage [December 2009].

Centers for Medicare and Medicaid Services. (2009b). *National Health Expenditure Projections 2008-2018.* Available: http://www.cms.hhs.gov/NationalHealthExpendData/downloads/proj2008.pdf [December 2009].

Centers for Medicare and Medicaid Services. (2009c). *NHE Web Tables.* Available: http://www.cms.hhs.gov/NationalHealthExpendData/downloads/tables.pdf [December 2009].

Chen, D., and Mintz, J. (2008). *Still a Wallflower: The 2008 Report on Canada's International Tax Competitiveness.* Toronto, Canada: C.D. Howe Institute. Available: www.cdhowe.org/pdf/ebrief_63.pdf [November 2009].

Clemans-Cope, L., Zuckerman, S., and Williams, R. (2009). *Changes to the Tax Exclusion of Employer-Sponsored Health Insurance Premiums: A Potential Source of Financing for Health Reform.* Washington, DC: Urban Institute.

Cline, W.R. (2009). Long-term fiscal imbalances, U.S. external liabilities, and future living standards. Chapter 2 in C.F. Bergsten, ed., *The Long-Term International Economic Position of the United States.* Washington, DC: Peterson Institute for International Economics.

Cogan, J., and Mitchell, O. (2003). Perspectives from on the President's Commission on Social Security reform. *Journal of Economic Perspectives, 17*(2), 149-172.

Cohen, J.T., Neumann, P.J., and Weinstein, M.C. (2008). Does preventive care save money?: Health economics and the presidential candidates. *The New England Journal of Medicine, 358*(7), 661-663.

Committee for a Responsible Federal Budget. (2009). *Comparing Health Care Plans: A Guide to Health Care Reform Proposals in the 111th Congress.* Washington, DC: Committee for a Responsible Federal Budget. Available: http://crfb.org/document/comparing-health-care-plans-guide-reform-proposals [December 2009].

Committee for Economic Development. (2007). *Quality, Affordable Health Care for All: Moving Beyond the Employer-Based Health-Insurance System.* Washington, DC: Committee for Economic Development.

Committee on Ways and Means, U.S. House of Representatives. (2004). *Green Book: Back-*

ground Material and Data on Programs Within the Jurisdiction of the Committee on Ways and Means. Washington, DC: U.S. Government Printing Office.

Committee on Ways and Means, U.S. House of Representatives. (2009). *America's Affordable Health Choices Act of 2009 (HR 3200).* House Report 111-299, Part 2, October 14. Washington, DC: U.S. Government Printing Office.

Committee on Ways and Means, Committee on Energy and Commerce, and Committee on Education and Labor, U.S. House of Representatives. (2009). *Affordable Health Care for America Act: Public Health Insurance Option.* Available: http://energycommerce.house. gov/Press_111/health_care/hr3962_PUBLIC_OPTION.pdf [December 2009].

Commonwealth of Australia. (2007). *Intergenerational Report 2007.* Canberra: Australian Government, The Treasury. Available: http://www.treasury.gov.au/igr/IGR2007.asp [December 2009].

Congressional Budget Office. (1994). *The Economic and Budget Outlook: Fiscal Years 1995-2004.* Washington, DC: U.S. Government Printing Office.

Congressional Budget Office. (1995). *Who Pays and When?: An Assessment of Generational Accounting.* Washington, DC: U.S. Government Printing Office.

Congressional Budget Office. (1996). *The Economic and Budget Outlook: Fiscal Years 1997-2006.* Washington, DC: U.S. Government Printing Office.

Congressional Budget Office. (1997). *The Economic Effects of Comprehensive Tax Reform.* Washington, DC: U.S. Government Printing Office.

Congressional Budget Office. (2000). *The Long-Term Budget Outlook.* Washington, DC: U.S. Government Printing Office.

Congressional Budget Office. (2001). *Social Security: A Primer.* Washington, DC: U.S. Government Printing Office.

Congressional Budget Office. (2005a). *The Long-Term Budget Outlook.* Washington, DC: U.S. Government Printing Office.

Congressional Budget Office. (2005b). *Long-Term Economic Effects of Chronically Large Federal Deficits.* Washington, DC: U.S. Government Printing Office.

Congressional Budget Office. (2006a). *Is Social Security Progressive?* Washington, DC: U.S. Government Printing Office.

Congressional Budget Office. (2006b). *Medical Malpractice Tort Limits and Health Care Spending.* Washington, DC: U.S. Government Printing Office.

Congressional Budget Office. (2007a). *Historical Effective Federal Tax Rates: 1979 to 2005.* Washington, DC: U.S. Government Printing Office.

Congressional Budget Office. (2007b). *The Long-Term Budget Outlook.* Washington, DC.

Congressional Budget Office. (2007c). *The Long-Term Outlook for Health Care Spending.* Washington, DC: U.S. Government Printing Office.

Congressional Budget Office. (2007d). *Medicare Advantage: Private Health Plans in Medicare.* Washington, DC: U.S. Government Printing Office.

Congressional Budget Office. (2008a). *Accounting for Sources of Projected Growth in Federal Spending on Medicare and Medicaid.* Washington, DC: U.S. Government Printing Office.

Congressional Budget Office. (2008b). *Budget Options, Volume 1: Health Care.* Washington, DC: U.S. Government Printing Office.

Congressional Budget Office. (2008c). *Evidence on the Costs and Benefits of Health Information Technology.* Washington, DC: U.S. Government Printing Office.

Congressional Budget Office. (2008d). *Geographic Variation in Health Care Spending.* Washington, DC: U.S. Government Printing Office.

Congressional Budget Office. (2008e). *Issues and Options in Infrastructure Investment.* Washington, DC: U.S. Government Printing Office.

Congressional Budget Office. (2008f). *Key Issues in Analyzing Major Health Insurance Proposals.* Washington, DC: U.S. Government Printing Office.

Congressional Budget Office. (2008g). *The Long-Term Economic Effects of Some Alternative Budget Policies.* Washington, DC: U.S. Government Printing Office.

Congressional Budget Office. (2008h). *Technological Change and the Growth of Health Care Spending.* Washington, DC: U.S. Government Printing Office.

Congressional Budget Office. (2009a). *The Budget and Economic Outlook: An Update.* Washington, DC: U.S. Government Printing Office.

Congressional Budget Office. (2009b). *Budget Options, Volume 2.* Washington, DC: U.S. Government Printing Office.

Congressional Budget Office. (2009c). *CBO's Long-Term Projections for Social Security: 2009 Update.* Washington, DC: U.S. Government Printing Office.

Congressional Budget Office. (2009d). *H.R. 3962, Affordable Health Care for America Act: Cost Estimate for the Bill as Introduced on October 29, 2009 and Incorporating the Manager's Amendment from November 3, 2009 (updated to reflect enactment of H.R. 3548).* Available: http://www.cbo.gov/doc.cfm?index=10710 [December 2009].

Congressional Budget Office. (2009e). *The Long-Term Budget Outlook.* Washington, DC: U.S. Government Printing Office.

Congressional Budget Office. (2009f). *Preliminary Analysis of the Affordable Health Care for Americans Act: Letter to the Honorable Charles B. Rangel.* Available: http://www.cbo.gov/doc.cfm?index=10688 [December 2009].

Congressional Budget Office. (2009g). *A Preliminary Analysis of the President's Budget and an Update of CBO's Budget and Economic Outlook.* Washington, DC: U.S. Government Printing Office.

Congressional Budget Office. (2009h). *Spending and Enrollment Detail for CBO's March 2009 Baseline: Medicaid.* Washington, DC: U.S. Government Printing Office.

Congressional Budget Office. (2009i). *Correction Regarding the Longer-Term Effects of the Manager's Amendment to the Patient Protection and Affordable Care Act: Letter to the Honorable Harry Reid.* Available: http://www.cbo.gov/doc.cfm?index=10870 [December 2009].

Congressional Budget Office. (2009j). Patient Protection and Affordable Care Act, Incorporating the Manager's Amendment: Cost Estimate for the Amendment in the Nature of a Substitute to H.R. 3590, Incorporating the Effects of Changes Proposed in the Manager's Amendment Released on December 19, 2009. Available: http://www.cbo.gov/doc.cfm?index=10868 [December 2009].

Conley, D. (2009). *Savings, Responsibility and Opportunity in America.* Washington, DC: New America Foundation.

Cook, P.J., and Tauchen, G. (1982). The effect of liquor taxes on heavy drinking. *The Bell Journal of Economics,* 13(2), 379-390.

Coulam, R., Feldman, R., and Dowd, B.E. (2009). *Competitive Pricing for All Medicare Health Plans.* Washington, DC: American Enterprise Institute.

Council of Economic Advisors. (2007). *Immigration's Economic Impact.* Washington, DC: U.S. Government Printing Office.

Council of Economic Advisors. (2009). *Economic Report of the President.* Washington, DC: U.S. Government Printing Office.

Cox, K., Ruffing, K., Horney, J., and Van de Water, P. (2009). *CBPP'S Updated Long-Term Fiscal Deficit and Debt Projections.* Washington, DC: Center for Budget and Policy Priorities.

Cromwell, J., Dayhoff, D.A., McCall, N.T., Subramanian, S., Freitas, R.C., Hart, R.J., Caswell, C., and Stason, W. (1998). *Medicare Participating Heart Bypass Demonstration: Final Report.* Baltimore, MD: Centers for Medicare and Medicaid Services.

Davidoff, A.J., and Johnson, R.W. (2003). Raising the Medicare eligibility age: Effects on the young elderly. *Health Affairs, 22*(4), 198-209.

DeCicca, P., and McCleod, L. (2008). Cigarette taxes and older adult smoking: Evidence from recent large tax increases. *Journal of Health Economics, 27*(4), 918-929.

DeCicca, P., Kenkel, D., and Mathios, A. (2008). Cigarette taxes and the transition from youth to adult smoking: Smoking initiation, cessation, and participation. *Journal of Health Economics, 27*(4), 904-917.

Dhaval, D., and Saffer, H. (2007). *Risk Tolerance and Alcohol Demand Among Adults and Older Adults.* NBER Working Paper No. W13482. Cambridge, MA: National Bureau of Economic Research.

Diamond, P., and Orszag, P. (2005). Saving Social Security: The Diamond-Orszag plan. Berkeley, CA. *The Economists' Voice, 2*(1), article 8.

Economos, C.D., and Irish-Hauser, S. (2007). Community interventions: A brief overview and their application to the obesity intervention. *Journal of Law, Medicine, and Ethics, 35,* 131-137.

Eddy, D.M. (1997). Balancing cost and quality in fee-for-service versus managed care. *Health Affairs, 6*(3), 162-173.

Edwards, C. (2003). Replacing the scandal-plagued corporate income tax with a cash-flow tax. *Policy Analysis, 484,* 1-43.

Edwards, C., and Mitchell, D.J. (2008). *Global Tax Revolution: The Rise of Tax Competition and the Battle to Defend It.* Washington, DC: Cato Institute.

Elmendorf, D. (2009). *The Effects of Health Legislation Beyond the Next Decade.* Congressional Budget Office Director's Blog, June 24. Available: http://cboblog.cbo.gov/?m=200907 [December 2009].

Engen, E.M., and Hubbard, R.G. (2004). *Federal Government Debt and Interest Rates.* NBER Working Paper No. 10681. Cambridge, MA: National Bureau of Economic Research.

European Commission. (2009). *VAT Rates Applied in the Member States of the European Community.* Brussels, Belgium: European Commission.

Evans, W.N., Farrelly, M.C., and Montgomery, E. (1999). Do workplace smoking bans reduce smoking? *American Economic Review, 89*(4), 728-747.

Fabrizio, S., and Mody, A. (2006). Can budget institutions counteract political indiscipline? *Economic Policy, 21*(48), 689-739.

Feldstein, M.A. (1995). The effect of marginal tax rates on taxable income: A panel study of the 1986 Tax Reform Act. *Journal of Political Economy, 103*(3), 551-572.

Feldstein, M.A. (2006). The effect of taxes on efficiency and growth. *Tax Notes,* 679-682.

Finkelstein, A. (2007). The aggregate effects of health insurance: Evidence from the introduction of Medicare. *Quarterly Journal of Economics, 122*(1), 1-37.

Fisher, E.S., Berwick, D.M., and Davis, K. (2009a). Achieving health care reform—How physicians can help. *The New England Journal of Medicine, 360*(24), 2,495-2,497.

Fisher, E.S., Bynum, J.P., and Skinner, J.S. (2009b). Slowing the growth of health care costs—Lessons from regional variation. *The New England Journal of Medicine, 360*(9), 849-852.

Fisher, E.S., McClellan, M.B., Bertko, J., Lieberman, S.M., Lee, J.J., Lewis, J.L., and Skinner, J.S. (2009c). Fostering accountable health care: Moving forward in Medicare. *Health Affairs,* w219-w231. Available: http://content.healthaffairs.org/cgi/reprint/hlthaff.28.2.w219v1 [December 2009].

Foster, J.D. (2008). *Tax Hikes, Economic Clouds, and Silver Linings: A Review of Deficits and the Economy.* Backgrounder No. 2095. Washington, DC: The Heritage Foundation.

Frank, R. (2005). *Macroeconomics and Behavior.* 6th ed. New York: McGraw-Hill.

Friedman, B. (1988). *Day of Reckoning: The Consequences of American Economic Policy Under Reagan and After.* New York: Random House.

Furman, J. (2005a). *An Analysis of Using "Progressive Price Indexing" to Set Social Security Benefits.* Washington, DC: Center on Budget and Policy Priorities.

Furman, J. (2005b). *Evaluating Alternative Social Security Reform Proposals.* Testimony of May 12, 2005, before the House Committee on Ways and Means. Serial No. 109-22. Washington, DC: U.S. Government Printing Office. Available: http://frwebgate.access. gpo.gov/cgi-bin/getdoc.cgi?dbname=109_house_hearings&docid=f:24732.pdf [December 2009].

Gentry, W.M., and Hubbard, R.G. (2004). *Success Taxes, Entrepreneurial Entry, and Innovation.* NBER Working Paper No. 10551. Cambridge, MA: National Bureau of Economic Research.

Ginsburg, P.B., and Grossman, J.M. (2005). When the price isn't right: How inadvertent payments drive medical care. *Health Affairs*, w5-376-384. Available: http://content. healthaffairs.org/cgi/reprint/hlthaff.w5.376v1 [December 2009].

Goetzel, R.Z., Baker, K.M., Short, M.E., Pei, X., Ozminkowski, R.J., Wang, S., Bowen, J.D., Roemer, E.C., Craun, B.A., Tully, K.J., Baase, C.M., DeJoy, D.M., and Wilson, M.G. (2009). First-year results of an obesity prevention program at the Dow Chemical Company. *Journal of Occupational and Environmental Medicine*, 51(2), 125-138.

Gokhale, J., and Smetters, K. (2003). *Fiscal and Generational Imbalances: New Budget Measures for New Budget Priorities.* Monograph. Washington, DC: American Enterprise Institute.

Gold, M.R., Sofaer, S.T., and Siegelbert, T. (2007). Medicare and cost-effectiveness analysis: Time to ask the taxpayers. *Health Affairs*, 26(5), 1,399-1,406.

Goldin, C., and Katz, L.F. (2008). *The Race Between Education and Technology.* Cambridge, MA: Harvard University Press.

Goldman, D.P., Zheng Y., Girosi, F., Michaud, P., Olshansky, S.J., Cutler, D., and Rowe, J.W. (2009). The benefits of risk factor prevention in american aged 51 years and older. *American Journal of Public Health*, 9(11), 1-6.

Goodman, J.C. (2005). *Health Care in a Free Society: Rebutting the Myths of National Health Insurance.* Washington, DC: Cato Institute.

Gordon, R. (2006). The Boskin Commission report: A retrospective one decade later. *International Productivity Monitor*, 12, 7-22.

Gortmaker, S.L., Peterson, K., Wiecha, J., Sobol, A.M., Dixit, S., Fox, M.K., and Laird, N. (1999). Reducing obesity via a school-based interdisciplinary intervention among youth: Planet health. *Archives of Pediatric and Adolescent Medicine*, 153(4), 409-418.

Gottlieb, S. (2009). *Promoting and Using Comparative Research: What Are the Promises and Pitfalls of a New Federal Effort?* Washington, DC: American Enterprise Institute.

Government Accountability Office. (1994). *Deficit Reduction: Experience of Other Nations.* GAO/AIMD-95-30. Washington, DC: U.S. Government Accountability Office.

Government Accountability Office. (2003). *Fiscal Exposures: Improving the Budgetary Focus on Long-Term Costs and Uncertainties.* GAO-03-213. Washington, DC: U.S. Government Accountability Office.

Government Accountability Office. (2005). *Government Performance and Accountability: Tax Expenditures Represent a Substantial Federal Commitment and Need to Be Reexamined.* Washington, DC: U.S. Government Accountability Office.

Government Accountability Office. (2007a). *State and Local Governments: Persistent Fiscal Challenges Will Likely Emerge Within the Next Decade.* GAO-07-1080SP. Washington, DC: U.S. Government Accountability Office.

Government Accountability Office. (2007b). *Long-Term Fiscal Challenge: Comments on the Bipartisan Task Force for Responsible Fiscal Action Act.* GAO-08-238T. Washington, DC: U.S. Government Accountability Office.

Government Accountability Office. (2009). *The Nation's Long-Term Fiscal Outlook: March 2009 Update*. Washington, DC: U.S. Government Accountability Office.

Gravelle, J. (2004). *Historical Effective Marginal Tax Rates on Capital Income*. Congressional Research Service Report for Congress. Washington, DC: U.S. Government Printing Office.

Hacker, J. (2006). *The Great Risk Shift*. New York: Oxford University Press.

Hacker, J. (2009). *Healthy Competition: How to Structure Public Health Insurance Plan Choice to Ensure Risk-Sharing, Cost Control, and Quality Improvement*. Institute for America's Future and the Center on Health, Economic and Family Security, University of California at Berkeley. Available: http://www.ourfuture.org/healthcare/hacker [December 2009].

Hadley, J., and Holahan, J. (2003). Is health care spending higher under Medicaid or private insurance? *Inquiry, 40*(3), 323-342.

Haines, D.J., Davis, L., Rancour, P., Robinson, M., Neel-Wilson, T., and Wagner, S. (2007). A pilot intervention to promote walking and wellness and to improve the health of college faculty and staff. *Journal of American College Health, 55*(4), 219-225.

Hall, R.E., and Jones, C.I. (2007). The value of life and the rise in health spending. *Quarterly Journal of Economics, 122*(1), 39-72.

Hayes, K.J., Pettengill, J., and Stensland, J. (2007). Getting the price right: Medicare payment rates for cardiovascular services. *Health Affairs, 26*(1), 124-136.

Heclo, H. (1998). *Political Risk and Social Security Reform*. Social Security Brief No. 1. Washington, DC: National Academy of Social Insurance.

Hillestad, R., Bigelow, J., Bower, A., Girosi, F., Meili, R., Scoville, R., and Taylor, R. (2005). Can electronic medical record systems transform healthcare? Potential health benefits, savings, and costs. *Health Affairs, 24*(5), 1,103-1,117.

Hines, J. (2006). *Do Tax Havens Flourish?* NBER Working Paper No. 10936. Cambridge, MA: National Bureau of Economic Research.

Holubowich, E.J., and Antos, J.R. (2008). Treading water: The no growth investment in health services research. *American Health & Drug Benefits, 6*, 34-42.

Holzer, H., and Martinson, K. (2008). *Helping Poor Working Parents Get Ahead: Federal Funds for New State Strategies in Systems*. Washington, DC: Urban Institute.

Hubbard, G. (1998). *The Impact on Individuals and Families of Replacing the Federal Income Tax*. Testimony before the House Committee on Ways and Means, April 15, 1997. Washington, DC: U.S. Government Printing Office. Available: http://www.docstoc.com/docs/19452859/Headline-THE-IMPACT-ON-INDIVIDUALS-AND-FAMILIES-OF-REPLACING-THE-FEDERAL-INCOME-TAX----House-Congressional-Hearing-105 [December 2009].

Hurd, M.D., and Rohwedder, S. (2008). *The Retirement Consumption Puzzle: Actual Spending Change in Panel Data*. NBER Working Paper No. 13929. Cambridge, MA: National Bureau of Economic Research.

Institute of Medicine. (2000). *To Err Is Human: Building a Safer Health System*. L.T. Kohn, J.M. Corrigan, and M.S. Donaldson, eds. Washington, DC: National Academy Press.

Internal Revenue Service. (2008). *National Taxpayer Advocate 2008 Annual Report to Congress, Volume 1*. Washington, DC: Internal Revenue Service. Available: http://ftp.irs.gov/pub/irs-utl/08_tas_arc_intro_toc_msp.pdf [December 2009].

Internal Revenue Service. (2009). *Statistics of Income*. Washington, DC: U.S. Department of the Treasury. Available: http://www.irs.gov/pub/irs-soi/06in02ar.xls [November 2009].

International Monetary Fund. (2007a). *Balance of Payments Statistics Yearbook*. Washington, DC: International Monetary Fund.

International Monetary Fund. (2007b). *World Economic Outlook Database*. Available: http://www.imf.org/external/pubs/ft/weo/2007/02/weodata/index.aspx [December 2009].

International Monetary Fund. (2009a). *Fiscal Implications of the Global Economic and Financial Crisis.* IMF Staff Position Note, SPN/09/13. Washington, DC: International Monetary Fund.

International Monetary Fund. (2009b). The state of public finances cross-country. *Fiscal Monitor,* November 3, SPN/09/25.

International Monetary Fund. (2009c). Transcript of a Conference Call with IMF Senior staffs on the Launch of *The State of Public Finances: A Cross-Country Fiscal Monitor,* July 30. Available: http://www.imf.org/external/np/tr/2009/tr073009a.htm [December 2009].

Isaacs, J. (2007). *Cost-Effective Investments in Children.* Washington, DC: Brookings Institution.

Johnson, D.S., Reed, S.B., and Stewart, K.J. (2006). Price measurement in the United States: A decade after the Boskin report. *Monthly Labor Review,* 129(5), 10-19.

Joint Committee on Taxation. (1997). *Tax Modeling Project and 1997 Symposium Papers.* Washington, DC: U.S. Government Printing Office.

Joint Committee on Taxation. (2005). *Macroeconomic Analysis of Various Proposals to Provide $500 Billion in Tax Relief.* JCX-4-05. Washington, DC: U.S. Government Printing Office.

Joint Committee on Taxation. (2008a). *Estimates of Federal Tax Expenditures for Fiscal Years 2008-2012.* Washington, DC: U.S. Government Printing Office

Joint Committee on Taxation. (2008b). *Tax Expenditures for Health Care.* Hearing before the Senate Committee on Finance. Available: http://finance.senate.gov/hearings/testimony/2008test/073108ektest.pdf [December 2009].

Joint Committee on Taxation. (2009). *Background Materials for the Senate Committee on Finance Roundtable on Health Care Financing.* Washington, DC: U.S. Government Printing Office.

Jones, D., Reed, S., and Stewart, K. (2006). Price measurement in the United States: A decade after the Boskin report. *Monthly Labor Review,* 129(5), 10-19.

Jorgenson, D.W., and Yun, K.-Y. (2002). *Investment, Volume 3: Lifting the Burden: Tax Reform, The Cost of Capital, and U.S. Economic Growth.* Cambridge, MA: MIT Press.

Joyce, P.G. (2008). Does more (or even better) information lead to better budgeting? A new perspective. *Journal of Policy Analysis and Management,* 27(4), 945-975.

Kahneman, D. (2002). *Maps of Bounded Rationality: A Perspective on Intuitive Judgment and Choice.* Princeton, NJ: Princeton University Press.

Kaiser Family Foundation and Health Research and Educational Trust. (2008). *Employer Health Benefits 2008 Annual Survey.* Available: http://ehbs.kss.org/images/abstract/7991.pdf [December 2009].

Kessler, D., and McClellan, M. (1996). Do doctors practice defensive medicine? *The Quarterly Journal of Economics,* 3(2), 353-390.

Kobes, D., and Rohaly, J. (2002). *Dynamic Scoring and Budget Estimations.* Washington, DC: Urban Institute. Available: http://www.urban.org/url.cfm?ID=310316 [December 2009].

Kotlikoff, L. (1993). *The Economic Impact of Replacing Federal Income Taxes with a Sales Tax. Policy Analysis.* Washington, DC: Cato Institute.

Kotlikoff, L. (2006). Is the United States bankrupt? *Federal Reserve Bank of St. Louis Review,* 88(4), 235-249.

Krugman, P. (2005). One nation, uninsured. *The New York Times.* Available: http://www.nytimes.com/2005/06/13/opinion/13krugman.html [December 2009].

Krugman, P., and Wells, R. (2005). The health care crisis and what to do about it. *The New York Review of Books,* 53(5). Available: http://www.nybooks.com/articles/18802 [December 2009].

Ku, L., and Broaddus, M. (2008). Public and private health insurance: Stacking up the costs. *Health Affairs*, 24(4), w318-w327. Available: http://content.healthaffairs.org/cgi/reprint/27/4/w318 [December 2009].

Lavery, J. (2009). *Social Security Finances: Findings of the 2009 Trustees Report*. Washington, DC: National Academy of Social Insurance.

Lewis-Beck, M.S., and Stegmaier, M. (2008). Economic voting in transitional democracies. *Journal of Elections, Public Opinion and Parties*, 18(3), 303-323.

Light, P. (1995). *Still Artful Work: The Continuing Politics of Social Security Reform*. Columbus, OH: McGraw-Hill.

Lindert, P. (2003). *Why the Welfare State Looks Like a Free Lunch*. NBER Working Paper No. 9869. Cambridge, MA: National Bureau of Economic Research.

Longman, P. (2007). *Best Care Anywhere: Why VA Health Care Is Better Than Yours*. Sausalito, CA: PoliPoint Press.

Lusardi, A., and Mitchell, O.S. (2007). Baby boomer retirement security: The roles of planning, financial literacy, and housing wealth. *Journal of Monetary Economics*, 54(1), 205-224.

Madrick, J. (2009). *The Case for Big Government*. Princeton, NJ: Princeton University Press.

Marmor, T. (2001). How not to think about Medicare reform. *Journal of Health Politics, Policy and Law*, 26(1), 107-117.

Mataloni, R. (2007). Operations of U.S. multinational companies in 2005. *Survey of Current Business*, 42-64.

Mathews, A. (2005). Reading fine print, insurers question studies of drugs. *Wall Street Journal*, August 24.

Mattke, S., Seid, M., and Sai, M. (2007). Evidence for the effect of disease management: Is $1 billion a year a good investment? *American Journal of Managed Care*, 13(12), 670-676.

McCall, N., Cromwell, J., Urato, C., and Rabiner, D. (2007). *Report to Congress: Evaluation of Phase I of Medicare Health Support (formerly Voluntary Chronic Care Improvement) Pilot Program Under Traditional Fee-for-Service Medicare*. Available: http://www.cms.hhs.gov/reports/downloads/McCall.pdf [December 2009].

McCully, C.P., Moyer, B., and Kenneth, S. (2007). A reconciliation between the consumer price index and the personal consumption expenditures price index. *Monthly Labor Review*. Available: http://www.bea.gov/papers/pdf/cpi_pce.pdf [December 2009].

McDevitt, R., Gable, J., Pickreign, J., Whitmore, H., and Brust, T. (2010). Group insurance: A better deal for most people than individual plans. *Health Affairs*, 29(1). Available: http://content.healthaffairs.org/cgi/reprint/hlthaff.2009.0060v1 [December 2009]

McGlynn, E.A., Asch, S.M., Adams, J., Keesey, J., Hicks, J., DeCrisofaro, A., and Kerr, E.A. (2003). The quality of health care delivered to adults in the United States. *The New England Journal of Medicine*, 348(26), 2,635-2,645.

Mercer Human Resources Consulting. (2007). *Primary Care Management in North Carolina*. Available: http://www.communitycarenc.com/PDFDocs/Mercer%20SFY05_06.pdf [December 2009].

Meyers, R. (2009). The ball of confusion in federal budgeting: A shadow agenda for deliberative reform of the budget process. *Public Administration Review*, 69(2) (March/April), 211-223.

Miller, R.H., and Luft, H.S. (2002). HMO plan performance update: An analysis of the literature, 1997-2001. *Health Affairs*, 21(4), 63-86.

Miller, T. (2008). *Hitting the Snooze Button on Our Medicare Fiscal Alarm Clocks*. Washington, DC: American Enterprise Institute.

Minarik, J. (2009a). *Health Care: Thinking Through a Public Option*. Washington, DC: Committee for Economic Development. Available: http://www.ced.org/commentary/65-commentary/362-health-care-thinking-through-a-public-option [December 2009].

Minarik, J. (2009b). *USGov Insurance, Inc.: A Bad Buy.* Washington, DC: Committee for Economic Development. Available: http://www.ced.org/commentary/65-commentary/330-usgov-insurance-inc-a-bad-buy [December 2009].

Minarik, J. (2010). *Tax Expenditures in OECD Countries.* Paris, France: Organisation for Economic Co-operation and Development.

Miranda, E., Penner, R.G., and Steuerle, C.E. (2002). *Social Security in Nine European Countries: A Portrait of Reform.* Washington, DC: Urban Institute.

Mitchell, O.S., and Phillips, J.W.R. (2006). Social Security replacement rates for alternative earnings benchmarks. *Benefits Quarterly, Fourth Quarter,* 37-47.

Mitchell, O.S., and Phillips, J.W.R. (2009). Hypothetical versus actual earnings profiles: Implications for Social Security reform. *Journal of Financial Transformation,* 24, 102-104.

Modigliani, A., and Modigliani, F. (1987). The growth of the federal deficit and the role of public attitudes. *Public Opinion Quarterly,* 51(4), 459-480.

Moore, N. (2009). *Entitlements Darken Long-Term Outlook for Federal Budget.* Washington, DC: Heritage Foundation. Available: http://www.heritage.org/research/budget/wm2510.cfm [December 2009].

National Institutes of Health. (2007). *Fact Sheet: Research into What Works Best.* Washington, DC: U.S. Government Printing Office.

National Research Council. (1997). *The New Americans: Economic, Demographic, and Fiscal Effects of Immigration.* Panel on the Demographic and Economic Impacts of Immigration, J.P. Smith and B. Edmonston, eds. Washington, DC: National Academy Press.

National Research Council. (2002). *At What Price?: Conceptualizing and Measuring Cost-of-Living and Price Indexes.* Panel on Conceptual, Measurement, and Other Statistical Issues in Developing Cost-of-Living Indexes, C. Schultze and C. Mackie, eds., Committee on National Statistics. Washington, DC: The National Academies Press.

Nemet, G.F., and Kammen, D.M. (2007). U.S. energy research and development: Declining investment, increasing need, and the feasibility of expansion. *Energy Policy,* 35, 746-755.

Nordhaus, W. (2008). *A Question of Balance, Weighing the Options on Global Warming Policies.* New Haven: Yale University Press.

Nyce, S., and Schieber, S. (2009). *Productivity Rewards and Pay Illusions Caused by Health and Retirement Benefit Cost Increases.* Watson Wyatt Worldwide. Available: http://www.watsonwyatt.com [August 2009].

Oberlander, J. (2003). *The Political Life of Medicare.* Chicago, IL: University of Chicago Press.

Oberlander, J., and White, J. (2009). Public attitudes toward health care spending aren't the problem: Prices are. *Health Affairs,* 28(5), 1,285-1,293.

Olshanksy, S.J., Goldman, D.P., Zheng, Y., and Rowe, J.W. (2009). Aging in America in the twenty-first century: Demographic forecasts from the Macarthur Research Network on an Aging Society. *The Milbank Quarterly,* 87(4), 842-862.

Organisation for Economic Co-operation and Development. (2007). *OECD Budget Practices and Procedures Data Base.* Paris, France: Organisation for Economic Co-operation and Development.

Organisation for Economic Co-operation and Development. (2008a). *Growing Unequal?: Income Distribution and Poverty in OECD Countries.* Paris, France: Organisation for Economic Co-operation and Development.

Organisation for Economic Co-operation and Development. (2008b). *Revenue Statistics 1965-2007.* Paris, France: Organisation for Economic Co-operation and Development.

Organisation for Economic Co-operation and Development. (2008c). *OECD Factbook 2009.* Paris, France: Organisation for Economic Co-operation and Development.

Organisation for Economic Co-operation and Development. (2009). *International Budget*

Practices and Procedures Database. Available: http://www.oecd.org/document/61/0,3343, en_2649_34119_2494461_1_1_1_1,00.html [December 2009].

Patashnik, E.M. (2000). *Putting Trust in the U.S. budget: Federal Trust Funds and the Politics of Commitment.* Cambridge, England: Cambridge University Press.

Paulus, R.A., Davis, K., and Steele, G.D. (2008). Continuous innovations in health care: Implications of the Geisinger experience. *Health Affairs, 27*(5), 1,235-1,245.

Pearson, S., and Littlejohns, P. (2007). Reallocating resources: How should the National Institute for Health and Clinical Excellence guide disinvestment efforts in the national health service? *Journal of Health Services Research & Policy, 12*(3), 160-165.

Penner, R. (2004). *Searching for a Just Tax System.* Washington, DC: Urban Institute.

Penner, R. (2007). *International Perspectives on Social Security Reform.* Washington, DC: Urban Institute.

Penner, R.G., and Steuerle, C.E. (2007). *Stabilizing Future Fiscal Policy: It's Time to Pull the Trigger.* Washington, DC: The Urban Institute.

Peterson, P. (2004). *Running on Empty, How the Democratic and Republican Parties Are Bankrupting Our Future and What Americans Can Do About It.* New York: Farrar, Straus, and Giroux.

Peterson-Pew Commission on Budget Reform. (2009). *Red Ink Rising: A Call to Action to Stem the Mounting Federal Debt.* Washington, DC: Peterson-Pew Commission on Budget Reform.

Phelps, E. (1961). The golden rule of capital accumulation. *American Economic Review, 51,* 638–643.

Piketty, T., and Saez, E. (2004). *Income inequality in the United States, 1913-2002.* Unpublished paper. Available: http://elsa.berkeley.edu/~saez/piketty-saezOUP04US.pdf [November 2009].

Proper, K.I., Hildebrandt, V.H., Van der Beek, A.J., Twisk, J.W., and Van Mechelen, W. (2003). Effect of individual counseling on physical activity, fitness, and health: A randomized controlled trial in a workplace setting. *American Journal of Preventive Medicine, 24*(3), 218-226.

Rawls, J. (2001). *Justice as Fairness, A Restatement.* Cambridge, MA: Belknap Press.

Reinhart, C.M,. and Rogoff, K.S. (2009). *This Time Is Different: Eight Centuries of Financial Folly.* Princeton, NJ: Princeton University Press.

Reno, V.P., and Lavery, J. (2009). *Fixing Social Security: Adequate Benefits, Adequate Financing.* Washington, DC: National Academy of Social Insurance.

Rivlin, A., and Sawhill, I., eds. (2004). *Restoring Fiscal Sanity: How to Balance the Budget.* Washington, DC: Brookings Institution.

Rohaly, J., Carasso, A., and Saleem, M.A., (2005). The Urban-Brookings Tax Policy Center microsimulation model: Documentation and methodology for version 0304. Washington, DC: Urban-Brookings Tax Policy Center.

Romer, P.M. (1986). Increasing returns and long-run growth. *Journal of Political Economy, 94*(5), 1,002-1,037.

Romer, P.M. (2001). *Growth Policy.* Policy brief, Stanford Institute for Economic Policy Research. Available: http://www.siepr.stanford.edu/papers/briefs/policybrief_oct01.html [December 2009].

Rubin, R.E., Orszag, P.R., and Sinai, A. (2004). Sustained Budget Deficits: Longer-Run U.S. Economic Performance and the Risk of Financial and Fiscal Disarray. Paper presented at the AEA/Allied Social Science Associations Annual Meeting. http://www.brookings.edu/papers/2004/0105budgetdeficit_orszag.aspx [December 2009].

Russell, L.B. (2007). *Prevention's Potential for Slowing the Growth of Medical Spending.* Washington, DC: National Coalition on Health Care. Available: http://www.nchc.org/documents/nchc_report.pdf [December 2009].

Russell, L.B. (2009). Preventing chronic disease: An important investment, but don't count on cost savings. *Health Affairs, 28*(1), 42-45.

Samuelson, P. (1954). The pure theory of public expenditure. *Review of Economics and Statistics, 36,* 387-389.

Schoen, C., Guterman, S., Shih, A., Lau, J., Kasimow, S., Gauthier, A., and Davis, K. (2007). *Bending the Curve: Options for Achieving Savings and Improving Value in U.S. Health Spending.* Commonwealth Fund Publication 80. Washington, DC: Commonwealth Fund.

Schick, A. (2005). Sustainable budget policy: Concepts and approaches. *OECD Journal on Budgeting, 5*(1), 107-125.

Schick, A. (2007). *The Federal Budget, Politics, Policy, Process.* Washington, DC: Brookings Institution Press.

Schultze, C. (1992). Is there a bias toward excess in U.S. government budgets or deficits? *The Journal of Economic Perspectives, 6*(2), 25-43.

Shekelle, P.G., Morton, S.C., and Keeler, E.B. (2006). *Costs and Benefits of Health Information Technology.* Evidence Report/Technology Assessment No. 132 (1-71). Prepared by the Southern California Evidence-based Practice Center under Contract No. 290-02-0003. AHRQ Publication No. 06-E006. Rockville, MD: Agency for Healthcare Research and Quality.

Shelton, A. (2008). *Reform Options for Social Security.* Washington, DC: AARP Public Policy Institute.

Sherman, A., Greenstein, R., Trisi, D., and Van der Water, P. (2009). *Poverty Rose, Median Income Declined, and Job-based Health Insurance Continued to Weaken in 2008, Recession Likely to Expand Ranks of Poor and Uninsured in 2009 and 2010.* Washington, DC: Center for Budget and Policy Priorities.

Smeeding, T. (2005). Public policy, economic inequality, and poverty: The United States in comparative perspective. *Social Science Quarterly, 86*(1), 955-983.

Smith, S., Newhouse, J., and Freeland, M. (2009). Income, insurance, and technology: Why does health spending outpace economic growth? *Health Affairs, 28*(5), 1,276-1,284.

Social Security Administration. (2009a). *Fact Sheet on the Old-Age, Survivors, and Disability Insurance Program.* Available: http://www.segurosocial.gov/OACT/FACTS/fs2009_06.pdf [December 2009].

Social Security Administration. (2009b). *Income of the Population 55 or Older, 2006.* SSA Publication No. 13-11871. Washington, DC: U.S. Government Printing Office.

Social Security Administration. (2009c). *Proposals Addressing Social Security Solvency.* Office of the Chief Actuary. Available: http://www.ssa.gov/OACT/solvency/index.html [December 2009].

Social Security Administration. (2009d). *The 2009 Annual Report of the Board of Trustees of the Federal Old-Age and Survivors Insurance and Federal Disability Insurance Trust Funds.* Washington, DC: U.S. Government Printing Office.

Social Security Advisory Board. (2005). *Social Security: Why Action Should Be Taken Soon.* Available: http://www.ssab.gov/documents/coverstatement.pdf [December 2009].

Stehr, M. (2007). The effect of Sunday sales bans and excise bans on drinking and cross-border shopping for alcoholic beverages. *National Tax Journal, 60*(1), 85-105.

Steuerle, C.E. (2006). Can we buy our way to health reform? *Tax Notes, 111,* 1,253. Available: http://www.taxmuseum.org/www/econpers.nsf/e172eb973c4c929485257173000cd0ff/85256dba007fa0928525718c00004ee2?OpenDocument [December 2009].

Steuerle, C.E., Spiro, C., and Carasso, A. (2000). *Measuring Replacement Rates at Retirement.* Series on Straight Talk on Social Security and Retirement Policy. Washington, DC: Urban Institute.

Trenchard, J., and Gordon, T. (1995). *Cato's Letters: Or Essays on Liberty, Civil and Religious, and Other Important Subjects, Volume 1.* Indianapolis, IN: Liberty Fund, Inc.

Ulla, P. (2006). Assessing fiscal risks through long-term budget projections. *OECD Journal on Budgeting*, 6(1), 177-178.

U.S. Department of the Treasury. (2008). *2008 Financial Report of the United States Government.* Washington, DC: U.S. Department of the Treasury.

U.S. Department of the Treasury. (2009). *Treasury Bulletin*, December. Washington, DC: U.S. Department of the Treasury. Available: http://www.fms.treas.gov/bulletin/index.html [December 2009].

U.S. Office of Management and Budget. (1997). *Budget of the United States, Fiscal Year 1998.* Washington, DC: U.S. Government Printing Office.

U.S. Office of Management and Budget. (2000). *Budget of the United States Government, Fiscal Year 2001: Analytical Perspectives.* Washington, DC: U.S. Government Printing Office.

U.S. Office of Management and Budget. (2009a). *Budget of the United States Government, Fiscal Year 2010: Analytical Perspectives.* Washington, DC: U.S. Government Printing Office.

U.S. Office of Management and Budget. (2009b). *Budget of the United States Government, Fiscal Year 2010: Appendix.* Washington, DC: U.S. Government Printing Office.

U.S. Office of Management and Budget. (2009c). *Budget of the United States Government, Fiscal Year 2010: Historical Tables.* Washington, DC: U.S. Government Printing Office.

Von Furstenberg, G.M. (1991). Taxes: A license to spend or a late charge? Part three of *The Great Fiscal Experiment*, R.G. Penner, ed. Pp. 155-191. Washington, DC: Urban Institute Press.

Weaver, R.K. (1986). The politics of blame avoidance. *Journal of Public Policy*, 6(4), 371-398.

White, C. (2007). Health care spending growth: How different is the United States from the rest of the OECD? *Health Affairs*, 26(1), 154-161.

White, J. (2009a). *Cost Control and Health Care Reform: The Case for All-Payer Regulation.* Available: http://www.ourfuture.org/files/JWhiteAllPayerCostControl.pdf [December 2009].

White, J. (2009b). *Implementing Health Care Reform with All-Payer Regulation, Private Insurers, and a Voluntary Public Insurance Plan.* Available: http://www.ourfuture.org/files/JWhiteAllPayerImplementing.pdf [December 2009].

Wilson, T. (2007). *A Critique of Baseline Issues in the Initial Medicare Health Support Report.* Available: http://www.dmalliance.org/dmblog/2007/07/national-expert-critiques-mhs-initial.html [December 2009].

World Bank and PricewaterhouseCoopers. (2007). *Paying Taxes 2008: The Global Picture.* Washington, DC: World Bank and PricewaterhouseCoopers.

Yang, C., and Oppenheimer, M. (2007). A "Manhattan Project" for climate change? *Climatic Change*, 80, 199-204.

Yankelovich, D. (1994). How changes in the economy are reshaping American values (Excerpted in *Values and Public Policy*). Washington, DC: Brookings Institution Press.

Appendixes

Appendixes A through G are not printed in this book; they can be found online at http://www.nap.edu/catalog.php?record_id=12808.

Appendix H

Biographical Sketches of Committee Members and Staff

John L. Palmer (*Cochair*) is a university professor and dean emeritus of the Maxwell School of Citizenship and Public Affairs at Syracuse University. He recently completed two presidentially appointed terms as a public trustee for the Medicare and Social Security programs. Previously, he has held positions both in and out of government, including Assistant Secretary for Planning and Evaluation of the U.S. Department of Health and Human Services, senior fellow at the Brookings Institution and the Urban Institute, and adjunct professor at Harvard University. His publications include 13 books and numerous professional and popular articles on economic, budgetary, and social policy issues. He has testified before Congress on many occasions and been a consultant to numerous government agencies, private foundations, and universities. He is a fellow of the National Academy of Public Administration and past president of the National Academy of Social Insurance. He has a B.A from Williams College and a Ph.D. from Stanford University.

Rudolph G. Penner (*Cochair*) is an institute fellow at the Urban Institute, holding the Arjay and Frances Miller chair in public policy. Previously, he was a managing director of the Barents Group, a KPMG company, a resident scholar at the American Enterprise Institute, and a professor of economics at the University of Rochester. His government posts include director of the Congressional Budget Office, Assistant Director for Economic Policy at the U.S. Office of Management and Budget, Deputy Assistant Secretary for Economic Affairs at the U.S. Department of Housing and

Urban Development, and senior staff economist at the Council of Economic Advisors. He received the Jesse Burkhead Award for the best article published in *Public Budgeting and Finance*. He is a past president of the National Economists Club, and he served on the board of directors of the National Association for Business Economics. He has a Ph.D. from Johns Hopkins University.

Joseph Antos is the Wilson H. Taylor scholar in health care and retirement policy at the American Enterprise Institute. He is also a commissioner of the Maryland Health Services Cost Review Commission and an adjunct professor at the School of Public Health of the University of North Carolina at Chapel Hill. Previously, he was Assistant Director for Health and Human Resources at the Congressional Budget Office. His research focuses on the economics of health policy, including Medicare reform, health insurance regulation, and the uninsured. He has written and spoken extensively on the Medicare drug benefit and has led a team of experienced independent actuaries and cost estimators in a study to evaluate various proposals to extend health coverage to the uninsured. He has an M.A. and a Ph.D. from the University of Rochester.

Kenneth S. Apfel is a professor at the School of Public Policy of the University of Maryland. Previously, he held many senior government positions, including the Commissioner of the Social Security Administration, Associate Director for Human Resources for the U.S. Office of Management and Budget, and Assistant Secretary for Management and Budget at the U.S. Department of Health and Human Services. He also worked as legislative director to Senator Bill Bradley and served as committee staff for the Budget Committee of the U.S. Senate. He is a fellow of the National Academy of Public Administration and the National Academy of Social Insurance. He has a B.A. from the University of Massachusetts at Amherst, an M.Ed. from Northeastern University, and an M.P.A. from the LBJ School of Public Affairs at the University of Texas at Austin.

Richard C. Atkinson is president emeritus of the University of California and professor emeritus of cognitive science and psychology at the University of California at San Diego. Prior to assuming the presidency of the University of California system, he was chancellor of University of California at San Diego. He is a former director of the National Science Foundation, past president of the American Association for the Advancement of Science, and was a long-term member of the faculty at Stanford University. His research has been concerned with problems of memory and cognition. He is a member of the National Academy of Sciences, the Institute of Medicine, the National Academy of Education, and the American Philosophical Society. He has a Ph.B. from the University of Chicago and a Ph.D. from Indiana University.

Alan J. Auerbach is a Robert D. Burch professor of economics and law and director of the Burch Center for Tax Policy and Public Finance at the University of California at Berkeley. Previously, he was a member of the Department of Economics at Harvard University and a professor of law and economics at the University of Pennsylvania. He has served as a research associate at the National Bureau of Economic Research and as the deputy chief of staff of the Joint Committee on Taxation of the U.S. Congress. He has authored numerous articles, books, and reviews and is the past or present associate editor of six journals. He is a member of the American Academy of Arts and Sciences. He has a B.A. from Yale University and a Ph.D. from Harvard University.

Rebecca M. Blank resigned from the committee in spring 2009 to accept the position of Under Secretary for Economic Affairs in the U.S. Department of Commerce. Before this appointment, she was the Robert V. Kerr senior fellow at the Brookings Institution. Previously, she was dean of the Gerald R. Ford School of Public Policy and professor of economics at the University of Michigan and codirector of the school's National Poverty Center; a professor of economics at Northwestern University and director of the Northwestern University/University of Chicago Joint Center for Poverty Research; and a professor at Princeton University. She served as a member of President Clinton's Council of Economic Advisers. She has served as president of the Association for Public Policy Analysis and Management, vice president of the American Economic Association, and president of the Midwest Economics Association. She is a fellow of the National Academy of Public Administration and a member of the American Academy of Arts and Sciences. She has a Ph.D. in economics from the Massachusetts Institute of Technology.

Andrea L. Campbell is associate professor of political science at the Massachusetts Institute of Technology. She studies American politics, political behavior, public opinion, political inequality, and social policy, particularly the interplay between political institutions and the political behavior and attitudes of mass publics. She is currently working on a study of taxes, public opinion, and the American fiscal state and on an examination of the politics of the Medicare Modernization Act of 2003. Her work has been published in the *American Political Science Review, Health Affairs, Political Behavior, Studies in American Political Development,* and *Comparative*

Political Studies. She was a Robert Wood Johnson scholar in health policy at Yale University. She has a B.A. from Harvard University and a Ph.D. from the University of California at Berkeley.

Chris Edwards is the director of tax policy studies at the Cato Institute and manages www.downsizinggovernment.org. Previously, he was a senior economist on the congressional Joint Economic Committee, a tax manager with PricewaterhouseCoopers, and an economist with the Tax Foundation. Edwards' articles on tax and budget policies have appeared in the *Washington Post*, the *Wall Street Journal*, the *Los Angeles Times*, *Investor's Business Daily*, and other newspapers. He has a B.A. in economics from the University of Waterloo and an M.A. in economics from George Mason University.

Dana P. Goldman is the director of the Leonard D. Schaeffer Center for Health Policy and Economics and professor and Norman Topping chair in medicine and public policy at the University of Southern California. He also serves as an adjunct professor of health services and radiology at the University of California at Los Angeles and as a research associate at the National Bureau of Economic Research. His current research focuses on the intersection of applied microeconomics and medical issues, with a special interest in the role that medical technology and health insurance play in determining health-related outcomes. He is a recipient of the National Institute for Health Care Management Research Foundation Award for Excellence in Health Policy. He has a B.A. from Cornell University and a Ph.D. from Stanford University.

Robert F. Hale resigned from the committee in February 2009 to accept the position of the Under Secretary (Comptroller) in the U.S. Department of Defense. Before this appointment, he was executive director of the American Society of Military Comptrollers, an 18,000-member association that provides professional development activities for defense financial managers. During the Clinton Administration, he served as the Assistant Secretary of the Air Force (financial management and comptroller). Prior to that appointment, he was head of the defense unit of the Congressional Budget Office. He is a former national president of the American Society of Military Comptrollers. He is a fellow of the National Academy of Public Administration. He has a B.S. and an M.S. from Stanford University and an M.B.A. from George Washington University.

Ellen Hughes-Cromwick is a director and the chief economist for Ford Motor Company. She has major responsibility for the company's global economic and automotive industry forecasts used to support business strategy, finance, and planning and leads a group effort on special industry studies and strategic issues. Previously, she was a senior economist at Mellon Bank, with major responsibilities that included the monthly U.S. macroeconomic forecast, credit markets outlook, and industry analysis. She has also held positions as an assistant professor of economics at Trinity College in Connecticut and as a staff economist on the President's Council of Economic Advisers during the Reagan Administration. She currently serves as a board member of the National Association for Business Economics and the NABE Foundation. She has an M.A. and a Ph.D. from Clark University.

Malay Majmundar served as the senior program associate for this study. His research interests center on social policy and public administration. He has a Ph.D. in public policy from the University of Chicago and a J.D. from Yale University.

Mark David Menchik served as senior program officer for this study. Previously, he held a variety of positions at the U.S. Office of Management and Budget, where he conducted special studies on price indexation, employment programs, and child care and performed budget, management, and regulatory reviews for transportation, housing, financial, retirement, and statistical programs. He has also held positions at the U.S. Advisory Commission on Intergovernmental Relations, the RAND Corporation, and the University of Wisconsin-Madison. He has an A.B. from Harvard and an M.A. in city and regional planning and a Ph.D. in regional economics from the University of Pennsylvania.

Joseph J. Minarik is the senior vice president and director of research at the Committee for Economic Development (CED), where he leads research projects on the economy and the federal budget, globalization, trade, early childhood education, campaign finance reform, and health care. Previously, he served as executive director of the Joint Economic Committee for chair Lee Hamilton and executive director for policy and chief economist of the Budget Committee of the House of Representatives for chair Leon E. Panetta. During the Clinton Administration, he served as associate director for economic policy at the U.S. Office of Management and Budget. He is the author of *Making Tax Choices* (Urban Institute Press) and many articles on fiscal issues. He is a fellow of the National Academy of Public Administration. He has a B.A. from Georgetown University and a Ph.D. from Yale University.

Olivia S. Mitchell is the International Foundation of Employee Benefit Plans professor and chair of insurance and risk management, executive director of the Pension Research Council, and director of the Boettner

Center on Pensions and Retirement Research, all at the Wharton School at the University of Pennsylvania. She is also a research associate at the National Bureau of Economic Research and codirector of the Financial Literacy Center. Her main areas of research and teaching are private and public insurance, risk management, public finance and labor markets, and compensation and pensions, both in the United States and internationally. She was a member of the Commission to Strengthen Social Security in the George W. Bush Administration. Her many speaking engagements have included the World Economic Forum and the International Monetary Fund, and she has provided testimony to committees of the U.S. Congress, the parliament of the United Kingdom, the Australian Parliament, and the Brazilian Senate. She has a B.A. from Harvard and a Ph.D. from the University of Wisconsin-Madison.

Sean O'Keefe is the chief executive officer of EADS North America. Previously, he was vice president and a corporate officer of the General Electric Company in the technology infrastructure sector, and he led Washington operations for the company's aviation business. He has been chancellor of Louisiana State University and has held faculty positions at Syracuse University and Pennsylvania State University. In the administration of George W. Bush he served as deputy assistant to the President, deputy director of the U.S. Office of Management and Budget, and administrator of the U.S. National Aeronautics and Space Administration. He also served as secretary of the Navy and as comptroller and chief financial officer of the U.S. Department of Defense in the administration of George H.W. Bush and, previously, as staff director of the Committee on Appropriations and the Defense Subcommittee of the U.S. Senate. He is a fellow of the National Academy of Public Administration and of the International Academy of Astronautics. He has a B.A. from Loyola University and an M.P.A. from the Maxwell School of Syracuse University.

Gilbert S. Omenn is professor of internal medicine, human genetics, bioinformatics, and public health at the University of Michigan. Previously, he served as executive vice president for medical affairs and as chief executive officer of the University of Michigan Health System. He also served as dean of the School of Public Health and professor of medicine and environmental health at the University of Washington in Seattle. His research interests include cancer proteomics, chemoprevention of cancers, public health genetics, science-based risk analysis, and health policy. During the Carter Administration he was associate director in the Office of Science and Technology Policy and associate director of the U.S. Office of Management and Budget. He is a former president of the American Association for the Advancement of Science. He is a member of the Institute of Medicine, the American Academy of Arts and Sciences, the Association of American Physicians, and the American College of Physicians. He has a B.A. from Princeton University, an M.D. from Harvard Medical School, and a Ph.D. from the University of Washington.

June E. O'Neill is the Wollman professor of economics at the Zicklin School of Business and the director of the Center for the Study of Business and Government in the School of Public Affairs at Baruch College of the City University of New York. She is also an adjunct scholar of the American Enterprise Institute. Her government service includes director of the Congressional Budget Office, director of policy and research at the U.S. Commission on Civil Rights, and senior economist at the Council of Economic Advisers in the Reagan Administration. She has also held positions as senior research associate at the Urban Institute and research associate at the Brookings Institution. Her published research includes wage differentials by race and gender, health insurance, tax and budget policy, and social security. She has a Ph.D. from Columbia University.

Paul L. Posner is the director of the Public Administration Program at George Mason University. Previously, he led the budget and public finance work of the U.S. Government Accountability Office, developing long-term models of the federal budget, outlining opportunities for reform in major federal programs, and recommending changes to the budget process to provide greater visibility to long-term issues. His work on the federal budget has earned him the James Blum Award from the Association of Budget and Program Analysis for outstanding public budgeting leadership and the S. Kenneth Howard Award from the Association for Budget and Financial Management. He has served as president of the Association for Budget and Financial Management and of the American Society for Public Administration. He is a fellow of the National Academy of Public Administration and chairs the Academy's Panel on the Federal System. He has a Ph.D. from Columbia University.

F. Stevens Redburn served as study director, and he is an adjunct professor in the School of Public Policy and Public Administration of George Washington University. He has previously directed studies for the National Academy of Public Administration, and he has served as chair or member of many of its study panels. In government he has more than 25 years of experience as a senior government official in the U.S. Office of Management and Budget and the U.S. Department of Housing and Urban Development. He also served as senior budget adviser on the Kosovo V project of the U.S.

Agency for International Development, advising on a wide range of budgeting issues and improved budget procedures. He is a fellow of the National Academy of Public Administration. He has a Ph.D. in political science from the University of North Carolina at Chapel Hill.

Robert D. Reischauer is president of the Urban Institute. Previously, he was a senior fellow at the Brookings Institution and the senior vice president of the Urban Institute. His government service includes the Congressional Budget Office, where he served as assistant director for human resources, deputy director, and director. His main research foci are the federal budget, Medicare, and Social Security, especially the effects of entitlement programs on the fiscal outlook and budget process. He served on the Medicare Payment Advisory Commission and as its vice chair. He has written widely and testified before congressional committees on a range of economic and welfare issues. He is a member of the Institute of Medicine and a fellow of the National Academy of Public Administration. He has a master of international affairs degree and a Ph.D. from Columbia University.

Jane L. Ross, who served as senior staff officer for this study, is director of the Center for Economic, Governance, and International Studies at the National Research Council. Previously, she was the deputy commissioner for policy at the Social Security Administration, serving as an adviser to the commissioner of Social Security on policy issues, as well as the leader of the policy analysis and research office. Her other government service includes director for income security issues and senior assistant director for Medicare and Medicaid issues at the U.S. Government Accountability Office. She is a member of the Association for Public Policy Analysis and Management and is a founding member of the National Academy of Social Insurance. She has a Ph.D. in economics from American University.

Kathy A. Ruffing served as a senior program officer for this study until October 2008. She is a senior policy analyst at the Center on Budget and Policy Priorities, specializing in federal budget issues. She spent 25 years at the Congressional Budget Office, where she analyzed a wide range of topics including interest costs and federal debt, federal pay, immigration, and Social Security. She also held positions at the U.S. Department of Labor and the Social Security Administration. She has a B.A. in economics and political science from the University of Pittsburgh and an M.A. in economics from George Washington University.

Margaret C. Simms is an institute fellow at the Urban Institute and director of its low-income working families project, a research initiative exploring the challenges faced by 9 million families and their 19 million children.

Previously, she held many positions at the Joint Center for Political and Economic Studies, including vice president for governance and economic analysis and interim president. She has also served as a faculty member at Atlanta University, at Clark College (Atlanta), and at the University of California at Santa Cruz. She has been editor of the *Review of Black Political Economy* and chair of the board of the Institute for Women's Policy Research. She has been a member of *Black Enterprise* magazine's board of economists and president of the National Academy of Social Insurance. She is a member of the American Academy of Arts and Sciences. She has an M.A. and a Ph.D. in economics from Stanford University.

William E. Spriggs resigned from the committee in spring 2009 to accept the position of Assistant Secretary for Policy at the U.S. Department of Labor. Before this appointment, he was a professor and chair of the Department of Economics at Howard University. He was also a senior fellow for the Community Service Society of New York. He served as chair of the Independent Health Care Trust for United Auto Workers (UAW) Retirees of Ford Motor Company, and he was on the board of the Retiree Health Administration Corporation, which administers the health care trusts for UAW retirees of Ford and General Motors, and he chaired the UAW Retirees of the Dana Corporation Health and Welfare Trust. During the Clinton Administration he served as a senior adviser and an economist and special adviser in the U.S. Department of Commerce. He has also served as executive director of the National Urban League's Institute for Opportunity and Equality. He is a member of the National Academy of Public Administration and the National Academy of Social Insurance. He has a B.A. from Williams College and a Ph.D. from the University of Wisconsin-Madison.

Thomas C. Sutton is the retired chairman and CEO of Pacific Life Insurance Company. He now serves on the boards of directors of Pacific Life, Edison International, Southern California Edison, and the Public Policy Institute of California, which he previously chaired; and he previously served as chair and director of the American Council of Life Insurers and the Association of California Life and Health Insurance Companies. He has previously served as director or trustee for a range of organizations, including the Irvine Company, the California Chamber of Commerce, the Orange County Performing Arts Center, the California Business Roundtable, and the South Coast Repertory Theatre. He has a B.S. from the University of Toronto and he completed the Advanced Management Program at Harvard University.

Susan Tanaka is the director of citizen education and engagement at the Peter G. Peterson Foundation. Previously, she was the associate director for communications and a senior analyst in the Budget Analysis Division of the

Congressional Budget Office. Other government work included the U.S. Office of Management and Budget, as a budget analyst and as a special assistant to the Assistant Director of Administration and Legislation, working on agencywide personnel and administrative issues. She has also been vice president of the Committee for a Responsible Federal Budget, directing its analytic work on issues related to the federal budget, including Social Security, health care programs, tax issues, and budget process and scorekeeping. She has an M.B.A. from the Yale School of Management and an M.A. from the Fletcher School of Law and Diplomacy of Tufts University.

Ruth A. Wooden is president of Public Agenda. Previously, Ms. Wooden was executive vice president and senior counselor at the international public relations firm of Porter Novelli, where she led the advertising and cause-related marketing practice. Other previous positions included volunteer president of the National Parenting Association and president of the Advertising Council. She currently serves as chair of the Board of Civic Ventures. She is also on the boards of the Family Violence Prevention Fund and Research!America and is a former director of CARE and the Edna McConnell Clark Foundation. She is a recipient of United Jewish Appeal's Maxwell Dane Humanitarian Award, the Advertising Woman of the Year Award, the Prudential Prize in Non-Profit Leadership, and the Matrix Award from New York Women in Communication. She has a B.A. in sociology and history from the University of Minnesota and an honorary Ph.D. from Northeastern University.